"SLICK WILLIE" II

"SLICK WILLIE" II

Why America *Still* Cannot Trust Bill Clinton

Deborah J. Stone and
Christopher Manion

Annapolis-Washington Book Publishers, Inc.
Annapolis, Maryland

© 1994 Annapolis-Washington Book Publishers, Inc.
Published May 1994
Printed in the United States of America
10 9 8 7 6 5 4 3 2 1

ISBN: 0-9634397-2-3

Annapolis-Washington Book Publishers, Inc.
P.O. Box 2365
Annapolis, MD 21404

Cover photograph courtesy of
UniPhoto

Jacket design by
the Gann Agency

CONTENTS

"SLICK WILLIE" DOES WASHINGTON

"Bill Clinton has been heaving aside his campaign commitments with the gay abandon of a stripper tossing her knickers into the cheap seats."[1]

— Jonathan Yardley,
Washington Post

"I'm just astonished and reeling and waiting for the next blow."[2]

— Sen. Daniel Patrick Moynihan,
on the Clinton administration's
"First 100 Days"

There is nothing like the gap between Bill Clinton's words and his actions.

"He talks all the time," observed Jeffrey Tulis, a University of Texas political scientist who studies presidential rhetoric.[3] And his *talk* resonates with most Americans. "Our democracy must be not only the envy of the world but the engine of our own renewal," said the 42nd President in his Inaugural address. "There is nothing wrong with America that cannot be cured by what is right with America."[4]

As the "Washington outsider," Clinton gave voice to Americans' frustration when he stood in front of the Capitol and railed on the city as a place where "powerful people maneuver for position and worry endlessly about who is in and who is out, who is up and who is down, forgetting those people whose toil and sweat sends us here and pays our way."[5] Clinton called for a "new season of renewal for America" and, declaring one of his first days in office a "National Day of Fellowship and Hope," said, "I stand humbly before God and ask for His guidance and blessings for our great nation."[6]

But as was characteristic throughout his student and adult careers and campaigns, Bill Clinton's words were betrayed by his actions. The pattern of deception and broken promises that earned him the notorious nickname, "Slick Willie," was, if anything, more pronounced once he arrived in Washington. Far from stopping or rising above the corruption in the nation's capital, Bill Clinton heads an administration that wallows in it.

"The Clintonites call their inauguration 'An American Reunion: New Beginnings, Renewed Hope,' " wrote the *Washington Post*'s Jonathan Yardley, "but all the evidence indicates that it's nothing more than the same old sleaze."[7]

INAUGURAL GLITZ

Though he campaigned as a man of the people, Bill Clinton revealed himself at his Inauguration to be a man of the beautiful people. It didn't matter that he captured only 43 percent of the vote—he captured Hollywood. "Friends of Bill" Harry Thomason and Linda Bloodworth-Thomason co-chaired the $25 million event that attracted Jack Nicholson, Kim Basinger, Michael Bolton, Sidney Poitier, Diana Ross, Michael Jackson, Sally Field and many other stars. "When was the last time you felt welcome in Washington?" Whoopie Goldberg asked a cheering crowd of glitterati at a pre-Inaugural party.[8]

It was nothing less than emotional euphoria for those who had waited 12 years to recapture the White House. "I haven't slept, I'm punch drunk," said Hollywood agent Karen Russell. "I'm in this place called Clinton-land."[9] "As far as governments go," said Canadian singer k.d. lang in an Inaugural week address to People for the Ethical Treatment of Animals, "this one looks good and I feel a really positive vibe in Washington."[10]

"We are in," cried Barbra Streisand exultantly, "I can't believe it."[11]

The Clintons sought consciously to invoke the Inauguration of John F. Kennedy. As Kennedy had invited Robert Frost to give an Inaugural reading of poetry, Clinton asked Maya Angelou to participate in his swearing-in ceremony. The North Carolina poet read her poem, "On the Pulse of Morning" and, in 115 lines, managed to laud the peace movement, multiculturalism, homosexuals, the homeless, anticapitalism, and environmentalism.

Meanwhile, crowds didn't know what to make of Hillary Rodham Clinton's outfit—the *New York Times* referred to the "blue unidentified flying object" sitting on top of her head.[12] And the level of informality throughout the Inaugural week was decidedly unKennedyesque. The most popular Inaugural Ball, for example, was the Music Television (MTV) dance, which rocked with performances by En Vogue, Boyz II Men, 10,000 Maniacs, Soul Asylum and the president's half-brother, Roger Clinton. "I think everyone here knows that MTV had a lot to do with a Clinton-Gore victory," beamed the President to his young supporters.[13] For the first time ever, homosexuals and lesbians had their own Inaugural Ball.

"This is Woodstock in a Tuxedo," said theologian Michael Novak of Inaugural week.[14] Indiana Congressman Stephen Buyer observed that the Black Horse Troop, an Indiana military high school unit that had marched in nine straight Inaugural parades for presidents of both parties, had been bumped by the Clinton crowd and replaced by a reggae band, two Elvis impersonators, and a homosexual chorus.[15]

All in all, events of Clinton's Inaugural week resembled a circus sideshow more than the transfer of power of the presidency of the United States. "The Co-Dependant White House is upon us," concluded the *New York Times* in a story that reported on the "diversity," "self-discovery," "therapy," and "inner-child" themes of Clinton's Inauguration.[16] Early in his term, Clinton invited his Cabinet to Camp David for a weekend of "human resource development" with the help of professional "facilitators." The top federal officials were asked to "share" something private about themselves. President Clinton, for example, told about how he suffered as a child when others teased him for being a "fat, little kid."[17]

PROMISES, PROMISES

Foremost among the pledges Bill Clinton made to the American people was his promise to stop the revolving door between Washington's lobbying firms and the federal government. Less than an hour after being sworn in, Clinton signed an executive order that banned members of his administration from lobbying the government for five years after leaving it.

Within the year, however, two top Clinton aides left the White House for high-paying lobbying jobs. Although this was precisely the kind of "cashing in" that Clinton had promised to forbid, the aides left without protest from the administration. Roy Neel, who had served as Clinton's Deputy Chief of Staff, took a $500,000 job as head of the lobbying firm U.S. Telephone Association. And Howard

Paster, Clinton's congressional liaison, became the million-dollar chairman of Washington's public relations giant, Hill & Knowlton.[18]

Another central Clinton promise was his insistence on "a cabinet that looks like America." And while Clinton achieved the superficial diversity in vogue among politically correct circles,* his Cabinet was nonetheless, in the words of the *National Journal*, made up of "veterans of federal service, Democrats awaiting another chance to work in government."[22] President Clinton "was going to turn government back to the people," wrote the *New Republic*'s Fred Barnes. "Instead, he's turned at least the cabinet back to millionaires and lawyers. The President's a lawyer, his wife's a lawyer. All four economic policy officials are lawyers. And the surprising thing is there are more millionaires in the Clinton cabinet than there were in the Reagan or Bush cabinet. This is not a populist administration at the cabinet level."[23]

Another broken Clinton promise concerned his agenda

---

*The attention paid by the Clinton administration to individuals' gender and skin color drew concern from many quarters as it hindered the selection process for executive government officials. Undersecretary of State for Management Richard M. Moose complained in a November 12, 1993 memo to Secretary Warren Christopher that he was unable to fill an important position at the Department because "White House personnel (probably Bruce [Lindsey]) is deeply entrenched against 'white male career officers.' " When asked about the memo by the *Washington Post*, Lindsey responded, "It's no secret we have been encouraging all departments to seek diversity. We are trying to push the State Department as well as others to seek minorities and women for senior positions."[19]

According to inside White House source Deepwater, the Clinton administration sought to record which executive personnel were homosexual in a job selection process that benefited those who were.[20] Moreover, the Department of Transportation sponsored a special "gay pride" program for employees, funded with $1,900 in taxpayer funds, in the summer of 1993. Transportation Secretary Federico Pena presided over the celebration, which featured homosexual Congressman Barney Frank (D-Mass.) as a special guest.[21]

with Congress. "If I'm elected," Clinton vowed during a campaign appearance on ABC's "Good Morning America," "I'll have the bills ready the day after I'm inaugurated."[24] At another campaign stop, Clinton said "We'll have a whirlwind set of early proposals . . . in the first hundred days."[25] But then just before his Inauguration, when a reporter asked if he was ready to send his outline to Congress, Clinton shot back, "I don't know who led you to believe that, but I'm the only one who's authorized to talk about that."[26] And when the proposals didn't materialize, White House spokesman Dee Dee Myers denied the promises: "People of the press are expecting to have some 100-day program. We never ever had one."[27]

From the gas tax to the White House staff cuts, from welfare reform to the line-item veto, and from Bosnia to Haiti, Clinton managed to renege on many, if not most, of his campaign pledges.

How many promises did Clinton break? Rep. Dick Armey (R-Tex.) and his staff tracked 120 promises broken during Clinton's first 100 days in office. According to Representative Armey, the president's 120th equivocation came on April 25, 1993, when he "assured us that he had 'only broken one campaign promise,' as far as he could remember."[28]

Bill Clinton did keep some promises. But they hardly seemed designed to spark "renewal" in America. Once sworn in, Clinton immediately moved to satisfy militant feminists and big labor. He announced a series of executive orders that allowed federally funded clinics to offer abortion counseling; allowed abortions at U.S. military hospitals abroad; increased prospects for importation of RU-486, the French abortion pill; and ended the ban on fetal tissue research. Clinton threw a bone to labor unions by revoking executive orders that required non-union contractors, employers, and their employees to be notified that they did not have to pay union dues, and that they may be entitled to a refund on dues already paid.

THE "GATES"

Within hours of taking office, President Clinton suffered his first major political scandal. The news broke that his nominee for Attorney General, Zoe Baird, had hired illegal aliens as housekeeper and chauffeur in violation of U.S. immigration laws. "Nannygate" had hit.

Apparently, President Clinton saw no problem in appointing to the nation's highest law enforcement office an individual who had violated the very laws she was being asked to uphold. But the public saw a big problem, and its outrage was compounded when it was learned that Baird had also failed to pay Social Security and other employment taxes on her servants' wages. Clinton nominated Baird on the condition that she pay all taxes owed and Baird complied, explaining, "I did not adequately perceive the significance of the matter here."[29] The public however, didn't fall for this fix-it scheme. Telephone lines to Capitol Hill jammed with record levels of calls from disgusted citizens opposing Baird, and she withdrew her nomination in disgrace.

Nonetheless, the Clinton White House didn't seem to learn anything from this episode. George Stephanopolous explained to reporters that having unreported nannies was "a very common situation,"[30] and indeed it seemed to be among individuals Clinton named to his administration. (Over the course of the next year, Clinton backed at least 27 individuals to work in his administration who were guilty of Nannygate infractions.)

The Nannygate scandal reached a height of ridiculousness 11 months later, when Clinton nominated Admiral

Bobby Ray Inman to replace Les Aspin as Secretary of Defense despite Inman's failure to pay Social Security taxes for the maid at his Austin, Texas home. Inman said he was aware from the Baird controversy that he was required to pay taxes for his houseworker but, according to White House spokesman Dee Dee Myers, he was "waiting to see if there would be changes in the law" so he would not have to pay.[31]* Only after he was nominated did Inman personally visit the Austin IRS office to pony up $6,000 in federal back taxes.[33] And, in a March 1994 Nannygate installment, Associate White House Counsel William Kennedy, who was in charge of checking Clinton appointees for ethical problems, admitted his own failure to pay taxes on his Little Rock nanny.[34]

"Will they ever stop putting 'gate' at the end of everything?" asked radio host G. Gordon Liddy of Watergate fame. "I have a proprietary interest in the suffix 'gate.' It's mine. Get your own!"[35] But Nannygate was just the beginning. Next to hit was "Scalpgate," also known as "Hair Force One," when President Clinton held up planes at Los Angeles International Airport for 45 minutes while luxuriating under the scissors and combs of Hollywood's Christophe. But perhaps no episode better illustrated the inexperience and poor judgment of the Clinton White House than "Travelgate," a travesty that truly deserved use of Liddy's prized suffix.

---

*Inman's reluctance to pay the taxes he owed should have been an indication that he was not up to the highly demanding job of Secretary of Defense. Moreover, Inman had maintained prior to his nomination that he wanted to leave Washington most weekends to visit his Austin, Texas and Aspen, Colorado homes.[32] That he was still nominated after twice revealing a lack of dedication to the post in question says more about Clinton's judgment than anything else. The issue died when Inman withdrew himself from consideration after being haunted by an imagined "conspiracy" against him between Senator Robert Dole and *New York Times* columnist William Safire.

The known facts about Travelgate are that a 25-year-old distant cousin of the President, Catherine Cornelius, who had directed press travel during Clinton's presidential campaign, wanted to take control of the White House travel office, which arranges travel for both the press and administration officials who accompany the president on various trips.

Cornelius suggested to David Watkins, Assistant to the President for Management and Administration, the possibility of mismanagement practices in the White House travel office, which was run by seven career veterans. To back up her request to take over, Cornelius copied documents and even took papers home during a month of internal spying on the travel office. Furthermore, Cornelius enlisted the help of Hollywood producer, and important "Friend of Bill," Harry Thomason. Thomason's interest piqued because he was a partner in an aviation firm that had been turned away from travel office bidding, and he mentioned the alleged problems in the travel office to both Clintons. Thomason further pushed Watkins to move on the matter and, after a meeting of Cornelius, Thomason, Watkins and Deputy White House Counsel Vincent Foster, a decision was made to notify Associate White House Counsel William H. Kennedy III* of Cornelius''s suspicions.

Kennedy swung into action. He called the FBI and asked for an official investigation. He threatened to call the IRS if the FBI failed to respond immediately to his requests.[36] Meanwhile, on May 19, 1993, Watkins fired the

---

*Hillary Rodham Clinton was kept apprised of these on-going discussions, raising suspicions that there was more to Travelgate than meets the eye, namely that the First Lady feared problems in the travel office might bring to light the huge expenses incurred by the hundreds of members of her secret health care task force who were routinely flown into Washington.

seven career officials without notice and without giving them the opportunity to defend themselves. White House spokesman Dee Dee Myers, apparently in an effort to justify the firings, told a reporter that the FBI was investigating possible wrongdoing by the travel office employees, although no such investigation was underway.

Under heavy media scrutiny, the White House issued a formal report on Travelgate, reassigned five of the travel office employees, and allowed the remaining two to retire. Chief of Staff McLarty took responsibility for the fiasco stating that the firings, the direct call to the FBI, and the announcement of the FBI investigation were wrong. "Mistakes were made," McLarty concluded, "mistakes of judgment, mistakes of inexperience, that included inappropriate actions with respect to the FBI, allowing the appearance that personal interest and favoritism could play a role in management decisions, and unfair treatment of White House employees."[37]

In the wake of the controversy and the official White House report, *Washington Post* columnist David Broder called Travelgate a "saga so shoddy, so saturated with petty manipulations, snooping and spying, rampant cronyism, and tacky deceits that it made you cringe. It also confirmed an abuse of the FBI's role . . . that makes you wonder if anyone on that young staff had learned the hard-earned lesson of Watergate. They did not seem to understand that nothing is more dangerous to the Constitution than a political police-state operation directed from the White House."[38]

"An embarrassing display of raw patronage," added the *New York Times*'s William Safire.[39] But despite the White House's own admission of fault, no Clinton officials received more than a slap on the wrist.

HRC

"Hillary!" Bill Clinton answered when asked whom he wanted in the room when he had big decisions to make. With a single word, reported the *New York Times,* Clinton shattered "200 years of Presidential protocol."[40]

One of the early indications that Hillary would be a major political player was her decision to start using her maiden name again. She reportedly agonized over whether to make it Rodham Clinton, or go "all the way" and revert to Hillary Rodham. (Hillary used only her maiden name in the early years of her marriage; she was known as Hillary Rodham. Then she changed her name to Hillary Clinton to help win votes in one of her husband's close re-election campaigns for governor. During the presidential campaign, Hillary used only the last name Clinton, but changed back to Rodham Clinton after arriving in Washington.)

As the first First Lady to have an office in the West Wing of the White House, Rodham Clinton has been heavily involved in personnel and policy decisions for her husband's administration, from choosing an Attorney General to formulating a health care proposal. Still, members of Congress and the media have been reluctant to challenge her on that level. "Foes of the administration's health plan," reported the *New York Times,* "seem to have decided that they cannot safely attack a First Lady."[41]

"Everybody, after all, goes around saying that Hillary Clinton is ultra-bright," wrote Christopher Hitchens in *Vanity Fair.* "But how do we know this? . . . Everybody also knows, or thinks he knows, that Ms. Hillary is stirred by deep tides of conscience and passion. I have no hard evidence of this either."[42]

Viewed by some as a saint, others as a Dragon Lady,

Rodham Clinton seemed most to confirm the latter with her health care task force work and her domestic management of the White House. Rodham Clinton oversaw a controversial redecoration of the White House that resulted in costly overruns, and she fired the White House chef. She also fired a White House usher merely because he had given computer advice to former First Lady Barbara Bush. "I'm at a loss to try to explain this," said Chris Emery, the fired usher and a father of four. Emery said that Bush had called him because he was the one who taught her how to use her laptop before she left the White House. "It was strictly for computer support," said Emery of the telephone conversations.[43] "Running afoul of the First Lady on issues of secrecy, policy and personnel is considered a ruinous career move," wrote a *Washington Post* reporter.[44]

But it was Rodham Clinton's turn to sit in the hotseat on March 18, 1994. On that day, the *New York Times* reported on Rodham Clinton's astounding foray into the commodities trading market. Between October 1978 and October 17, 1979, the *Times* reported, Rodham Clinton made close to $100,000 trading cattle futures, exiting the market just as it started to collapse.[45] How did the young Rodham Clinton, with no savvy in the financial world, parlay this sizable fortune from a mere $1,000 investment? That was the question on many people's minds when it was disclosed that, among her profits, Rodham Clinton made $5,300 the day after she opened her small account.

To have "made $5,300 [in one] day," wrote economist Paul Craig Roberts, "Mrs. Clinton would have needed to hold at least 12 contracts valued at more than a quarter of a million dollars. To speculate on that level, she would have needed $14,400 in her account. Her $1,000 investment would not have supported even one contract. Someone was obviously bending the rules for her, if not giving her money outright."[46]

Former IRS career attorney David Brandon wrote, "From my standpoint . . . [with] extensive experience in these matters, Mrs. Clinton's windfall in the late 1970s has all the trappings of prearranged trades."[47] Rodham Clinton's commodities advisor was James Blair, then a powerful lawyer for Arkansas food giant Tyson Foods Inc. (Both Blair and Donald Tyson, chairman and CEO of Tyson Foods, Inc., were strong political supporters of Bill Clinton, and Tyson typically received excellent treatment from the state during Clinton's tenure as governor.[48]

When the cattle dust settled, Rodham Clinton paid $14,615 owed in back taxes and interest on these unreported profits. "It was an oversight, I don't know how it happened," said a White House official.[49] Concerned citizens were left scratching their heads over Hillary Rodham Clinton's financial windfall in the world of wealth, power, and greed—a world she so harshly condemns.

HOMOSEXUALS IN THE MILITARY

No less controversial than his administrative disasters and his powerful wife were President Clinton's early policy initiatives. Foremost among these was the question of homosexuals in the military.

"We call for an immediate repeal of the ban on gays and lesbians serving in the United States armed forces," promised a Clinton campaign document.[50] "We have too much to do to endure quaint little rules," said Clinton of the ban.[51]

Once in office, however, Clinton changed his tune: "I was frankly appalled that we spent so much time . . . on gays in the military."[52] But the problem was one of Clinton's own making. It was he who had promised to remove the ban on homosexuals in the military, and he who made it an issue of major importance at the outset of his administration.

In fact, Bill Clinton is the first American president to have actively and enthusiastically courted homosexual voters in his bid for the White House. David Mixner, a homosexual activist who was an Oxford friend of Clinton's, became the campaign's chief adviser on homosexual issues. In May 1993, Mixner organized a high-profile Hollywood fund-raiser for Clinton that raised $100,000, "the biggest chunk of money Clinton, or any other candidate for that matter, ever got from queers at one time," wrote one homosexual writer.[53] "I have a vision and you're part of it," Clinton told his eager constituents.[54]

Following this landmark event, the *Los Angeles Times* reported, "Almost anything Arkansas Governor Bill Clinton said to the audience of gay and lesbian activists who turned out at a fund-raiser for his campaign in Hollywood seemed less important than the simple fact that he was there."[55]

Candidate Clinton made many promises to homosexual groups. He pledged to sign a national "gay rights" bill, support a federal "Manhattan Project" to develop a cure for AIDS, support condom distribution programs, and appoint open homosexuals to positions throughout his administration. Most important to many homosexual activists, Clinton vowed to end the ban on homosexuals in the military during his first 100 days in office.

"I have spent the last year of my life telling [the homosexual] community that our agenda will be accomplished through this administration," said Mixner, who put the total dollar figure for homosexual contributions to Clinton at $3-4 million.[56]

But Clinton's love affair with homosexuals died down

soon after he took office. Apparently for the first time, Clinton listened to the military opposition to ending the ban on homosexuals. The concerns of men and women in the armed forces included religious and moral opposition to homosexuality, the privacy rights of soldiers, health factors, and the strongly held belief that open homosexuals would undermine the unit cohesion and combat readiness of America's fighting forces.

Under pressure from both sides, Clinton postponed his decision on ending the ban for six months, perhaps hoping things would cool down. But homosexual groups started upping their demands. They wanted "sensitivity training," for example, for all members of the armed forces. Meanwhile, U.S. soldiers registered massive opposition to the homosexual agenda. "We have always perceived that the threats to our honor were external to our borders, and could be countered with courage, zeal, and competence," wrote Maj. Arthur J. Corbett in *Marine Corps Gazette*. "We never suspected that the threat to our ethos would come from within our Nation and be sanctioned, however indirectly, by the American people . . . For such an un-deserved indignity to be heaped upon such a noble insti-tution, with but a whimper of protest, would betray the untold thousands who bought with their blood the honor we enjoy."[57]

Retired National Guard Chaplain Jim Hutchens, a Brig-adier General, summed up the concerns of many military chaplains who feared lifting the ban would serve as an invitation to homosexual chaplains to join the military: "Surely the soldier lying on the battlefield with a sucking chest wound and calling for a chaplain has the right to expect the solace, comfort and ministry of a chaplain whose presence and touch is not morally offensive or phys-ically repulsive. A wounded or dying soldier deserves something better than the morally compromised musings of a homosexual chaplain."[58]

Homosexuals argued that discrimination against them was analogous to the prejudice against blacks, and pointed to President Truman's desegregation of the military as the example that Bill Clinton should follow. America's highest-ranking black military officer, however, disagreed. "Skin color is a benign, non-behavioral characteristic," said Gen. Colin Powell, then-Chairman of the Joint Chiefs of Staff. "Sexual orientation is perhaps the most profound of human behavioral characteristics. Comparison of the two is a convenient but invalid argument."[59]

Senator Sam Nunn (D-Ga.), chairman of the Armed Services Committee, proceeded with hearings on the issue, inviting retired Army Gen. H. Norman Schwarzkopf to testify in May 1993. "The armed forces' principal mission is not to be instruments of social experimentation," the hero of Operation *Desert Storm* told Congress. "The first, foremost and all-eclipsing mission of our military is to be ready to fight our nation's wars and, when called upon to do so, to win those wars . . . Whether we like it or not, in my years of military service I've experienced the fact that the introduction of an open homosexual into a small unit immediately polarizes that unit and destroys the very bonding that is so important for the unit's survival in time of war."[60]

Nonetheless, on July 19, President Clinton announced his "Don't ask, Don't tell" policy, ending the military's practice of asking recruits if they're homosexual. In a classic hair-splitting maneuver Clinton said: "Service men and women will be judged based on their conduct not their sexual orientation,"[61] making the distinction between homosexual "status" and homosexual "conduct." "I never said I would be in favor of changing any of the rules of *conduct*," he insisted. "You can go back through every statement I have made."[62] Despite further congressional action, statements from Clinton, and on-going court challenges, the issue of homosexuals in the military remains undecided.

"During the campaign, when money and volunteers from the gay community were moving Clinton's way, his argument for lifting the 40-year prohibition [against homosexuals in the military] was unequivocal," reported the *Chicago Tribune*.[63] But following Clinton's election, homosexual activists learned the lesson that so many others had before them: Bill Clinton is not a man of his word. Although Clinton caved somewhat on his promise to abolish the ban on homosexuals in the military, he did pursue other items on the homosexual agenda with zeal.

AN EXOTIC SOCIAL AGENDA

When Bill Clinton stood "humbly before God," and called for "renewal in America," probably not many Americans conjured up images of dancing condoms in their heads. Neither did they likely envision homosexual couples adopting children as a remedy for societal decline. But these are among the answers Bill Clinton and his top officials push on the whole nation. Leading the charge for Clinton's exotic social agenda have been Surgeon General Joycelyn Elders, AIDS Czar Kristine Gebbie, Assistant Secretary for fair housing at the Department of Housing and Urban Development (HUD) Roberta Achtenberg, and Health and Human Services (HHS) Secretary Donna Shalala.

As America's new AIDS Czar, Kristine Gebbie admonished citizens for "couch[ing] messages around sexuality in terms of don'ts and diseases," and described America as a "Victorian society that misrepresents information, denies sexuality early, denies homosexual sexuality, especially in teens, and leaves people abandoned with no place to go."[64]

Gebbie was outdone, however, by Clinton's Assistant HUD Secretary, Roberta Achtenberg, the first open homosexual ever to be confirmed by the U.S. Senate. Achtenberg had a history of not only talking about perverse sexual liberation, but flaunting it in front of cameras. It turned out that Achtenberg had participated in San Francisco's 1992 "Gay Pride" parade with her lesbian lover, whom she kissed openly, and their son, who was conceived through artificial insemination.[65] So proud was Achtenberg of her girlfriend that she later introduced her at her Senate confirmation hearings.

Apparently, Achtenberg's role as public lesbian was her prime qualification for nomination to the Clinton administration. "I'm not a fair housing expert," she admitted to the *Washington Times*.[66] But Achtenberg was considered an important voice of radicalism. As a United Way Board member, Achtenberg had voted to bar $1.2 million in donations to the Boy Scouts because they barred homosexual scoutmasters. "Do we want children learning the values of an organization . . . that provides character-building exclusively for straight, God-fearing male children?" she asked in an interview with the *San Francisco Chronicle*.[67]

Another vocal critic of the Boy Scouts has been Surgeon General Joycelyn Elders, who came to Washington having served as Clinton's health commissioner in Arkansas. To Elders, homosexual sex is "wonderful," "normal," and "healthy," certainly not something that should disqualify men from serving as role models for young Boy Scouts.[68] Moreover, Elders recommends that homosexual couples be allowed to adopt children.

In a series of stunning statements on heterosexual practices, Elders has sought to deaden Americans' instincts of traditional family values and moral responsibility. Specifically, Elders condescends to pro-lifers, barking that they should get over their "love affair with the fetus."[69] When asked by *Newsweek* whether it is immoral for people to have children out of wedlock, Elders replied, "No. Everyone has different moral standards."[70] Elders believes that sex education should start in kindergarten, and she says she tells "teenage girls often that you should never go out on a serious date without a condom in your purse."[71] Her advice to parents is to teach teenagers not only "what to do in the front seat of the car," but "what to do in the back seat" as well.[72]

"If I could be the 'condom queen,' " Elders declared with a smile on her face, "and get every young person who is engaged in sex to use a condom, I would wear a crown on my head with a condom on it. I would."[73]

Joining Elders in the government push for condom use has been HHS Secretary Donna Shalala, who officially spearheads the Clinton administration's national television and radio condom campaign, at a cost to taxpayers of $800,000 thus far. Shalala described "the great challenge of the campaign" as convincing young people "to use latex condoms . . . correctly and consistently."[74]

Although announced as an important political triumph, Clinton's condom campaign has drawn criticism from many quarters. "Is it progress that we now are able to enjoy government-sponsored sexual advice on television?" asked *U.S. News & World Report* columnist John Leo. "The whole idea of relying on Madison Avenue to change national sexual behavior is so breathtakingly naive that probably only the federal government would try it."[75]

Meanwhile, homosexual groups complained because the ads failed to advocate water-based lubricants over oil-based lubricants, apparently an important distinction concerning condom durability. Still others have criticized the ads for exaggerating the effectiveness of condoms in combatting AIDS. In fact, the campaign relies on statistics for condom effectiveness provided by two European studies, while overlooking U.S. studies that indicate higher failure rates in protection against AIDS.[76]

Another complaint of homosexual activists was that the television commercials seemed to feature mostly heterosexual couples. Not so, said Secretary Shalala during a CNN interview about the ads: "In fact," Shalala beamed, "I would suggest that if you look at the ads," which show a couple under bed sheets, "you'd have to guess whether someone was gay or straight."[77]

When the Clinton condom campaign was initiated, one of the radio spots featured rock star Anthony Kiedis, who is known for undressing on stage during performances. "I'm Anthony Kiedis of the Red Hot Chili Peppers," the singer said in the taxpayer-funded ad. "I've been naked on stage. I'm naked whenever I have sex. But now I'm on the radio. So I might as well get naked again. Now I'm naked. With a condom. Wear a condom if you're gonna have sex."[78]

Following release of the Kiedis ads it came to light that he had been convicted of sexual battery and indecent exposure in April 1990. The conviction sprang from an encounter with a female student at George Mason University, following one Kiedis's campus performances. At the end of the show, the student called to band members from outside their dressing rooms to make sure they had rides back to their hotel. When Kiedis heard the student, he emerged from his dressing room and asked her if she would perform oral sex on him. Kiedis next unzipped his pants and made a rude gesture toward the young woman with his penis.[79]

Upon learning of Kiedis's conviction, Secretary Shalala deemed him an "inappropriate" advocate of condom use, and the government cancelled his radio ad.[80] But a certain irony soon emerged over the Kiedis story . . . Bill Clinton, Americans would soon learn, had allegedly pulled a similar stunt during his days as Governor of Arkansas. The story of Bill Clinton and Paula Jones, and their encounter at Little Rock's Excelsior Hotel, came to light as part of yet another Clinton presidential scandal, putting the president's radical social campaign in a whole new perspective.

1. Jonathan Yardley, "Influence Reigns on this Parade"; *Washington Post*; January 18, 1993.
2. Sen. Daniel Patrick Moynihan (D-N.Y.), quoted in Editorial; *Washington Times*; April 29, 1993.
3. Jeffrey Tulis, quoted by Marshall Ingwerson in "Clinton Posts Renewal as Theme for Presidency"; *Christian Science Monitor*; January 22, 1993.
4. Bill Clinton, Inaugural Address; January 20, 1993.
5. *ibid.*
6. Bill Clinton, quoted by Jack Nelson in "Time for Sacrifice"; *Los Angeles Times*; January 21, 1993.
7. Jonathan Yardley, *supra* endnote 1.
8. Whoopie Goldberg, quoted by John Taylor in *New York* magazine; February 1, 1993.
9. Karen Russell, quoted by Maureen Dowd and Frank Rich in "The Inauguration"; *New York Times*; January 21, 1993.
10. k.d. lang, quoted by Karen Tumulty in "Inaugural Notebook"; *Los Angeles Times*; January 22, 1993.
11. Barbra Streisand, quoted by John McCaslin in "Inside the Beltway"; *Washington Times*; January 21, 1993.
12. Maureen Dowd and Frank Rich, *supra* endnote 9.
13. Bill Clinton, quoted by Rebecca Patterson in "MTV Ball Salutes Impact of Young"; *St. Petersburg Times*; January 21, 1993.

14. Michael Novak, quoted by Larry Witham in "Inaugural Fuels Church-State Debate"; *Washington Times*; January 19, 1993.

15. Rep. Stephen Buyer (R-Ind.), "MacNeil-Lehrer NewsHour"; January 19, 1993.

16. Michael Kelly and Maureen Dowd, "The Company He Keeps"; *New York Times*; January 17, 1993.

17. Charles Paul Freund, "Getting His Heads Together"; *Washington Post*; February 7, 1993.

18. W. John Moore, "Connections Still Count"; *National Journal*; January 8, 1994.

19. Thomas W. Lippman, "State Department Jobs Stuck in Search for Diversity"; *Washington Post*; November 22, 1993.

20. Interview with Deepwater, see Appendix A.

21. John McCaslin, "Inside the Beltway"; *Washington Times*; June 18, 1993.

22. James A. Brown, et. al., "A Familiar Look"; *National Journal*; January 2, 1993.

23. Fred Barnes, *The New Republic*, February 28, 1994.

24. Stephen Moore and David J. Byrd, "Bill Clinton: 'The Great Equivocator'; House Republican Conference; Rep. Dick Armey (R-Tex.), Chairman.

25. *ibid*.

26. *ibid*.

27. *ibid*.

28. *ibid*.

29. Zoe Baird, quoted by John Omicinski in "Does Zoe Baird Show a Clinton Double Standard?"; Gannett News Service"; January 21, 1993.

30. George Stephanopolous, quoted by John Omicinski, *supra* endnote 29.

31. Dee Dee Myers, quoted by Ruth Marcus and John Lancaster in "Inman Failed to Pay Housekeeper's Tax"; *Washington Post*; December 21, 1993.

32. Ruth Marcus and John Lancaster, *supra* endnote 31.

33. *ibid*.

34. Bruce Ingersoll, "Kennedy, Clinton's Ethics Gatekeeper, Hadn't Paid Taxes on Nanny's Wages"; *Wall Street Journal*; March 22, 1994.

35. G. Gordon Liddy, quoted by Lloyd Grove in "It Isn't Easy Being Right"; *Washington Post*; February 14, 1994.

36. Editorial, *Wall Street Journal*; June 7, 1993.
37. Thomas McLarty and Leon Panetta, "White House Travel Office: Management Review"; July 2, 1993.
38. David S. Broder, "Talk is not Enough"; *Washington Post*; July 14, 1993.
39. William Safire, "Scalpgate's Poetic Justice"; *New York Times*; May 24, 1993.
40. Michael Kelly and Maureen Dowd, "The Company He Keeps"; *New York Times;* January 17, 1993.
41. Adam Clymer, *New York Times;* October 11, 1993.
42. Christopher Hitchens; *Vanity Fair;* Sepember, 1993.
43. *Washington Post;* March 12, 1994.
44. Ann Devroy, *Washington Post;* April 3, 1993.
45. Dean Baquet, Jeff Gerth, Stephen Labaton, "Top Arkansas Lawyer Helped Hillary Clinton Turn Big Profit", *New York Times;* March 18, 1994.
46. Paul Craig Roberts, "Why Whitewatergate Remains Important"; *Washington Times;* April 11, 1994.
47. David L. Brandon, "The Mystery of Hillary's Trades"; *Wall Street Journal;* April 7, 1994.
48. Dean Baquet, Jeff Garth, Stephen Labaton, *supra* endnote 45.
49. Paul Bedard, "Hillary Pays Back Taxes on Unreported Profits"; *Washington Times;* April 12, 1994.
50. Stephen Moore and David J. Byrd, *supra* endnote 24.
51. Bill Clinton, quoted by Steve Daley in "Clinton's Retreat Latest Broken Vow"; *Chicago Tribune*; July 21, 1993.
52. Stephen Moore and David J. Byrd, *supra* endnote 24.
53. Tommi Avicolli Mecca, *Between Little Rock and a Hard Place*; Williams; Portland, Oregon; 1993; page 59.
54. ibid.
55. Ronald Browstein, *Los Angeles Times*, quoted in Tommi Avicolli Mecca, *supra* endnote 53.
56. Peter Freiberg, "Gays Now Part of Governing Coalition"; *Washington Blade*; November 6, 1992.
57. Arthur J. Corbett, "Disband the Corps"; *Marine Corps Gazette*; January 1993; pages 22-23.
58. Chaplain (Brig. Gen.) Jim Hutchens, U.S. Army National Guard, Ret., in testimony before the House Republican Research Committee; March 24, 1993.

59. Gen. Colin Powell, then-chairman, Joint Chiefs of Staff, in letter to Rep. Patricia Schroeder (D-Colo.).

60. Gen. H. Norman Schwarzkopf, U.S. Army, Ret.; in testimony before the Senate Armed Services Committee; May 11, 1993.

61. Bill Clinton, quoted by Reuter; *Washington Post*; July 20, 1993.

62. Bill Clinton, quoted by Ann Devroy in "President Opens Military to Gays"; *Washington Post*; July 20, 1993.

63. Steve Daley, *supra* endnote 51.

64. Kristine Gebbie, quoted by Frank Murray; *Washington Times*; October 22, 1993.

65. Joyce Price, "Strident Activism Steps on Toes"; *Washington Times*; May 24, 1993.

66. Roberta Achtenberg, quoted by Joyce Price, *supra* endnote 65.

67. Roberta Achtenberg, quoted by Patrick J. Buchanan in "Senate Ducks the Achtenberg Challenge"; *Courier-Journal*; June 2, 1993.

68. Joycelyn Elders, quoted by Joyce Price in "Elders Calls Gay Sex 'Wonderful' "; *Washington Times*; March 19, 1994.

69. Brian Robertson, "Clinton Crosscurrents Cloud Social Policies"; *Insight*; January 31, 1994; page 18.

70. Joycelyn Elders, quoted by Joe Klein in "The Out-of-Wedlock Question"; *Newsweek*; December 13, 1993.

71. Joycelyn Elders, quoted on the Carrie Gordon Report; Family News in Focus Radio; February 21, 1994.

72. Dr. Paul Reisser's Commentary; Family News in Focus Radio; April 13, 1994.

73. Joycelyn Elders, quoted in *Chicago Tribune*; February 15, 1994.

74. Donna Shalala, in interview with Judy Woodruff; CNN News; January 4, 1994.

75. John Leo, "Condom Campaign Promotes Promiscuity Problem"; *Washington Times*; January 12, 1994.

76. Joyce Price, "How Safe are They?"; *Washington Times*; January 28, 1994.

77. Donna Shalala, *supra* endnote 74.

78. Anthony Kiedis, quoted by Philip J. Hilts in "Narrator's Sex Charge Sinks Condom Ad"; *New York Times*; January 8, 1994.

79. Joyce Price, "Red-hot Officials Pull Condom Ad"; *Washington Times*; January 8, 1994.

80. Philip J. Hilts, *supra* endnote 78.

"FORNIGATE"

"When I see him now, President of the United States, meeting world leaders, I cannot believe it . . . I still have this picture of him wearing my black nightgown."[1]

—Sally Perdue, former "Miss Arkansas," with whom Bill Clinton allegedly had an affair.

"It was common practice that he [Bill Clinton] would see someone in a crowd, someone he was sexually attracted to. He would say 'God, she's got big t*ts. Find out who she is; find out if she's married.' He'd do things like that."[2]

—Arkansas state trooper Roger Perry, who worked on Governor Clinton's security detail for five years

When Bill Clinton ran for president in 1992, rumors swirled about his womanizing. His own staff complained about "bimbo eruptions" after nightclub singer Gennifer Flowers admitted her affair with Clinton: "I was Bill Clinton's lover for 12 years, and for the past two years I have lied to the press about our relationship to protect him . . . Well, I'm sick of all the deceit, and I'm sick of all the lies."[3] Flowers backed up her allegations with audio tapes of telephone conversations between her and Bill Clinton. These tapes captured Bill Clinton worrying that he would be "blown out of the water" because of their affair; he reassured Flowers that no one could prove anything "if they don't have pictures."[4] In another taped conversation, Flowers reported that her apartment had been broken into. Clinton asked, "Do you think they were trying to look for something on us?"[5]*

When the Flowers allegations jeopardized Clinton's candidacy, his campaign went on red alert. Jack Palladino, a San Francisco private investigator, was hired to put a lid on women's stories of their encounters with Clinton. Records show the Clinton campaign paid Palladino $93,000.[6]

Having assembled an expert damage control team, Bill Clinton sought to convince the public of his worth as husband and father. The turning point came during a CBS "60 Minutes" interview, when Bill Clinton said that although he had "caused pain" in his marriage, he and his wife still loved each other. He denounced Gennifer Flowers's stories as "false" and he left the impression that while he may have committed some minor indiscretions in his past, they were exaggerated. He claimed that he and Hillary Rodham Clinton had a loving and enduring marriage and the American voters seemed to believe him.[7]

But important facts have emerged since Bill Clinton's election that corroborate Gennifer Flowers's story and indicate she was only one of many Clinton paramours. Much of the new information comes from the testimonies of Arkansas state troopers who worked in Governor Clinton's security detail. In addition, other women have come

*For a full transcript of the Bill Clinton-Gennifer Flowers telephone conversations, see "SLICK WILLIE": *Why America Cannot Trust Bill Clinton*; 1992.

forward with stories of affairs and sexual harassment. Clinton's wild promiscuity, moreover, was just part of the scandal. Credible charges have surfaced that Bill Clinton used Arkansas state troopers and state vehicles, and the influence of his office, to facilitate his sexual affairs. State troopers further allege that Bill Clinton, while president, tried to orchestrate an illegal cover-up of these stories.

The mainstream media balked at the lurid accounts of Bill Clinton's private life. One White House aide moaned, "Not this [expletive] all over again."[8] But the Bill Clinton sex scandal *has* surfaced all over again—this time, with more detail and more corroboration than before. Some in the media have aptly named the scandal "Fornigate."

THE TROOPERS SPEAK OUT

During the presidential campaign, attention focused briefly on the Arkansas state troopers who provided Governor Clinton's security. Surely if Clinton were leading a wild double life, everyone reasoned, the troopers would know about it. But the troopers wouldn't talk, so the issue died. Clinton became president.

Then, in December 1993, four Arkansas state troopers dropped a bombshell: the rumors of Bill Clinton's extraordinary extramarital behavior were true. "The bottom line," said trooper Larry Patterson, "is that the American people have a right to know the man that is the seated president—the leader of the free world—to know what kind of man he really is."[9]

Investigative journalist David Brock broke the troopers' stories in the *American Spectator* magazine.* Reporters

---

*During the period in which David Brock researched his story, offices of the *American Spectator* were burglarized three times. The magazine's Arlington, Virginia, office was burglarized twice, and an apartment the magazine maintains

William C. Rempel and Douglas Frantz of the *Los Angeles Times* also met extensively with the troopers and secured signed affidavits from two of them before publishing stories containing their allegations.

David Brock conducted more than thirty hours of interviews with the four troopers in August, September, and October 1993. Brock interviewed the troopers on tape, separately and in groups, to test for any inconsistencies in their stories. Two of the troopers, Larry Patterson and Roger Perry, spoke on the record. Patterson had served on governor's security detail from 1987 to 1993, and Perry served from 1977 to 1979 and then again from 1989 until December 1993. Bill Clinton was Governor of Arkansas for most of the time Patterson and Perry worked in governor's security.* The other two troopers, Danny Ferguson and Ronnie Anderson, spoke off the record, but confirmed Patterson and Perry's reports.

The state troopers told of Bill Clinton's sexual liaisons while he was Governor of Arkansas and President-elect of the United States. They also revealed that Bill Clinton used them and state vehicles to arrange his sexual encounters. And, perhaps most significantly, they reported Bill Clinton's attempts from the White House to manipulate their stories by offering them federal jobs.

When asked why they waited so long before going public

---

in New York City was rifled through once. The Virginia burglaries were quite sophisticated; the thieves cut holes through the walls of other office suites to break into the *American Spectator* office. The thieves took few valuables, and the magazine's expensive computers were untouched, but office files were searched. The *American Spectator* has been in existence since 1968. Its offices had never been burglarized previously.[10]

*See Appendix B for an interview with Arkansas troopers Larry Patterson and Roger Perry.

with their information, the troopers responded that during the 1992 presidential campaign, they never imagined Bill Clinton would actually win the election. They thought he would lose and remain Governor of Arkansas—that is, their boss. In addition, as detailed below, the troopers had veiled and direct threats not to mention Clinton's dark side. They struggled for months before finally deciding to speak out publicly.

First among the stories corroborated by the troopers was Bill Clinton's longtime affair with Gennifer Flowers. Larry Patterson said he had driven then-Governor Clinton to Gennifer Flowers's condominium on several occasions and waited while Clinton went inside for anywhere from 40 minutes to two and one-half hours. He also charged that Governor Clinton used his influence to have Flowers hired as an administrative assistant for the Arkansas Board of Review, which handles state unemployment compensation cases.[11]

Larry Patterson told the *Los Angeles Times* that he was driving Governor Clinton in 1991 when Clinton called Bill Gaddy, Director of the Arkansas Employment Security Department, to ask Gaddy for help getting Gennifer Flowers a job. Gaddy has denied receiving such a call, but did admit making a favorable recommendation that helped Flowers secure her state job. An Arkansas state grievance panel has ruled that Flowers's hiring was improper, since, among other things, she ranked ninth out of 11 candidates who took a merit test for the position.[12]

Roger Perry, for his part, said that Bill Clinton talked to him about Gennifer Flowers in a way that suggested Clinton was sexually involved with her. Perry said Clinton once joked that Flowers could "suck a tennis ball through a garden hose."[13]

GOVERNOR ON THE LOOSE

According to the Arkansas troopers, Gennifer Flowers was just one of many women with whom Bill Clinton had ongoing, often simultaneous affairs. David Brock reported that these women included "a staffer in Clinton's office; an Arkansas lawyer Clinton appointed to a judgeship; the wife of a prominent judge; a local reporter; an employee at Arkansas Power and Light, a state-regulated public utility; and a cosmetics sales clerk at a Little Rock department store."[14]

The troopers claimed that many of Governor Clinton's trysts occurred in late-night hours. They said that Clinton would wait until Hillary Rodham Clinton had fallen asleep before sneaking out of the Governor's Mansion. He would then borrow one of the troopers' unmarked police cars, "we were told to keep our cars clean for this purpose" Perry said,[15] and instruct the security personnel on duty to call him on his cellular telephone if any lights went on in the mansion.

Perry recalled that one time, when Hillary Rodham Clinton woke in the middle of the night and found her husband gone, she called down to the guard house and was told that he was on a late-night drive. "That sorry d*mn s*n of a b*tch!" she screamed. Perry quickly located Governor Clinton at the home of another woman and reported that Rodham Clinton was awake and angry. According to Perry, Bill Clinton cried, "Oh god, god, god. What did you tell her?"[16]

"When Clinton arrived soon after," Brock reported, "Hillary was waiting in the kitchen, where, not unexpectedly, a wild screaming match ensued. When Perry entered the kitchen after the dust had settled, the room was a wreck, with a cabinet door kicked off its hinges."[17]

In addition to his late-night forays, Governor Clinton

would sometimes invite women into the basement of the Governor's Mansion in the early morning, or arrange to meet them on his morning jogs. Roger Perry reported that on mornings when Clinton met women during his "jogs," he would visit the troopers' bathroom upon his return and drench himself with water to make it seem like he was sweating.

Patterson reported that Governor Clinton sometimes met one particular woman in an elementary school parking lot. While Patterson was standing guard during one of their late-night rendezvous, a Little Rock police car approached, apparently suspecting trouble in the school parking lot. Patterson said he flashed his I.D. and told the Little Rock officer that everything was okay.[18]

Another time, when Patterson was driving Governor Clinton to a Harrison County Chamber of Commerce reception in a Little Rock hotel, Clinton asked him to make a detour into the school parking lot to meet the same woman. Patterson said, "I could see Clinton get into the front seat and then the lady's head go into his lap. They stayed in the car for 30 to 40 minutes."[19]

Patterson also reported that he witnessed the same woman and Bill Clinton engage in a sex act in a pickup truck outside the Governor's Mansion. Patterson said he witnessed this encounter through one of security's remote-controlled surveillance cameras: "I pointed it [the camera] right at the truck," Patterson explained. Patterson watched the encounter on a 27-inch video screen.[20]

Los Angeles Times reporters tracked down records of some of the telephone calls Bill Clinton made on his official cellular line between 1989 and 1990. These records show that Clinton made 59 telephone calls to one of the women identified by troopers Patterson and Perry as a regular paramour, including 11 calls to her on July 16,

1989. In August 1989, while on a trip to Charlottesville, Virginia, Clinton called this woman at 1:23 a.m. for 94 minutes; the next morning, he called the same number at 7:45 a.m. for 18 minutes.[21]

Other than this discovery by the *Los Angeles Times*, reporters have been unable to find Bill Clinton's telephone records from his years as governor. Trooper Perry suspects that many records were removed during the 1992 campaign: "We had kept records of anybody that came in and out of the grounds, and all phone calls . . . There were boxes of these records, 4 or 5 boxes, and they were taken down to the old maintenance house. Well, after we got started talking about going forward with the allegations, Ronnie Anderson was curious about those phone records and he went down to the maintenance house. They were gone."[22]

In addition to his ongoing affairs with several women, Bill Clinton, according to the troopers, had many one-time sexual encounters, usually with women he picked up at receptions. In fact, Clinton often used the troopers to send messages to women he wished to proposition.

Clinton also ordered the troopers to pick up gifts for his various girlfriends at women's stores such as Victoria's Secret and Barbara Jean (a Little Rock women's clothing store). Roger Perry told David Brock that Clinton "told us to make sure they [the presents] were kept in the trunk of the cars and never bring them into the house where Hillary might see them."[23]

According to the troopers, Governor Clinton would even ask them to make arrangements with hotels to open a room for him, under the pretext that he needed a private place to accept an important phone call from the White House. Instead, the Governor would use the rooms to meet with women.

Hillary Rodham Clinton knew of her husband's rampant promiscuity, said the troopers. Larry Patterson says that while on duty at the guard house, he heard Rodham Clinton complaining that her husband gave all his attention to other women. "I need to be f****d more than twice a year!" Patterson said she shouted at the Governor.[24]

Finally, the troopers said that Bill Clinton did not end his adulterous behavior when he became a presidential candidate, or even when he was President-elect. When asked if they knew whether Bill Clinton continued his affairs after his 1992 "60 Minutes" interview, Patterson and Perry laughed at the question. Perry related an episode that occurred at approximately 4:45 a.m. at the Governor's Mansion the very day President-elect Clinton left Little Rock for Washington: "He snuck a woman by Secret Service, took her to the basement, [and] made a trooper go stand on the top of the stairs between the basement and the main level of the house. . . . He had sex with this woman in the basement while the trooper was standing in the stairway, then snuck her back by Secret Service." Perry said he learned of this incident from trooper Danny Ferguson, who had arranged the woman's entry into the mansion and had stood guard on the stairs.[25]

The troopers also reported that Hillary Rodham Clinton had an affair with Vincent Foster, her fellow Rose Law Firm partner who became Deputy White House Counsel and died in July 1993. "It was common knowledge around the mansion that Hillary and Vince were having an affair," Larry Patterson told David Brock.[26] The troopers said they drove Vincent Foster and Hillary Rodham Clinton to the Rose Law Firm's rustic mountain cabin in Heber Springs, Arkansas. They also reported that whenever Bill Clinton left town, Foster came to the Governor's Mansion.

THE ATTEMPTED COVER-UP

When rumors starting circulating about Gennifer Flowers during Bill Clinton's presidential campaign, he instructed her to deny the charges: "If they [the media] ever hit you with it just say 'no' and go on, there's nothing they can do."[27]

Larry Patterson reports that when Gennifer Flowers made public her affair with Bill Clinton in 1992, Clinton was furious. "What does that whore think she's doing to me?" the governor fumed.[28] Patterson said that his boss, Raymond L. "Buddy" Young, who was the chief of security for Governor Clinton, was asked to make sure that no other women came forward. "Buddy Young specifically told me that he was trying to keep a lid on the other women," Patterson told Brock. "If one more came out, they knew Gennifer would be credible." Young also kept an eye on troopers in the security detail: "If you're smart," he told them, "you won't talk to the press."[29]

Because his operatives were able to "keep a lid" on the tales of his sexual exploits in 1992, Bill Clinton won the presidency, and Buddy Young wound up as head of a regional office of the Federal Emergency Management Agency in Texas—a position that pays $92,300 a year.

All was quiet on the "bimbo" front until the summer of 1993, when the four Arkansas state troopers initiated plans to make their stories public. Upon learning of the troopers' plans from President Clinton himself, Buddy Young swung back into action. Trooper Roger Perry reported that Young called him and said, "I represent the President of the United States. Why do you want to destroy him over this?" Young added, "This is not a threat, but I wanted you to know that your own actions could bring about dire consequences."[30]

Larry Patterson, for his part, received a note, along

with an article, from Buddy Young expressing concern about Patterson's health—a note he interpreted as a threat to his well-being. Patterson said the article was about artery clogging, and was accompanied by Young's home phone number. "I would love to visit with you," Young wrote at the bottom of the note, according to Patterson.[31]

Young confirmed to the *Los Angeles Times* that he called three of the troopers after President Clinton relayed his concern that the troopers were going to reveal what they knew.[32] Young also said he met personally with President Clinton in Washington and verified that the troopers were going to tell their stories to the press. Young also reported to President Clinton that one trooper, Danny Ferguson, was considering withholding any public statements.

Following the Buddy Young briefing, President Clinton called Danny Ferguson. According to Roger Perry, with whom Ferguson discussed this phone conversation, President Clinton offered Ferguson a federal job and told Ferguson that Perry could have one too.[33] Ferguson told Perry that President Clinton promised, "Roger can have whatever he wants." According to Perry, Clinton told Ferguson: "If you tell me what stories Roger [Perry] and Larry [Patterson] are telling, I can go in the back door and handle it and clean it up."[34]

President Clinton admits calling Ferguson, but denies offering the troopers federal jobs.

PRESIDENT CLINTON RESPONDS TO "FORNIGATE"

When the *American Spectator* and the *Los Angeles Times* published their stories, President Clinton did not say the stories were untrue. He only denied the offer of a federal job in return for Danny Ferguson's silence.

In a press conference on December 22, 1993, Peter

Maer, a reporter for Mutual-NBC Radio, asked President Clinton, "So none of this ever happened?" President Clinton stammered: "I have nothing else to say. We, we did, if, the, the, I, I, the stories are just as they have been said. They're outrageous and they're not so."[35]

When asked by news reporters "to deny the sexual misconduct charges in simple, straightforward language," President Clinton refused to do so: "Well, I think we have cleared it up. I've told you that, you know, I just think the statement speaks for itself and I think what I have said today on the points that you've raised perhaps reinforces it and that's fine with me. I just think it is not appropriate in a situation like this for me to do much more than I am doing. What I need to do is just keep working at my job and keep going on. Apparently, in the world we live in, things like this happen."[36]

While the Clintons sought to defuse the situation in Washington, Betsey Wright, the former Clinton aide who ran damage control for the 1992 campaign, flew to Little Rock and confronted trooper Danny Ferguson. According to an anonymous source quoted by the *Los Angeles Times,* Wright found trooper Ferguson on duty at the Governor's Mansion within days of publication of the *American Spectator* story. The *Times* source said Wright showed Ferguson a copy of David Brock's article and told him, "Don't worry about this infidelity stuff. We can handle that. But this [the part where Ferguson alleged President Clinton made job offers] could get the man impeached."[37]

Although trooper Ferguson initially refused Betsey Wright's requests publicly to recant his off-the-record statements to reporters, he finally agreed to have his lawyer, Robert Batton, issue an affidavit modifying his accusation that President Clinton offered the troopers federal jobs in return for silence. Batton's affidavit read, in part: "My client [Danny Ferguson] does not wish to converse with any member of the media and, therefore, has authorized me to say on his behalf that President Clinton never offered or indicated a willingness to offer any trooper a job in exchange for silence or help in shaping their stories."[38]

While this statement appears authoritative, it is in fact meaningless. Danny Ferguson did not sign the statement and therefore *he* swore to nothing. And Robert Batton only swore that Danny Ferguson had told him a single, specific statement. This convoluted stratagem ensured that Danny Ferguson could appear to deny Perry's story while doing no such thing. In fact, Ferguson confirmed his original story to the *Los Angeles Times* after Batton had released the affidavit. Trooper Ferguson told the *Times* only that President Clinton "didn't say those words [the exact words in the affidavit]."[39]

Arkansas attorney Timothy F. Watson, Jr., wrote to the *Wall Street Journal* that President Clinton "has engaged in trickery and deception in the matter of the affidavit of Danny Ferguson. Bill Clinton is not known as Slick Willie for nothing. The 'affidavit' is a farce, and was evidently executed for the sole purpose of deceiving the public and the press."[40]

MORE WITNESSES COME FORWARD

Testimony regarding Bill Clinton's sexual exploits mounted in the wake of the revelations by the Arkansas state troopers. Sally Perdue, a former "Miss Arkansas" who had first come forward with her story during the presidential campaign, only to be ignored by the mainstream media, revealed more information about her affair with Bill Clinton—and about threats she had received during the 1992 campaign.

In a front-page story in the *Sunday Telegraph*, a leading British newspaper, Perdue recounted her affair with Bill Clinton between August and December 1983, stating that on at least a dozen occasions official vehicles brought him to her house for trysts. The cars, according to Perdue, would "pull up in a wooded area about 30 feet from the house and wait there. When Bill was ready to come out, he would signal using my patio light, flicking it on and off."[41]

Bill Clinton "had this little boy quality that I found very attractive," Perdue told the *Telegraph*. "I was going through a second divorce at the time; I was vulnerable . . . When I see him now, President of the United States, meeting world leaders, I can't believe it . . . I still have this picture of him wearing my black nightgown, playing the sax badly; this guy, tiptoeing across the park and getting caught on the fence."[42] Perdue has also reported that Clinton smoked marijuana when he visited her apartment. "He said it enhanced his sexual pleasure," said Perdue.[43]

Perdue contended she, too, was offered a federal job in return for silence. After appearing on the "Sally Jessy Raphael" show in July 1992, she said she was approached by a man named Ron Tucker, who said he represented the Democratic party. According to Perdue, Tucker said that there were "people in high places who were anxious about me and they wanted to know about me and they wanted me to know that keeping my mouth shut would be worthwhile . . . If I was a good little girl, and didn't kill the messenger, I'd be set for life: a federal job, nothing fancy, but a regular paycheck, level 11 or 12 [about $60,000 a year]. I'd never have to worry again." Perdue said that Tucker then threatened that "they" knew Perdue jogged by herself, and that he "couldn't guarantee what would happen to [her] pretty little legs."[44]

Perdue declined Tucker's federal job offer and one of her work colleagues who overheard the conversation reported the incident to the FBI. The FBI won't comment on what they call their "on-going investigation," but Perdue's story has additional corroboration. "Ron Tucker told me that somebody from the Democratic party in St. Louis had asked him through a friend to get to this woman and get her to shut up," said John Newcomb, Tucker's former employer.[45]

Shortly after her encounter with Ron Tucker, Perdue was fired from her job as a clerk in the admissions office of Lindenwood College, a small private school near St. Louis. Even worse, Perdue found a shotgun shell on the front seat of her Jeep and the car's back window shattered. She also received a threatening note that read, "I'll pray you have a head-on collision and end up in a coma . . . Marilyn Monroe got snuffed. It could happen."[46]

Perdue told British reporter Ambrose Evans-Pritchard that she wanted to tell her story to the American media after the Arkansas state troopers came forward. But she said, "I've had it with the American press. I think it's going to take a foreign paper to bring this whole thing out, because the powers here are so strong."[47]

Perdue confirmed the troopers' stories and said Larry Patterson was one of the troopers who drove Governor Clinton to her townhouse. "One evening when Bill came over to my place," Perdue said, "I was anticipating the visit, looking out my back window to where his car would drop him off and wait for him. I saw the car approach and stop just 50 feet from my door. The interior light of the car came on and I saw a man in the front seat. Not until I saw pictures of Mr. Patterson on TV did I know who he was."[48]

Another witness went public in February 1994 to tell of Bill Clinton's sexual advances.* Paula Jones came forward because the *American Spectator* article on the troopers reported that she and Bill Clinton had met in a hotel room in 1991. Jones wanted to correct the implication that she had been sexually involved with Clinton. Jones (then Paula Corbin) claimed that on May 8, 1991, she was working at a registration booth for the Arkansas Industrial Development Commission (AIDC) at the Excelsior Hotel in Little Rock when state trooper Danny Ferguson approached her and asked her to go upstairs to meet with then Governor Clinton. Jones, who was in her mid-20s at the time, explained she was surprised that the Governor wanted to meet with her because she had only been working for the state of Arkansas for two months. But, being curious, she went up to the room.

After she arrived, Jones said, Clinton asked her to perform oral sex on him. "He took my hand," she said, and "he was loosening his tie."[49] Jones reported that Clinton touched her leg and told her, "You have nice curves, I love the way your hair goes down your body."[50] Jones said that she rebuffed the Governor's advances and left the room approximately 15 minutes after arriving.[51]

Trooper Danny Ferguson confirmed to the *Los Angeles Times* that it was he who escorted Paula Jones to the hotel room where Clinton waited on May 8, 1991. Ferguson further reported that Clinton instructed him to arrange with hotel management to open a room for the Governor,

*See Appendix C for Paula Jones's affidavit.

under the pretense that he needed a place to take an important call from the White House.[52]

Jones, who was engaged at the time, said she found the experience in the hotel room "humiliating."[53]

In addition to Danny Ferguson's corroboration of these events, two other individuals have testified to the truth of Paula Jones's story. Pamela Blackard was Jones's co-worker at the AIDC; they manned the booth together at the Excelsior Hotel on May 8, 1991. Blackard has issued a sworn statement that trooper Ferguson approached Jones at the booth and asked her to meet Governor Clinton in a room upstairs.* Blackard said she agreed to tend the booth while Jones went to Clinton's room. Blackard further stated that Jones returned to the booth approximately 15 to 20 minutes later and told her that Clinton had made unwelcome sexual advances.[54]

A friend of Paula Jones, Debra Ballantine, also issued a sworn statement concerning Jones's experience. Ballantine said that she met Jones in the late afternoon of May 8, 1991, and that Jones at that time recounted her story of being approached by trooper Ferguson and sexually harassed by Bill Clinton. Ballantine said Jones told her that Clinton made three unwelcome sexual advances towards her.[55]

On May 6, 1994, Paula Jones filed suit against Bill Clinton, alleging her civil rights had been violated and that she had suffered emotional distress. "This case is about the powerful taking advantage of the weak," Jones said.[56] Jones's lawsuit added details to her earlier accounts, specifically that she could identify "distinguishing character-

---

*See Appendix D for Pamela Blackard's affidavit.

istics in Clinton's genital area." Jones said that when she was in the hotel room with Clinton, he "lowered his trousers and underwear, exposing his erect penis, and asked Jones to 'kiss it.' " Jones said that as she left the room in disgust, Clinton said, "You are smart. Let's keep this between ourselves."[57]

When asked for comment on the Jones lawsuit, President Clinton said, "I'm not going to dignify this by a comment . . . I'm going back to work."[58]

Yet another witness came forward after Paula Jones made her revelations. State trooper L.D. Brown, who served on then-Governor Clinton's security detail from 1982 to 1985, told his story to the *American Spectator* in spring 1994. Brown's revelations were especially damaging because he had been so close to Clinton. Brown frequently traveled with Governor Clinton, and Brown's wife had worked as Chelsea Clinton's nanny.

Trooper Brown reported that he had solicited women for Clinton more than one hundred times and that he drove Clinton to meet women on state time, in state vehicles. He corroborated the stories of Gennifer Flowers, Sally Perdue, Larry Patterson, and Roger Perry. Brown admitted that he often pursued women with Clinton, and that they graded women on a scale of 1 to 10.[59]

Brown recalled several incidents to *Spectator* reporter Daniel Wattenberg. Once, for example, while visiting a Boca Raton disco, Brown says that Clinton pointed to a woman and said, "Go ask that one if she wants to dance with the Governor of Arkansas." Brown said that they not only danced, but that he had to follow Clinton when Clinton left the disco with the woman in her car. "We drive up the road and they pull off," for a sexual encounter, Brown recalled.[60]

Brown also reported that Hillary Rodham Clinton had

an affair with Vincent Foster. "Bill knew what was going on between Hillary and Vince," he said.[61]

BILL CLINTON AS MORAL LEADER

"This is not about sex," explained attorney Cliff Jackson in the wake of statements made by his clients, Patterson and Perry. "It's about the exploitation of people, including women and state personnel."[62]

For some Americans, this *is* about sex. Many voters would oppose having the country's highest office occupied by an individual who practices the kind of uncontrolled promiscuity and adultery that has come to light in the allegations about Bill Clinton.

This is certainly about exploitation: what do Bill Clinton's reckless conquests say about his regard for the women and the troopers he used? Further, what does Clinton's abuse of his state office, the state troopers, and the state vehicles say about his respect for the law? What does the "Fornigate" scandal say about Bill Clinton's honesty? Bill Clinton lied to Americans on national television when he said in his "60 Minutes" interview that Gennifer Flowers's allegations were "false." And he disingenuously implied that his marriage to Hillary Rodham Clinton was one of love and trust and fidelity.

And what does the "Fornigate" scandal say about Bill Clinton's credibility and his sense of responsibility and judgment? Lecturing junior high schoolers in the wake of the trooper revelations, President Clinton said sex "is not a sport," but "a solemn responsibility."[63] Is Bill Clinton qualified to give this advice to America's young people? Was it responsible for Bill Clinton to have sex in cars in elementary school parking lots? Or to sneak women into the Governor's Mansion, including one on the day he was preparing to travel to Washington to take his oath as President of the United States? *Detroit News* columnist Tony Snow offered this bit of homespun wisdom: "When people elect a president, they not only want a person who promotes good policies, but also someone on whom they can depend. They like to think they're electing a Lincolnesque figure—and not a Caligula of the Ozarks. Without trust, our democracy collapses."[64]

1. Ambrose Evans-Pritchard, "I Was Threatened After Clinton affair"; *Sunday Telegraph*; January 23, 1994.
2. Interview with Larry Patterson and Roger Perry; February 12, 1994.
3. Gennifer Flowers's recorded conversation with Bill Clinton, published in Floyd Brown's "SLICK WILLIE": *Why America Cannot Trust Bill Clinton*; Annapolis-Washington Book Publisher; 1992; page 149.
4. *ibid.*, pages 152-153.
5. *ibid.*, page 157.
6. Michael Isikoff, "Back Doing The Wright Stuff For the President"; *Washington Post*; December 25, 1993.
7. CBS "60 Minutes"; January 26, 1992.
8. Ben Wattenberg, *Washington Times*; December 23, 1993.
9. Patterson/Perry interview, *supra* endnote 2.
10. Stephen Robinson, "Burglaries At Magazine in Clinton Affair"; *Daily Telegraph*; December 24, 1993.
11. Patterson/Perry interview, *supra* endnote 2.
12. William C. Rempel and Douglas Frantz, "Troopers Say Clinton Sought Silence"; *Los Angeles Times*; December 21, 1993.
13. David Brock, "Living With the Clintons"; *American Spectator*; January, 1994; page 29.
14. *ibid.*, page 26.
15. *ibid.*
16. *ibid.*, page 28.
17. *ibid.*
18. Rempel and Frantz, *supra* endnote 12.
19. Brock, *supra* endnote 13, page 27.
20. Patterson/Perry interview, *supra* endnote 2.

21. Rempel and Frantz, *supra* endnote 12.
22. Patterson/Perry interview, *supra* endnote 2.
23. Brock, *supra* endnote 13, page 27.
24. *ibid.*, page 28.
25. Patterson/Perry interview, *supra* endnote 2.
26. Brock, *supra* endnote 13, page 28.
27. Gennifer Flowers's recorded conversations with Bill Clinton, *supra* endnote 3.
28. Brock, *supra* endnote 13, page 30.
29. *ibid.*, pages 29-30.
30. *ibid.*, page 22.
31. Patterson/Perry interview, *supra* endnote 2.
32. Rempel and Frantz, *supra* endnote 12.
33. *ibid.*
34. Brock, *supra* endnote 13, page 22.
35. Bill Clinton, quoted in Editorial, *Washington Times*; January 10, 1994.
36. Bill Clinton, quoted by William C. Rempel and Douglas Frantz, "Did Nothing Wrong, Clinton Says"; *Los Angeles Times*; December 23, 1993.
37. William C. Rempel and Douglas Frantz, "Little Rock A Battleground of Credibility"; *Los Angeles Times*; December 26, 1993.
38. Affidavit of Robert Batton, undated.
39. Rempel and Frantz, *supra* endnote 37.
40. Letters to the Editor, *Wall Street Journal*; January 11, 1994.
41. Evans-Pritchard, *supra* endnote 1.
42. *ibid.*
43. Daniel Wattenberg, "Love and Hate in Arkansas"; *American Spectator*; April/May, 1994.
44. Evans-Pritchard, *supra* endnote 1.
45. *ibid.*
46. *ibid.*
47. *ibid.*
48. Floyd G. Brown, *ClintonWatch*; February 1994.
49. Reuters News Service; "Woman Makes Allegations Against Clinton"; February 11, 1994.
50. Michael Hedges, "Woman Accuses Clinton of Sexual Advances in '91"; *Washington Times*; February 12, 1994.
51. Affidavit of Paula Jones; February 7, 1994.

52. Robert Shogan, "Ex-Arkansas State Worker Says Clinton Harassed Her"; *Los Angeles Times*; February 12, 1994.
53. Hedges, *supra* endnote 50.
54. Affidavit of Pamela Blackard; February 7, 1994.
55. Affidavit of Debra Ballantine; February 7, 1994.
56. Michael Hedges, "Sexual Harassment Suit Filed against President"; *Washington Times*; May 7, 1994.
57. ibid.
58. John Aloysius Farrell, "Clinton Is Sued; Assault Alleged"; *Boston Globe*; May 7, 1994.
59. Daniel Wattenberg, *supra* endnote 43.
60. *ibid.*
61. *ibid.*
62. Laura Blumenfeld, "Bill Clinton's Worst Friend"; *Washington Post*; December 30, 1993.
63. "Sex is Not a Sport," *Chicago Sun-Times*; February 4, 1994.
64. Tony Snow, "Judging Clinton's Honor"; *Washington Times*; January 3, 1994.

NOTES ON THE
"DECADE OF GREED"

"For twelve years, the Republicans have raised taxes on the middle class. It's time to give the middle class tax relief."[1]

>   —Bill Clinton
>   Announcement Speech
>   October 3, 1991

"I have news for the forces of greed and the defenders of the status quo: your time has come—and gone. It's time for a change in America."[2]

>   —Bill Clinton
>   "A New Covenant"
>   July 16, 1992

"There's almost no enthusiasm [for middle-class tax cuts] now compared to what existed last year in New Hampshire . . . I don't think there's anybody now that thinks it's a very good way of getting the economy up."[3]

>   —President-elect Bill Clinton

As part of his 1992 campaign effort to define himself as a "new Democrat," Bill Clinton repeatedly promised voters a middle-class tax cut. "I believe you deserve more than 30-second ads or vague promises," Clinton said in his first campaign advertisement. "That's why I offered a comprehensive plan to get our economy moving again . . . it starts with a tax cut for the middle class and asks the rich to pay their fair share again."[4] In his book *Putting People First*, Clinton wrote, "We will lower the tax burden on middle-class Americans."[5]

Bill Clinton predicated his attack against Presidents Reagan and Bush, and his call for "change," on the notion that the 1980s were America's "Decade of Greed." In a Democratic presidential debate during the primaries, Clinton thundered that he "fail[ed] to see what is courageous about telling people who have already been plundered in the 1980s that they should not get a tax cut, while rolling over for those 'at the top of the totem pole' who made a killing in the 80s."[6] Continuing this bold misstatement of history, Clinton told an audience at his alma mater, Georgetown University, that "Ronald Reagan and George Bush pushed through programs that raised taxes on the middle class. I think it's time to cut them. And in my administration, I will offer middle income tax cuts that will cut rates on the middle class . . . and I won't finance it with increasing the deficit."[7]

As they say in film production: "Cut!"

HISTORICAL REMINDERS

Two things need to be clarified before considering the specifics of President Clinton's economic proposals. First, Clinton's own economic record as governor of Arkansas: in 1980, a 33-year-old Governor Clinton shocked Arkansas voters by pushing their state tax burden to nearly $1 billion. Voters dubbed him "Billion-Dollar Bill," and voted him out of office. But when Clinton recaptured the governorship in 1982, he was back raising taxes: he raised the sales tax; he doubled the gasoline tax;

and he levied taxes on used cars, mobile homes, and property renters. The Clinton taxes hit middle and lower-class Arkansans hardest; and with the average family of four paying an extra $1,500 by 1990, Clinton even abandoned his campaign promise to remove the sales tax on *food*.[8]*

Second, Bill Clinton claimed that the 1980s were a time in America when "the rich" benefited at the expense of "the poor." Throughout his presidential campaign, Clinton and his spokesmen cleverly employed this class-baiting scheme. The slogan "It's the economy, stupid!" reflected the campaign's strategy to breed class-based resentment among voters. "[George Bush] has *raised* taxes on the people driving pickup trucks, and *lowered* taxes on people riding in limousines," Clinton claimed.[9]

Those who criticize the 1980s as the "Decade of Greed" contend that during the Republican reign "the rich got richer and the poor got poorer." Big tax cuts for the rich were pushed through Congress, they say, in a program of "trickle-down" economics, in which the poor got a few dribbles of money as the rich spent their ill-gotten gains on high living and useless luxuries. In sum, the complaint goes, the Reagan tax cuts were reckless and resulted in ballooning deficits that became the nation's biggest problem.

This caricature of the 1980s became a staple of Clinton's campaign oratory, and was officially enshrined in his "Vision of Change for America" budget proposal: "Throughout the eighties," the proposal charged, "people at the bottom of the income scale actually lost ground."[10] But

---

*A full discussion of Bill Clinton's tax-and-spend record as governor of Arkansas is included in Floyd Brown's "SLICK WILLIE": *Why America Cannot Trust Bill Clinton,* published by Annapolis-Washington Book Publishers, 1992.

any honest examination of recent history exposes Clinton's assertions as false.

The economic policies of the Jimmy Carter administration unquestionably triggered economic catastrophe in America: double-digit inflation, gasoline shortages, stagflation, job losses, a shift of the tax burden to the poor, and a free-fall in incomes of the poor. In 1981, President Reagan persuaded Congress to cut taxes and trim waste and regulation, ushering in a period of unparalleled economic expansion:

> The policies of Reaganomics—sound money, low tax rates, regulatory relief, and budget control— transformed an era of economic crisis into a decade of industrial revival and prosperity. From 1982 to 1989 GNP grew by nearly one-third—a real increase of more than $1 trillion in eight years.
>
> Industrial production expanded 32 percent between 1982 and 1989. Employment growth was brisk with 18 million new jobs created and the unemployment rate tumbling in Reagan's last year in office to 5.3 percent—its lowest level in 20 years. Contrary to popular mythology, all income groups shared in the prosperity. Average middle class family income rose by 12 percent during the 1982-89 period; and even the poorest fifth in income enjoyed a 10 percent income rise.[11]

Ignoring this record, candidate Clinton called for an America "in which middle class *incomes*—not middle class taxes—are going up. An America, yes, in which the wealthiest few—those making over $200,000 a year—are asked to pay *their fair share*."[12]

WHO PAYS?

Clinton's rebuke of the wealthy begs the question: what is a "fair share" of the tax burden to ask them to pay? Under the Carter administration, the top marginal tax rate in America was 70 percent, and the top five percent of taxpayers—that is, those who earned $200,000 or more— paid 35 percent of the tax burden.

Then Ronald Reagan took office and slashed tax rates dramatically. While all taxpayers benefited from these cuts, the wealthy benefited especially because they were the ones who had suffered the astronomically high 70 percent top tax rate. As a result of the Reagan cuts, the wealthy saw their maximum tax rate fall to 28 percent. And it's true, the tax burden in America did shift as a result: the "rich" shouldered *more* of the total tax bill! Those in the highest income category went from paying 35 percent of America's taxes under Carter, to paying almost 46 percent in 1988.*

Reagan's tax cuts, far from "raping" the poor and middle class, turned out to be to their advantage. For the bottom 50 percent of taxpayers, the average tax payment fell 26 percent. The total share of the tax bill paid by the poor declined from 7.4 percent to 4.7 percent.[13] Moreover, the Republicans removed hundreds of thousands of low-income taxpayers from the tax rolls entirely by lifting the minimum income required to file taxes.

Not surprisingly, the burden borne by the middle class, those in income percentiles 51-95, also declined after these tax cuts. Ronald Reagan gave the middle class a real break, not only in tax rates, but in burden sharing. The middle-

---

*See Appendix E for official Internal Revenue Service (IRS) statistics that show how the tax burden shifted toward the wealthy from 1981-1990.

class tax burden declined from 57 percent in 1981 to only 49 percent in 1988.[14]

To repeat: the "rich," or the top five percent of income earners in America, paid 46 percent of the cost of government when Ronald Reagan left office in 1988. The middle class paid 49 percent. The "poor" paid only 5 percent of the cost of government.[15]

But how was it that the wealthy "paid more" by "paying less?"

The answer is that few wealthy individuals actually paid Jimmy Carter's confiscatory rates. They found ways to avoid paying the high income taxes through loopholes that legally sheltered their wealth from the IRS. This practice introduced major distortions into the economy, and increased incentives to invest in non-productive or marginal activities rather than in enterprises that would create jobs or stimulate economic growth. Moreover, much of the rich's income is discretionary. When tax rates are high, they can hold on to their assets. They can look for non-productive "shelters" to shield funds from high tax rates.

In other words, attempts to "soak the rich" actually result in their paying fewer taxes, and the middle-class citizens, who cannot afford costly tax advisors and fancy tax-avoidance schemes, pay more. Worse, when tax rates rise, the rich become reclusive, foregoing new investment activities and postponing expansion of production facilities—moves that harm the middle and lower classes.

One question remains: given the success of the Reagan tax cuts, why has the country been plagued with massive deficits? The answer is that during the 1980-1993 time period, when receipts to the government rose $631 billion, its spending rose $884 billion.[16] In other words, tax cuts didn't cause the deficit; *spending* did. The difference in the amount of taxes raised, and the amount government spends, has been a measure of the inability of the Democratic Congress to control its spending.

And the problem of out-of-control congressional spending and ballooning deficits was made worse by the tax hikes of 1986 and 1990. Of course, these tax increases were passed in the name of "deficit reduction." But the reality is that whenever Congress raises taxes, it doesn't apply the new revenues to previous deficits, it just spends more money on current and future programs. In fact, for every dollar raised through increased taxes, Congress spends $1.59.[17] The bottom line is, raising taxes has never reduced the deficit. It just encourages politicians to spend more.

CLINTON'S FIRST BUDGET

There was a world of difference between the calls for middle-class tax cuts Bill Clinton made on the campaign trail in New Hampshire, and the massive tax increases he proposed in his budget on February 17, 1993. By the time he was in power, Bill Clinton no longer needed middle-class voters; they were stuck with him. Instead, he listened to elite advisors who were eager to expand the role of government in directing the economy.

In the first major action of his administration, Clinton presented his budget to a joint session of Congress. He spoke for an hour about a "new direction" for America—about "creating jobs," "cutting waste," "improving productivity," "reducing the debt" and "cutting the federal bureaucracy." But President Clinton showed his true colors when he said, "Tonight I want to talk with you about what government can do, because I believe government must do more."[18] Instead of encouraging Americans to be self-reliant, Clinton wanted to increase Americans' dependence on the state.

The federal budget any president presents has three

types of expenses. The first is the cost of servicing the national debt, which is the accumulation of previous deficits. This cost expands when interest rates go up, so the total amount for these national interest payments depends upon other policies of the government that affect interest rates generally.

The second part of the budget is also difficult to estimate because it consists of "entitlements," or benefit programs based on formulas, like Social Security, federal retirement programs, Medicare, Medicaid, and welfare programs. Any citizen who qualifies under the formulas is "entitled" to these benefits. But nobody really knows how much entitlements will cost because, for example, nobody really knows how many parents of dependent children will apply for funds under Aid for Families and Dependent Children. Nobody can predict how many people will apply for federal unemployment compensation, because nobody knows how many will be unemployed. Nobody knows how many will be unemployed because nobody knows how many jobs will be lost after the new taxes to pay for more unemployment insurance are enacted.

Entitlement programs amount to nearly two-thirds of the federal budget. If more eligible persons apply than expected, Congress has to appropriate extra money, no matter how big the deficit might be. Yet, for political reasons, Congress doesn't want to alter these benefit formulas, or limit the number of persons eligible. Entitlements are programs that Congress won't touch.

The third part of the budget constitutes the "discretionary" programs. This is the part of the budget where Congress is free to authorize and appropriate whatever sums it desires, so it is the only part where significant cuts can be made. Discretionary programs include such familiar functions as defense, foreign affairs, transportation, energy, and space projects.

But most of the discretionary programs continue to grow. Very few are ever eliminated, and when the President or Congress talks about "cutting" these programs, they usually are talking about cutting the *rate of increase,* not the actual amount spent. To these politicians, "cutting" a program usually means spending more than last year, but less than the government agency hoped to get.

When any President presents a budget to Congress, it's just the opening gambit in a months-long process. The federal budget is normally presented in January, or, for a new President, in February. It doesn't take effect until October 1.

THE FEDERAL BUDGET PROCESS

The Federal budget process consists of four steps. Step one occurs when the President presents his budget to Congress. This will not turn out to be the real budget.

Inspired either to accept or reject the President's proposals, each House of Congress proceeds to step two, namely, passing a budget resolution of its own. Then both Houses confer, tinker with each other's wish list, and agree on a common document.

However, the budget resolution is not the real budget either. It's just a blueprint, stating in general terms how much money can be authorized for each government function, such as agriculture, foreign affairs, or defense. Each authorizing committee will be directed to limit its spending to a certain over-all amount, but each committee can divide that amount as it sees fit. Tax-writing committees, meanwhile, are charged with writing bills to raise the prescribed revenue.

Step three occurs as each committee works on the specifics in its area of jurisdiction, comes up with programs, and names specific costs for the programs.

Step four begins when all these differences are brought back to the floor of both the House and the Senate in the annual Budget Reconciliation Act. Both House and Senate pass separate drafts of the budget, and there is a conference between selected members of the House and the Senate to reconcile the differences into one last bill, the conference report, which must pass a final vote in each House.

Any member of Congress who wants to add a new program during this process has to find offsetting "savings" somewhere else. To get his or her own pork-barrel program approved, someone else's has to be killed. Or a new tax has to be invented. Some of these sessions can get pretty grisly.

PRESIDENT CLINTON'S 1994 BUDGET

When President Clinton announced his first budget he said it would, "by 1997, cut $140 billion in that year alone from the deficit. A real spending cut, a real revenue increase, a real deficit reduction."[19] Clinton's budget called for the abolition of only one program, saving $17 million a year.[20]

Instead of "a real spending cut" as promised, however, discretionary spending would only cut the rate of increase, resulting in billions more being spent each year until 1998. And instead of cutting entitlement spending, Clinton proposed an $18.3 billion increase over four years in the Earned Income Tax Credit, a sum, called a "refund," that is paid to low wage-earners even if they pay no taxes.

Moreover, Clinton's "spending cuts" were weighted to cut the rate of spending increases most heavily in the last years of the 1994-98 period. So small, painless reductions would take place in 1994, when members of Congress would be voting on the overall plan; but to meet the proclaimed goals, the reductions in the rate of spending increases would double and triple in 1996, 1997, and 1998, *after* the next presidential election. However, since Congress votes every year on the President's four-year plans, everything after 1994 was a non-binding promise. Congress can, and often does, decide that the grand promises of two or three years ago are ancient history best forgotten.

On the other hand, President Clinton really meant the part about the "real revenue increase." Unlike the ephemeral spending "cuts," the tax increases were scheduled to begin right away. In fact, Clinton even convinced Congress to make some of the tax hikes retroactive. Taxes on wealthy individuals and corporations, and increased estate taxes, took effect as of January 1, 1993—20 days *before* Clinton even took office.* Radio talk show hosts around the country howled that the President was raising taxes on "the rich" and the dead. Senator Bob Dole reported in the wake of these tax hikes, "If there's one issue that has people calling my office hopping mad, it's this retroactive tax increase. They don't think it's fair."[22]

Although during his campaign Bill Clinton talked about taxing only "the wealthy," his budget proposal asked every family making more than $30,000 to pay more. The official

*According to economist Paul Craig Roberts, President Clinton's retroactive taxation violates Article I, Section 9 of the Constitution. Furthermore, Roberts asks, why did President Clinton make these taxes retroactive? "The answer," he wrote, "is simple. Clinton and the Democrats know that higher marginal income-tax rates will not raise the predicted revenues if they are prospective. In order to raise revenues, the higher tax rates have to be applied to income already earned."[21]

figures he presented to Congress showed that he wanted to collect the following additional amounts from each income group:

Family Income	Added Taxes
$30,000 to $50,000	$4.4 billion
$50,000 to $75,000	$7.6 billion
$75,000 to $100,000	$5.9 billion
$100,000 to $200,000	$8.0 billion
$200,000 and more	$34.3 billion[23]

These figures show that Clinton's sock-it-to-the-rich program actually worked out to a plan to collect $13 billion more from the middle class, $13.9 billion more from the upper middle class, and $34.3 billion more from the wealthy.

Judging from history, of course, the $34.3 billion figure will not materialize; it is based on the idea that people earning more than $200,000 will continue to earn income at those levels, even if they have to pay more taxes on it. Moreover, politicians who set out to tax "the rich" ignore the fact that most of the tax returns reporting income of more than $200,000 come from partnerships and small businesses, which create most of the new jobs and wealth in America.

The most controversial proposal in Clinton's plan was a new comprehensive tax on energy, including coal, oil, gas, and nuclear power, based upon energy output (measured in British thermal units, or BTUs). In addition, Clinton demanded a 14-cent per gallon increase in the federal gasoline tax. Fortunately, in the end, he could not get Congress to approve the energy taxes because members feared the wrath of the millions of voters who would be forced to pay more to heat and cool their homes, or drive to work.

Moreover, there were billions of dollars in new taxes that Clinton called "user fees." These included not only admissions fees to national parks, airport fees added to the cost of airline tickets, and customs charges, but also taxes that directly burdened regional industries with new costs for such essential services as grazing rights, water rights, and river barge transportation.

In addition, President Clinton proposed to save billions of dollars in Medicare and Medicaid expenditures by arbitrarily limiting payments to physicians and hospitals—a proposal, by the way, that should be kept in mind when considering his health care plan. While this maneuver may reduce the budget, it hurts private citizens, because when the government refuses to pay the normal cost for services to patients, physicians and hospitals have to make up their losses by charging more to patients who don't get government subsidies. This cost-shifting has been a major reason why health insurance premiums keep rising. So the medical caps that President Clinton included in his budget proposal will become an indirect tax on working men and women in the form of increased insurance premiums.

While some of President Clinton's proposals for "savings" were shaky at best, his calls for spending were firm: some $100 billion in new programs. President Clinton called his spending proposals "investments." In ordinary language, of course, an investment is a capital expenditure that positions the investor to make money. Not so in the "great national journey" Bill Clinton leads.

President Clinton's increased spending proposals included $8.4 billion for highways, bridges, railroads, transit, and airports; $15 billion a year for "investment" in summer jobs, infant nutrition, and preschool education;

$1.5 billion for wetlands restoration; and $3 billion on solar energy, electric vehicles, and so-called "clean technology."

Still, President Clinton told Congress that his package would trim the deficit by $493 billion over five years. He claimed that these "savings" would be achieved by $247 billion in spending cuts and $246 billion in tax increases over the same period. But the day after his speech, Clinton made a correction. He had forgotten to include $149 billion in new spending in his projections, funds intended as a "stimulus" to the economy. So the $247 billion in net spending cuts became $98 billion overnight—just a mistake.

CLINTON'S FAILED STIMULUS PACKAGE

There was another matter that, strictly speaking, was not part of President Clinton's 1994 fiscal year budget proposals. Because he just couldn't wait for the budget to kick in on October 1, he announced that the economy needed an immediate stimulus, and he asked Congress to approve an emergency spending bill totalling $16.3 billion, plus authority to spend $3.2 billion from trust funds outside the budget. White House strategists expected the Democrat-controlled Congress to pass this emergency stimulus bill within a week, just to show that Republican gridlock was over. They confidently scheduled Congress to vote on it before the budget, in order to lock in new spending before having to vote on tax increases and program cuts. It was a policy of "apple pie now and castor oil later."

But the more the rank-and-file troops in the Democratic trenches thought about it, the more they were afraid of voter backlash. That word "emergency" on the bill title began to look a little too cynical when applied to a pork barrel.

In the end, even the Democratic fat-cats wouldn't back President Clinton in his mission to bust budget ceilings and add $19.5 billion to the deficit in the name of deficit reduction. They were afraid angry taxpayers would rebel. These legislators hadn't ridden in on Clinton's coattails, and they were skeptical of his 43 percent "mandate."

Meanwhile, the budget resolution itself ran into tough sledding, and was approved in late March only by party line votes of 243-183 in the House, and 54-45 in the Senate. Not a single Republican voted for the budget in either House on final passage. Of course, the budget resolution did not, in itself, actually legislate tax increases or spending cuts. Nonetheless, after its passage at the end of March, Democrats eagerly returned to discussion of the emergency stimulus bill.

But Republicans mercilessly exposed the stimulus package as a pork barrel for key Democratic constituencies. They pointed out how money would go for swimming pools, jogging trails, graffiti removal, recreation centers, and energy-efficient overhauls of federal buildings. In the House, only three Republicans deserted principle and voted for the increased spending. In the Senate all 43 Republicans joined in a filibuster.

Senate Majority Leader George Mitchell failed in four attempts to break the filibuster, and, after the Easter recess, he quietly removed the Clinton "emergency stimulus" bill from consideration, conceding defeat.

When the budget process resumed, the Democrats had more trouble. Step three of the budget process, the reconciliation bill, requires a lot of specific decisions on specific items in the budget. President Clinton's new BTU tax was sticking in the throats of Congressmen who knew it would devastate consumers, producers, and energy-intensive industries.

With two seats vacant, the 435-seat House needed 217 votes for passage. No Republican was going to vote in favor, and two days before the vote on May 27, the Democrats had only 150 votes for the Clinton bill. So President Clinton put in days of intense lobbying, contacting every conceivable interest group not supporting the reconciliation bill. The lobbying by the President and his cabinet continued not only up to the last minute, but even after the voting began. Finally, to get his last handful of votes, Clinton agreed to make concessions on the BTU tax. It was too late to change the bill, but he promised the tax would be reduced before the Senate vote.

This concession put House Democrats in a quandary: they were being asked to vote for provisions that might harm their re-election chances, while Senators would get off scot-free. In the end, 219 House Democrats voted with the President, but 38, including 10 subcommittee chairmen, did not.

In the Senate, the reconciliation bill passed with only one vote to spare, and that was after Clinton's BTU tax, with which he intended to collect $72 billion over five years, was reduced to a 4.3 cents-per-gallon gasoline tax, projected to bring in only $23 billion.[24]

Still, the drama was not over. The House bill and the Senate bill had to go to a conference committee to iron out their differences, and the conference threatened to deadlock. House and Senate conferees had to put in more spending programs to satisfy the hold-outs. When the conferees finished their work, even many Democrats were appalled. They were convinced that the bill relied too much on boosting spending and taxes, and too little on slashing programs. Each house had to vote again to approve the work of the conference. Once again so many Democrats were defecting that the White House was panic-stricken by the possibility of defeat.

The problem was politically serious for Clinton, who by July had achieved very little as president. A Conference Report cannot be amended; it has to be accepted or rejected as is. So President Clinton responded to the threatened defections with desperate deal-making: if Democrats promised to vote for the Conference Report now, he said, they could salve their consciences by voting for additional spending cuts when Congress returned from its August recess. President Clinton told the leader of the spending cutters, Rep. Timothy J. Penny (D—Minn.), that he would support a new anti-spending bill in the fall to cut an additional $5 to $10 billion, and that Penny's allies could propose even more amendments.

On August 5, 1993, the House voted 218-216 to approve the conference version of the budget. Some 41 Democrats voted against it, and a shift of just one vote would have meant its defeat. The next day, August 6th, the Senate vote on the Conference Report turned out to be another cliff-hanger. With the vote tied at 50-50, Vice President Al Gore performed the rare constitutional function of tie-breaker.

So, by one vote in the House and one vote in the Senate, Clinton's budget reconciliation conference report was approved. It was one of the few times in history that a majority party has passed important legislation without a single vote from the minority party.

The bill broke another record as well. "The President's plan is the largest tax increase in the history of the world," said Senator Dole, "[It] does not eliminate a single federal program. It does not tell government bureaucrats to spend less money. It says, 'Government programs will be increased, but the increase will not be quite as big as expected.' . . . [and] the so-called spending cuts are only promised for sometime in the future."[25]

1. Bill Clinton; Announcement Speech; October 3, 1991.
2. Bill Clinton, "A New Covenant" address to the Democratic National Convention; New York City; July 16, 1992.
3. Bill Clinton, quoted in *Wall Street Journal*; December 18, 1992.
4. Bill Clinton, quoted by Mark Stencil; *Washington Post*; January 15, 1993.
5. Bill Clinton, *Putting People First*; Times Books; page 15.
6. Dan Balz, *Washington Post*; February 28, 1992.
7. Dan Balz, *Washington Post*; June 23, 1992.
8. Floyd Brown, "SLICK WILLIE": *Why America Cannot Trust Bill Clinton*; Annapolis-Washington Book Publishers 1992; pages 39-46.
9. Bill Clinton, *supra* endnote 2.
10. Minority View, *The 1993 Joint Economic Report*; April 19, 1993; page 135.
11. *ibid.*, page 94.
12. Bill Clinton, *supra* endnote 2.
13. Minority View, *supra* endnote 10, pages 148-151.
14. *ibid.*, page 151.
15. *ibid.*
16. *ibid.*, page 109.
17. *ibid.*, page 118.
18. Bill Clinton, Address by the President to the Joint Session of Congress; February 17, 1993.
19. Bill Clinton, Joint Address to Congress; February 17, 1993.
20. *Congressional Quarterly*; February 20, 1993; page 370.
21. Paul Craig Roberts, "Retroactive Taxation Picks on Rich, the Dead and Constitution"; *Star Tribune*; August 11, 1993.
22. *Congressional Quarterly*; August 7, 1993; page 2127.
23. *Congressional Quarterly*; February 20, 1993; page 416.
24. *Congressional Quarterly*; July 31, 1993; page 2024.
25. *Congressional Quarterly*; August 7, 1993; page 2184.

THE DEPARTMENT
OF INJUSTICE

"You [have] demonstrated that you will be a formidable advocate for the vulnerable people in our society and especially for our children."[1]
—Bill Clinton to Janet Reno
at her swearing-in ceremony

"In Monday's fiery end to the 51-day standoff at . . . Waco, 24 children are believed to be dead. 'It is obvious with the Clinton crew that some people's rights are more important than others.' "[2]
—Doug Bandow
The Cato Institute

"They created her [Reno], and, much like Frankenstein, they're not sure what to do about it."[3]
—A "key Justice Department official,"
quoted in the *Washington Times*

Most Americans expect the Department of Justice, as the nation's top law enforcement agency, to lead the country's attack on crime. But instead of confronting America's crime problems, Bill Clinton and Janet Reno have reworked the department to make it "politically correct."

With serious consequences for the American people,

Clinton and Reno have neglected crime fighting to pursue projects ranging from pet environmental and social programs, to race and gender "crimes," to children's television content. They have welcomed homosexual agents into the FBI and pushed gun control. "Am I now employed by the Justice Department, or the Department of Social Work?" asked one veteran drug prosecutor.[4]

Moreover, despite promises to rise above political shenanigans, Clinton and Reno have tarnished the Justice Department's integrity. Their blatantly political mass firing of U.S. attorneys and their bloody raid at Waco, Texas, showed incompetence and malfeasance remarkable even by government standards.

Finally, the Clinton Justice Department has suffered major personnel debacles, from the President's inept selection of nominees who couldn't even survive the Senate confirmation process to the unsettling departures of top Justice officials. One year after Janet Reno's appointment, the number two and three men at Justice, Philip B. Heymann and Webster L. "Webb" Hubbell, were forced to tender their resignations. Heymann's mysterious departure was attributed by Reno to "bad chemistry." And Hubbell left under a cloud of suspicion concerning alleged ethical misconduct at the Rose Law Firm in Little Rock.

THE "RODHAM CLINTON
JUSTICE DEPARTMENT"

The Justice Department was marked for trouble from Day One of the new administration. Washington insiders were soon calling it the "Rodham Clinton Justice Department" because it was widely known that Hillary Rodham Clinton had insisted on implementing her own personnel choices and policy decisions there. First on Rodham Clinton's list of demands was that the new Attorney

General be a woman—an important political milestone in the minds of many feminists, and a statistic the "diversity"-conscious Clinton administration wanted to tout.

President Clinton tried twice in vain to comply with the feminist standards. First, he nominated Zoe Baird, general counsel of the giant Aetna Insurance Company. This immediately raised eyebrows because, although a competent business attorney, Baird had never litigated a criminal case in her life. But this failing was soon overshadowed by the revelation that Baird herself had disobeyed the law: she had hired illegal immigrants to work in her home and had failed to report their income and pay the appropriate taxes.

Clinton's next choice for Attorney General was Kimba Wood, a U.S. District Court judge from New York. It was "déjà vu all over again" when it was learned that Wood had hired an illegal alien for domestic help.* As the search for the first woman Attorney General resumed, the nation waited.

Finally, Clinton settled on Janet Reno, a little-known Dade County, Florida, prosecutor. Single and childless, Reno looked like the perfect solution to Clinton's embarrassing situation.† Senate Judiciary Committee Chairman Joe Biden called her nomination "a home run."[6]

But before long, what seemed like a home run curved foul. As initial fascination with the six-foot-plus daughter

---

*Although Judge Wood apparently did not break any law in her "Nannygate" episode, her babysitter was in the United States illegally. This alone proved disqualifying in the wake of the Zoe Baird disaster.

†While Reno met the feminist gender requirement, she was lacking a key qualification shared by most top members of the Rodham Clinton team: she was neither a "Friend of Bill" (FOB), nor a "Friend of Hillary" (FOH). This problem was remedied, however, by Webb Hubbell's presence as Associate Attorney General. Although technically the number three man on the totem pole, Hubbell wielded the real power as "Hillary's eyes and ears at the Justice Department."[5]

of an alligator wrestler wore off, reporters started looking
at Reno's record. Seven months into her tenure, the *New
York Times* reported: "Interviews with . . . former and
current lawyers at the [Justice] department indicate that
in contrast to the public image of competence and com-
passion, Ms. Reno's stewardship has resembled a shake-
down cruise under a novice captain."[7]

THE POLITICIZATION OF JUSTICE
Without a thought to the Clinton campaign promise of
nonpartisan government, Janet Reno and Bill Clinton
have created one of the most biased, politicized Justice
Departments in American history.

Petty politicking was evident from the start. In a transition meeting between Bush and Clinton officials, soon-
to-be Assistant Attorney General Eleanor Dean Acheson,
a "Friend of Hillary," complained about the large portraits of conservative Supreme Court Justices William
Rehnquist and Antonin Scalia hanging in the Office of
Legal Counsel, where both men had previously served.
Refusing to sit facing the portraits, Acheson swung around
to face the window and snarled, "You can guess how long
those will stay after January 20!"[8]

For her part, Janet Reno promised the day she was
sworn in "to do everything I can to make sure that politics
is not a part of the Justice Department."[9] No sooner said than
she joined President Clinton in a "joint decision" to fire all
93 United States attorneys.* The maneuver was so crude that
it was dubbed the "March Massacre" by one columnist.[10]

One obvious target of this unprecedented firing was Jay
B. Stephens, the U.S. attorney in the District of Columbia

---

*The U.S. attorneys investigate and prosecute federal crimes on behalf of the
U.S. government in all 50 states and the District of Columbia.

who was investigating federal criminal allegations against one of President Clinton's most important allies on Capitol Hill: House Ways and Means Committee Chairman Dan Rostenkowski (D-Ill.). Having investigated Rostenkowski for 19 months, Stephens was reportedly just weeks away from bringing an indictment. By getting rid of Stephens, Clinton assured that the powerful Rostenkowski would be around long enough to grease the congressional skids for new taxes and socialized health care.*

Although President Clinton claimed the mass firing was routine, this was not so. From 1977 on, incoming administrations have allowed U.S. attorneys to complete their four-year terms before replacing them, a custom that helps preserve public confidence in impartial justice. When Clinton and Reno broke with this tradition, the *New York Times* lamented, "Any hope that the Clinton administration would operate a Justice Department free of political taint . . . [has grown] dim."[11] The *Times* solemnly warned that "until the White House gets its fingerprints off the Department, there can be no start on the promised regime of justice above politics at Justice."[12]

The firing of the U.S. attorneys was not the only political chicanery at the Justice Department. Members of the Clinton administration also tried to intervene in the jury selection for the trial of Rep. Harold Ford (D-Tenn.), who had been indicted on federal corruption charges. Hoping to save the black Democrat from jail, they instructed the U.S. attorney in Tennessee to arrange for a more "diverse" jury than had been picked. But this power play

---

*Rostenkowski has since reimbursed the federal Treasury for $82,000 in taxpayer money that he had used, among other things, to purchase expensive chairs as gifts for friends and financial supporters. The Congressman also allegedly paid an "invisible staff" with public funds. The firing of Jay Stephens left Rostenkowski free to secure renomination from his Illinois district.

collapsed when the U.S. attorney resigned, and the indignant federal judge overseeing the case retained the original jury.*

Observed columnist Paul Craig Roberts: "Jury tampering is a serious crime, and no less so when attempted by the Justice Department. . . . it will be difficult in the future to condemn the Mafia, or local drug gangs, for jury tampering when the Justice Department attempts to do the same thing itself."[13]

CLINTON AND RENO: SOFT ON CRIME

Although Bill Clinton uses tough rhetoric in speeches about crime, it has been another case of "all talk, no action."

Shrugging off his poor record of law enforcement in Arkansas, Bill Clinton promised to escalate the fight against crime as President: "The Clinton-Gore national crime strategy will use the powers of the White House to prevent and punish crime."[14]

Once in office, however, Clinton called for cutbacks of 1,523 law enforcement positions—including federal prosecutors, and agents from the FBI and the Drug Enforcement Agency—and recommended a 30 percent cut in federal prison construction.[15] At the same time, Clinton laid not a finger on other bloated sectors of the federal bureaucracy.

Unsurprisingly, during Clinton's first year in the White House, law enforcement lagged: in 1993, the number of federal criminal prosecutions *decreased* by more than three percent, and drug prosecutions *decreased* by seven percent.[16]

Again undeterred by his weak record, Clinton contin-

*Rep. Ford was ultimately acquitted.

ued to use strong rhetoric. In his 1994 State of the Union address, Clinton sought to create a law-and-order image of himself by endorsing the "three strikes and you're out" plan. But the Senate had already passed a "three strikes and you're out" proposal. U.S. Sen. Orrin G. Hatch (R-Utah) praised the Senate's work as "the finest anti-crime package in history,"[17] but, as the *New York Times* reported, Clinton "had virtually nothing to do with the compromises that made its passage possible."[18]

Unlike Bill Clinton who talks tough on crime but does nothing, Janet Reno doesn't even like to *talk* tough. Reno's indulgence stems from her 1960s-style philosophy about the "root causes" behind violent acts. She seems more concerned with "understanding" crime than with stopping it. "If the Attorney General can think about pre-natal care before she thinks about more prisons," she says self-righteously, "that's got to tell you something."[19]

When interviewed on national television the morning she was confirmed as Attorney General, Reno was asked what her priorities would be. Her answer? Enforcement of *civil* rights. Reno also wanted "to protect our land, our air, our water, to protect this nation's environment, which we all love."[20] (But not, apparently, to protect the ordinary citizen from violence.)

She continued, "I want to use the laws of America in the right way, to give children a chance to grow as strong, constructive human beings."[21] (Still nothing about crime.)

"My highest priority," admitted Reno on another occasion, "is not to convict criminals, but to protect their rights."[22]* In pursuit of which, Reno (1) overturned a Bush

---

*Floridians weren't surprised by Janet Reno's lack of commitment to real crime fighting. She had taken fewer cases to trial, won fewer guilty verdicts, and

administration policy that forbade federal prosecutors from plea bargaining with criminals; (2) attacked mandating minimum prison sentences in the federal system, which makes federal criminal laws tough; (3) discouraged building new prisons and encouraged the release of more prisoners to reduce overcrowding; and (4) twisted Supreme Court precedent by maintaining that the death penalty for drug kingpins is unconstitutional.

Finally, like her President, Janet Reno was nowhere to be found when both houses of Congress were considering landmark crime legislation. "The Justice Department's silence has been deafening," one congressional aide told journalist Anthony Lewis. "They've been nowhere— zilch. There has been no leadership."[26]

THE BRADY BILL

There was one "crime" proposal that both Attorney General Reno and President Clinton pushed: the Brady Bill. Named after Press Secretary James Brady, who was injured in the 1981 assassination attempt on President Ronald Reagan, the legislation requires a five-day waiting period before handgun buyers may pick up weapons they have purchased.

In November 1993, Reno accompanied Sarah Brady, wife of James Brady and spokesman for the bill, on a lobbying tour of Capitol Hill. President Clinton got in-

---

obtained fewer prison sentences than her fellow state prosecutors.[23]

"She's a very good politician," explained former Miami Police Chief Kenneth Harms, "but in terms of putting bad guys in jail, I'm not at all comfortable with her record."[24]

Instead of locking up criminals in Florida, Reno directed grand juries to investigate homelessness, public housing, and treatment of minorities. Meanwhile, Dade County's crime rate skyrocketed about 50 percent, almost double the rate of increase for the whole state.[25]

volved when a Senate filibuster threatened to kill the bill, and Vice-President Al Gore lobbied Congress incessantly. The administration's full treatment worked: although the Brady Bill had been dismissed for years as a glitzy public relations ploy, Reno and Clinton pushed it through Congress as their answer to crime.

But even proponents of the Brady Bill conceded *after its passage* that it was only "symbolic." The truth soon emerged—no one really expected results from the legislation. The *New York Times* reported, for example, that in the 22 states that have waiting periods similar to the Brady Bill's, there "has been no sign of their having any overall impact on crime."[27]

What really happened with passage of the Brady Bill was that gun control advocates finally got a foot in the door of Congress and public opinion. Sarah Brady herself admitted that the legislation was just a political "first step" in keeping guns out of the hands of citizens. "Once we get this," she said, "I think it will become easier and easier to get the laws we need passed."[28]

If Clinton and Reno had truly wanted to get tough on crime, they could have enforced gun laws *already on the books*, laws that are tougher than the Brady Bill, such as longer jail terms for individuals who carry firearms when they commit felonies. But Clinton took the easy opportunity for political grandstanding by pushing this politically-correct legislation. (The presence of Sarah and James Brady at Clinton's first State of the Union address certainly added drama.)

THE RIGHT TO BEAR ARMS

The truth that Bill Clinton and Janet Reno either do not or will not see, is that while gun control *cannot stop criminals*, gun availability *can protect innocents*. And with rising crime rates and the Clinton cutbacks in prosecutors and prisons, the need for Americans to defend themselves is becoming greater and greater.

The right to self-defense and to defend others is rooted in American tradition and the U.S. Constitution. But the campaign to ban guns is a relatively new phenomenon: "It's a fairly recent idea that guns aren't a good thing," University of California history professor Jon Weiner observed.[29]

Perhaps it is difficult for the political elite to grasp the dangers that are unfortunately common for many Americans. They don't seem to understand that ordinary citizens need to protect themselves. Although the wealthy can live in exclusive neighborhoods with expensive home security systems, many Americans cannot afford these luxuries. They should not therefore be denied the opportunity to defend themselves, whether from burglars, rapists, or oppressive government agents.

When America was founded, the Founding Fathers understood that citizens needed to keep and bear arms, and not only to protect against robbers. It was, after all, King George and the British who tried to strip colonists of their arms. James Madison criticized European despots as "afraid to trust the people with arms," and added that his fellow American countrymen need not fear their government because they have "the advantage of being armed."[30]

Whose side are Bill Clinton and Janet Reno on?

THE WACO, TEXAS ASSAULT

Sunday, February 28, 1993, seemed like just another day for members of David Koresh's religious cult. "I picked up the Sunday paper, went upstairs to my room, and started reading," recalled 77-year-old Catherine

Matteson, one of the survivors of the government's 51-day siege on the Branch Davidian compound outside Waco, Texas. Matteson said she had seen some trucks approaching the compound and figured it was some kind of delivery. "Next," said Matteson, "bullets came through the roof. I could hear the helicopters overhead, I got under my bed."[31]

Matteson was wrong about the delivery trucks. What was really underway was a government raid. The Bureau of Alcohol, Tobacco, and Firearms (ATF), in the biggest raid in its history, had arrived to serve search and arrest warrants on David Koresh for suspected gun violations.*

---

*The validity of the ATF warrants is questionable. Much of the information relied on by the warrants was eight months old or older, whereas a search warrant should properly show reason to suspect *current*, or at least *ongoing*, criminal activity.[32] The warrants also depended on information from anonymous sources. Furthermore, the reasons cited for issuing the warrants included suspected child abuse, which was later determined not to be a problem, and was out of ATF jurisdiction anyway—a fact that raises suspicions that the Clinton administration was really just after the guns.[33]

Finally, ATF officials based their warrants on a Texas state official's April 6, 1992, visit with Koresh, during which Koresh warned that "the riots in Los Angeles would pale in comparison" to events that would accompany Koresh's revelation of himself as a "Messenger from God." The ATF never confirmed the official's statements. They couldn't have: the L.A. riots occurred on April 29, 1992, 23 days *after* the official's meeting with Koresh.[34]

One can only speculate about the motivations behind the ATF raid. Circumstantial evidence points to some rather cynical explanations. In January 1993, for example, one month before the initial raid on the Branch Davidian compound, CBS's "60 Minutes" aired embarrassing accusations against the ATF from female agents who claimed they were sexually harassed by male colleagues.[35] What better way to prove themselves after the "60 Minutes" exposé than to raid some "religious gun nuts" in Texas? Moreover, the ATF actively sought publicity for their raid. Agents offered a local newspaper "front-row seats,"[36] and the show of 100 heavily armed agents arriving to serve a warrant seemed designed to draw media attention.

It should also be noted that the ATF raid occurred just days prior to an annual appropriation hearing that would be crucial to determining the agency's

Based on information from delivery drivers and disaffected members of the religious group, the ATF had grown concerned that Koresh was illegally converting semiautomatic weapons to fully automatic machine guns. David Koresh had a history of cooperating with the law, however, that made the ATF's show of force completely out-of-whack.*

To serve the warrants, the ATF arrived at the Branch Davidian compound with truckloads of heavily armed agents and helicopter backup. The government agents, according to the *Waco Tribune-Herald*, "leaped out of the cattle trucks, throwing concussion grenades and screaming, 'Come Out!' "[39]

Wayne Martin, a Harvard-trained attorney who belonged to Koresh's group, called 911 from inside the compound for help: "There's 75 men around our building and they're shooting at us! Tell 'em there's women and children in here and to call it off!" Martin asked the police at least 25 times to stop the ATF attack.[40] The voice of another Branch Davidian captured on the 911 tape yelled,

---

budget—a well-executed raid could only have enhanced the agency's prospects for funding.

*In 1992, Koresh had escorted sheriff's deputies and child-abuse investigators through the ranch house after they had called to say they were coming. Koresh invited one of the deputies to come back and fish in their lake. "He was real nice," said Sheriff Jack Harwell, "real congenial . . . They were like living in another little country out there," he said. "They had their property line, and they were basically good people. All of 'em were good people."[37]

In a 1987 incident, Koresh was charged with attempted murder, a far more serious charge than weapons violations. In this case, the sheriff simply picked up the telephone and called Koresh down to his office. Koresh turned himself in quietly, and a hung jury later voted 9-3 to acquit him.[38] In this instance, the judicial process ran its course peacefully.

The 1993 ATF raid, in contrast, was a violent perversion of measured justice and the rule of law.

"Another chopper . . . more guns going off. They're firing! That's them, not us!"[41]

Wayne Martin said, "I have a right to defend myself. They started firing first."[42]

Catherine Matteson reported that there was mass confusion inside the compound during the initial government assault. She added that most of the Davidians' guns were packed up in boxes in preparation for a gun show in Austin: "Nobody could find anything," she said.[43]

Following the February 28 shootout that left four ATF agents dead and an unknown number of Branch-Davidians dead or wounded, a bizarre stand-off began. At this point, the FBI and the Department of Justice took control of the operation from the Department of Treasury's ATF. This transfer of responsibility put Attorney General Janet Reno in direct control of the Waco operation.

As weeks passed, the FBI alternately harassed and tried to negotiate with Koresh. They cut off power and communication to the Branch Davidians, focused bright spotlights on the compound at night, and pumped loudspeakers with sounds of dental drills and screaming rabbits being slaughtered.[44]

During the standoff, adults and children who wished to leave the compound did so, unhindered by Koresh.* Texas caseworkers who examined the children for signs of abuse found none. "Despite accusations by former cult members that Mr. Koresh sexually abused girls," the *New York Times* reported, "there is considerable evidence that the children were, in at least some important respects, well cared for. None show any signs of physical abuse."[46]

---

*This fact was ignored by President Clinton when he later wrongly charged that Koresh had "destroy[ed] himself and murder[ed] the children, *who were his captives.*"[45]

Inside the Justice Department, FBI officials debated strategy. Their behavioral experts offered contradictory advice about the possibility of mass suicide. Some warned it was probable. Others argued the standoff would end peacefully. Attorney General Reno ordered a report on the standoff but, as later noted in a Justice Department summary, she "did not read the prepared statement carefully, nor did she read the supporting documentation."[47]

Ultimately, despite the lack of evidence of child abuse, Reno used the charge to justify the final, lethal assault. On April 19, 51 days after the initial ATF attack, an FBI "negotiator" telephoned the Branch Davidians at 5:59 a.m.: "We're in the process of delivering a non-lethal tear gas into the compound," he said. "This is not an assault. Do not fire your weapons."[48]

As tanks rolled toward the house and commenced attack, Janet Reno and other top Justice officials gathered in a windowless room at the J. Edgar Hoover building in Washington to monitor the scene via a special television transmission.[49]

At 6:04 a.m., the tanks began punching holes in the house and inserting O-chlorobenzalmalononitrile (CS gas).* Within 30 minutes, a white flag appeared waving outside a window of the compound.[52] But an exchange of gunfire took place anyway, and FBI tanks inserted more CS gas while FBI marksmen fired canisters of tear gas into the compound.†

---

*CS gas is designed for outdoor use and CS grenades are notorious for starting fires.[50] Moreover, CS gas is banned under the Paris chemical weapons convention, to which the United States is a party as of January 1993.[51]

†At the trial of the Branch Davidians, one FBI marksman testified that he fired 70 to 75 canisters of tear gas into the compound and that at least three other agents had as well, for a total of approximately 300 canisters.[53]

At 9:07 a.m., the Branch Davidians displayed a banner that read, "We want our phones fixed." Eight minutes later, a government tank rammed through the front door.[54] With walls and ceilings falling in around them, and stinging gas filling the compound, Koresh told his followers to "Stay calm" and use their gas masks. (The children had no gas masks.)[55]

At 11:47 a.m., another tank assault was launched.[56] Minutes later, fire burst out and spread quickly. The compound was filled with bales of hay, ammunition, propane gas tanks, and the flammable CS gas—a fire waiting to happen.[57] As the first flames flared, television networks broke programming to carry live coverage of the assault.

How the fire started has remained a point of dispute. FBI snipers reported that they saw individuals inside the compound start the fire. But surviving Branch Davidians disagree; they say the fire started when a tank, ramming into the compound, knocked over a lantern.[58]

However the fire started, it caused mass panic among the people inside. FBI officials heard screams, but waited in vain for families to run out. Such escape was difficult, if not impossible, with smoke, flames, and blinding gas everywhere. Moreover, when tanks battered the compound, they destroyed stairways on which some inhabitants would have relied for their escape.[59] As the entire building went up in flames, a handful of Branch Davidians emerged from the building, some of them on fire. Inside, 60 adults and 25 children were incinerated.

At 12:12 p.m., the FBI called the Waco Fire Department. Ten minutes later, when fire engines reached FBI checkpoints miles away from the compound, they were held up for 15 minutes.[60] By the time they arrived at the compound, the building was gone and vultures were already circling the skies overhead.[61]

Two days later, authorities began removing bodies from the area. "As you can imagine, it's a very gruesome scene," reported a spokesman for the Texas Department of Public Safety to the *New York Times*. "We're talking charred bodies."[62] A medical examiner said that at least one small child appeared to have died in its mothers arms.[63]

"For the first time in history," one magazine editor observed, "a President attacked American children with tanks and got away with it."[64] *Lonesome Dove* author Larry McMurtry wrote that the "most Orwellian aspect of the final day was the FBI's attempt to convince the Branch Davidians that they weren't under assault, even as tanks were knocking the compound to splinters and pumping in the gas."[65]

In the wake of the disaster, Janet Reno justified the attack as a way to redress child abuse and relieve weary FBI officials. Clinton laid the blame on Koresh, calling him "dangerous, irrational, and probably insane." The President charged that *Koresh* had "murder[ed] the children."[66]

Both the Treasury and Justice Departments ordered official reports on the events at Waco. The Treasury investigation determined that ATF agents had engaged in lies and cover-ups.[67] ATF Director Stephen E. Higgins and five other Treasury officials were fired.

In contrast, the official Justice Department report found "no place for fault," not surprising, given that the firm of the report's author had clients with matters pending at the Justice Department.[68]

The Justice report did conclude, however, that there was no evidence of child abuse at the Branch Davidian compound, a point passed off by Reno as though it were a minor detail. "I now understand that nobody in the bureau told me that [child abuse] was ongoing," she said. "We were briefed, *and I misunderstood.*"[69]

Alan Stone, a Harvard University professor of psychiatry and law retained by the Justice Department to review the Waco incident, concluded, "It is difficult to understand why a person whose primary concern was the safety of the children would agree to the FBI's plan."[70]

In the end, the government's defense of its actions crumbled before a San Antonio jury, which acquitted all 11 Branch Davidian defendants on murder and conspiracy charges in the deaths of the four ATF agents. The jury acquitted four of the defendants of all charges; the other seven defendants were found guilty of lesser charges including weapons violations and abetting voluntary manslaughter.

For some reason, Janet Reno was consoled by these acquittals: "This clearly indicates that the killing of these four agents was not justified," she said.[71] Responded the *New York Times*, "Just about the only person who does not view the [San Antonio] verdict as a rebuke to the massive and unnecessary police action is Attorney General Janet Reno."[72]

IN BED WITH A CHILD PORNOGRAPHER

Janet Reno pledged that as Attorney General she would make protection of children a top Justice Department priority. But following the deaths of 25 Branch Davidian children, Reno caused another uproar when she sided with convicted pornographer Stephen Knox in a now notorious legal appeal of *Knox v. United States*.

Unlike the events at Waco, the *Knox* case involved genuine child abuse. At issue were three videotapes federal officials had seized from Knox, a graduate student at Pennsylvania State University. (A former grade school teacher, Knox had been convicted previously of receiving pornography.) The tapes in question showed girls aged 10 to 17 in leotards, bathing suits, or panties, spreading their legs. The tapes focused on the girls' genital areas and were accompanied by a newsletter that said the girls' clothing was so revealing it was as if they were naked. "Designed to pander to pedophiles," concluded the Justice Department.[73]

Nonetheless, Knox's lawyers argued at his 1991 trial that the tapes were not pornographic because the girls, technically, were clothed. But the judge and jury were not convinced; Knox was convicted on two counts of knowingly receiving child pornography through the mail, and the jury sentenced him to five years in prison. This decision was upheld on its first appeal.

When the Knox conviction was ultimately appealed to the U.S. Supreme Court, the Bush administration sided with the prosecution *against* Knox. But in September 1993, Janet Reno reversed the Bush position and sent her Solicitor General to the Supreme Court to side with the defense *for* Knox. Reno's Justice Department insisted that, in order to qualify as pornography, material "must depict a child lasciviously engaging in sexual conduct (as distinguished from lasciviousness on the part of the photographer or viewer)."[74] Under that standard, the Clinton administration's lawyers argued, Knox would be not guilty.

Because the Justice Department's Solicitor General was now siding with the pornographer, the Supreme Court could not schedule an argument. There was no one to present the government's case.

Angry Congressmen jumped on the Clinton Justice Department for reinterpreting child pornography statutes to benefit the criminals. "The Justice Department brief is an outrage," charged Sen. William V. Roth (R-Del.).[75] In November 1993, the Senate voted *100-0* to chastise Reno for her failure "to protect children's rights to be free from exploitation."[76]

The following month, a bipartisan group of more than 200 lawmakers asked President Clinton to order Reno to prosecute child pornographers vigorously, noting, "It has become increasingly clear that despite the Clinton administration's rhetoric about protecting children from exploitation and abuse, the administration's recent actions pose a real threat to the general welfare of our children."[77]

Finally, embarrassed, not to say cornered, Clinton fired off a terse letter to Reno. But instead of asking Reno to change her position on the existing law, Clinton asked her to submit *new* legislation to deal with child pornography. Just as he had done with the problem of gun violence, Clinton failed to enforce adequate existing laws, and instead sought a political victory by calling for new laws. "The President is absolutely off base in calling for new legislation," said Pat Trueman, the government's former top child pornography fighter. "We have the strongest child pornography law in the Western world. What we need is an Attorney General and an administration willing to protect children by merely applying [that] law."[78]

But Janet Reno was already busy on a new effort: clamping down on television violence. "I want to put in a pitch for children," she sanctimoniously told U.S. Senators in her October 1993 testimony. "I don't relish the prospect of government action," Reno said, "but if immediate, voluntary steps are not taken . . . government should respond [to TV violence with censorship] and respond immediately."[79] Evidently, the Attorney General preferred censoring America's television and movie executives to punishing convicted child pornographers.

"It is a pity," wrote *Wall Street Journal* culture critic Dorothy Rabinowitz, that "no one pointed out that the greatest instance of TV violence in the past year came in the April 19 assault on the Waco compound housing David Koresh's followers."[80] The irony was lost on Janet Reno.

1. Bill Clinton in remarks at Janet Reno's swearing-in ceremony; March 12, 1993.
2. Doug Bandow, quoted by Michael Hedges and Jerry Seper; *Washington Times*; April 21, 1993.
3. "Key Justice Department official," quoted by Jerry Seper in "Now that Hubbell's Out, Who's Minding the Store at Justice?"; *Washington Times*; March 16, 1994.
4. "Anonymous drug prosecutor," quoted by Alicia Mundy in "Attorney General of Social Work"; *Wall Street Journal*; January 5, 1994.
5. Wesley Pruden, "The All-White Refuge at the Country Club"; *Washington Times*; May 14, 1993.
6. U.S. Sen. Joseph R. Biden, Jr., quoted by Gwen Ifill in "Reno is Confirmed in Top Justice Job"; *New York Times*; March 12, 1993.
7. David Johnston with Stephen Labaton, "Doubts on Reno's Competence Rise in Justice Department"; *New York Times*; October 26, 1993.
8. Anonymous; interview with the authors; March 1994.
9. Janet Reno, appearing on "CBS This Morning"; March 12, 1993.
10. Paul Craig Roberts, "Clout Behind the Scenes at Justice"; *Washington Times*; March 31, 1993.
11. Editorial, "Backsliding at the White House"; *New York Times*; March 26, 1993.
12. *ibid.*
13. Paul Craig Roberts, *supra* endnote 10.
14. Bill Clinton and Al Gore, *Putting People First*; Times Books; 1992; page 71.
15. Statement of U.S. Sen. Orrin G. Hatch, "Capitol Hill Hearing Testimony"; Federal Document Clearing House; March 16, 1994.
16. *ibid.*
17. U.S. Sen. Orrin G. Hatch, quoted by Clifford Krauss in "Senate

Approves Broad Crime Bill"; *New York Times*; November 20, 1993.

18. Clifford Krauss, *supra* endnote 17.
19. Janet Reno, quoted by Rich Lowry in "Gambling on Reno"; *National Review*; November 15, 1993.
20. Janet Reno, *supra* endnote 9.
21. *ibid.*
22. Janet Reno, quoted in "ClintonWatch"; Volume 1, Number 2; May 1993.
23. Larry Rohter, "Debate Arises on Record of Justice Department Nominee"; *New York Times*; March 9, 1993.
24. Former Miami Police Chief Kenneth Harms, quoted by Larry Rohter, *supra* endnote 23.
25. Rich Lowry, *supra* endnote 19.
26. Anthony Lewis, "Abroad at Home: Where is Janet Reno?"; *New York Times*; November 22, 1993.
27. Clifford Krauss, "Much Ado, Little Done"; *New York Times*; November 23, 1993.
28. Sarah Brady, quoted by Erik Eckholm in "A Little Gun Control, A Lot of Guns"; *New York Times*; November 23, 1993.
29. Jon Weiner, quoted by Anne Thompson in "The Executive Life; Post-Riot L.A.'s Gun-Toting Liberals"; *New York Times*; June 28, 1992.
30. Morgan O. Reynolds and W.W. Caruth III in "Myths about Gun Control"; published by the National Center for Policy Analysis as Report No. 176; December 1992; page 29.
31. Catherine Matteson, quoted from August 30, 1993, interview with Gun Owners of America in Larry Pratt's "Special Report: Could a Search Warrant Be Your Death Warrant?"; Gun Owner's Foundation; Springfield, Virginia; page 8.
32. Daniel Wattenberg, "Gunning for Koresh"; *The American Spectator*; August 1993; page 33.
33. Dirk Johnson, "Death in Waco"; *New York Times*; April 22, 1993.
34. Daniel Wattenberg, *supra* endnote 32, page 32.
35. *ibid.*, page 39.
36. Debra Gersh Hernandez, "Government at Odds with SPJ Report"; *Editor & Publisher*; October 30, 1993.
37. Jack Harwell, quoted by Daniel Wattenberg, *supra* endnote 32.
38. Daniel Wattenberg, *supra* endnote 32, page 32.

39. *Waco-Tribune Herald*, cited in note 18 of Larry Pratt, *supra* endnote 31; page 6.
40. William P. Chesire, "Gonzo Justice and the Branch Davidians"; *Arizona Republic*; March 3, 1994.
41. Branch Davidian caller to 911, quoted in Larry Pratt, *supra* endnote 31.
42. Wayne Martin, quoted in Larry Pratt, *supra* endnote 31.
43. Catherine Matteson, quoted in Larry Pratt, *supra* endnote 31.
44. William P. Chesire, *supra* endnote 40.
45. Bill Clinton, quoted in "Clinton Says Koresh to Blame for the Carnage"; Compiled by *Times* Wires; *St. Petersburg Times*; April 21, 1993 (emphasis added).
46. Sam Howe Verhovek, "In Shadow of Texas Siege, Uncertainty for Innocents"; *New York Times*; March 8, 1993.
47. William Safire, "Waco, Reno, Iraqgate"; *New York Times*; October 14, 1993.
48. FBI Negotiator Byron Sage, quoted by Dirk Johnson in "Last Hours in Waco"; *New York Times*; April 26, 1993.
49. Dirk Johnson, *supra* endnote 48.
50. Larry Pratt, *supra* endnote 31, page 9.
51. Simon Tisdall, "FBI Rumors Obscured Fatal Mistakes at Waco"; *The Guardian*; April 26, 1993.
52. Dirk Johnson, *supra* endnote 48.
53. "Jurors in Sect's Murder Trial View Photos of FBI Assault (Special to the *New York Times*); *New York Times*; February 8, 1994.
54. Dirk Johnson, *supra* endnote 48.
55. *ibid.*
56. *ibid.*
57. J. Michael Kennedy, "Waco Cult Set Fire"; *Los Angeles Times*; April 27, 1993.
58. *ibid.*
59. Kathy Fair, "Expert Says Tanks Cut off Cult Escape; Crushed Stairwell Could Have Taken Women, Children to Safety"; *Houston Chronicle*; August 27, 1993.
60. Dirk Johnson, *supra* endnote 48.
61. *ibid.*
62. Texas Department of Public Safety spokesman Mike Cox, quoted by Dirk Johnson, *supra* endnote 33.
63. Dirk Johnson, *supra* endnote 48.
64. Robert Posch, *Direct Marketing Magazine*; June 1993.

65. Larry McMurtry, "Return to Waco"; *The New Republic*; June 7, 1993; page 18.
66. Bill Clinton, quoted by *St. Petersburg Times Wires, supra* endnote 45.
67. Howard Chua-Eoan, "Tripped Up by Lies"; *Time*; October 11, 1993.
68. Stephen Labaton, "Report on Assault on Waco Cult Contradicts Reno's Explanations"; *New York Times*; October 9, 1993.
69. Janet Reno, quoted by Michael Isikoff in "FBI Clashed over Waco"; *Washington Post*; October 9, 1993.
70. Dr. Alan Stone, quoted by Stephen Labaton in "Harsh Criticism of FBI in Review of Cult Assault"; *New York Times*; November 16, 1993.
71. Janet Reno quoted by Pierre Thomas in "Verdicts"; *Washington Post*; February 27, 1994.
72. Editorial, "A Jury Judges Waco"; *New York Times*; March 1, 1994.
73. Justice Department statement issued in March 1993, quoted by Joan Biskupic in "Administration Redefines Child Pornography Case"; *Washington Post*; November 2, 1993.
74. Justice Department brief quoted by U.S. Sen. William V. Roth (R-Del.) in "Protecting the Child Victims of Porn"; *Washington Post*; March 2, 1994.
75. U.S. Sen. William V. Roth (R-Del.), quoted in interview with Carl Ramsey; Family News in Focus Radio; October 29, 1993.
76. Jerry Seper, "Hill Sounds Alarm on Kiddie Porn"; *Washington Times*; December 16, 1993.
77. *ibid.*
78. Pat Trueman, quoted in interview with Carl Ramsey; Family News in Focus Radio; November 15, 1993.
79. Janet Reno, in her October 20, 1993, testimony before the Senate Commerce, Science and Transportation Committee.
80. Dorothy Rabinowitz, "The Attorney General as Scriptwriter"; *Wall Street Journal*; November 1, 1993.

FOREIGN POLICY DISASTERS

"Bill Clinton's foreign policy experience is limited to having had breakfast at the International House of Pancakes."
> —Patrick J. Buchanan
> Columnist and Radio-TV commentator,
> during the 1992 campaign

"For the Clinton team, implementing the decisions of the U.N. Security Council and the secretary general . . . is our foreign policy."[1]
> —Former U.N. Ambassador
> Jeane Kirkpatrick

Foreign policy disaster. These three words became synonymous with Bill Clinton's international agenda during his first year in office—at enormous cost to the United States.

In just one year, the new president ceded U.S. authority to the United Nations and provoked America's traditional allies. He squandered the historic opportunity to take advantage of the collapse of Communism by propping up old-guard bureaucrats and rejecting the aspirations of Eastern European countries who wanted to join NATO. His policy of appeasement encouraged Communist North Korea to pursue a nuclear capability, and his unsophisticated diplomacy toward China put America in a lose-lose situation with the biggest country on earth. Clinton has risked alienating a critical Middle East ally by touting anti-Israeli Strobe Talbott as a top advisor. And that's for starters.

After flip-flopping on his Haitian refugee policy, Clinton made an embarrassing effort to support Haitian president-in-exile Aristide, whose human rights record is appalling. On the Bosnian issue, Clinton's waffling destroyed his credibility with friend and foe alike. And in Somalia, Clinton escalated the U.S. role in such an irresponsible fashion as to lead to the deaths of 18 American soldiers.

Moreover, Clinton's breaches of protocol in Washington and his undignified behavior at international summits raised eyebrows among world leaders. Clinton barely pulled off a tea with the King of Spain and, after 15 months in office, he still had no ambassador to India. He did manage to coddle terrorists, contradicting years of American toughness.*

To call President Clinton's foreign policy weak would be generous. But is anyone surprised?

POST COLD WAR WHINING

Bill Clinton avoided foreign policy during his presidential campaign. Defense and foreign affairs issues made him uncomfortable. As a draftdodger, Clinton was run-

---

*In addition to admitting Irish terrorist Gerry Adams into the United States over the strenuous objections of the British government, Clinton has instructed the State Department—and presumably the CIA—to train the bodyguards of African National Congress/South African Communist party (ANC) leaders, even though the Defense Department lists the ANC as a terrorist group. Clinton also ordered the State Department to train the bodyguards of Palestine Liberation Organization (PLO) leader Yasser Arafat, who is personally responsible for terrorist attacks on American citizens, including the murder of the American ambassador to Sudan.

ning for president against George Bush, who had flown combat missions as the Navy's youngest pilot in World War II, and Naval Academy graduate Ross Perot, whose search for American prisoners of war in Southeast Asia and hostage rescue efforts in the Middle East had earned him wide admiration. Clinton was lucky: foreign policy issues drew little attention in the 1992 presidential campaign because the Reagan and Bush administrations had successfully pursued a platform of "Peace through Strength." Americans had grown accustomed to the firm, able presence of men and women such as Caspar Weinberger, Jeane Kirkpatrick, Dick Cheney, and General Colin Powell.

The Reagan and Bush administrations protected against, and ultimately defeated, Soviet Communism. Ronald Reagan took decisive, principled actions to establish America as the strongest military power in the world. He called the Soviet Union an "evil empire" and forced Mikhail Gorbachev to tear down the Berlin Wall.

But Bill Clinton brought weakness and uncertainty to the White House. In his Inaugural address, President Clinton's foreign policy priorities were "the world environment, the world AIDS crisis, [and] the world arms race."[2] Once ensconced in the White House, Clinton complained about the complexity of contemporary international challenges. He even joked to the *Washington Post*, "Gosh, I miss the Cold War,"[3] forgetting both the tragic costs of communist expansionism and the bitter divisions in America over how to handle the Soviet Union.

The personnel and policies that had opposed the "Peace through Strength" campaign in the 1980s found a new home when Bill Clinton took office. Where Republicans had stood for decisive policies and unilateral action in America's interest, the Clinton team pursued multinational planning. Foremost among this group was Clinton's Secretary of State Warren Christopher, who had played a prominent role in the Panama Canal giveaway by the Carter administration. On his first trip as U.S. Secretary of State, Christopher visited the United Nations and had a private lunch with U.N. Secretary General Boutros Boutros-Ghali. A State Department spokesman explained that this trip "underscored the importance the new administration attaches to the role of the United Nations in the international arena."[4] Clinton appointed Anthony Lake as his National Security Advisor. Like Christopher, Lake had served in the Carter State Department, where he worked to accommodate the Communists in Nicaragua.

Former U.N. Ambassador Jeane Kirkpatrick identified this transformation in American foreign policy: "This is not the first time an American administration has brought to U.S. foreign policy-making a global perspective and tendency to prefer universal needs to national interests. Many of the same people now making foreign policy for the Clinton administration tried these ideas first when they served in the Carter administration."[5] In Clinton's first year as president, this "global perspective" produced failure after failure.

CRYING WOLF ON AID TO BOSNIA

The breakup of Yugoslavia in 1992 left Bosnia, the heart of the former Communist state, torn among contending Serb, Croat, and Bosnian Muslim troops fighting each other. The communist Serbs launched a vicious offensive against Croatia and invented a new expression for genocide—"ethnic cleansing." The world watched in horror as shellings, starvation and rape ravaged the country.

As a candidate, Bill Clinton had loudly denounced this carnage and faulted the Bush administration for tolerating it. But once in office, Clinton did no more than bluster—he made threat after threat of U.S. air strikes against the Serbs, but he never made good on any of them. Clinton became the international "boy who cried wolf." Far from helping the Bosnians, Clinton's indecisiveness emboldened the Serbian aggressors and their allies to conquer more territory and kill tens of thousands more civilians. It also encouraged Russian hard-liners to make a comeback in the Balkans by sending in their own troops, unilaterally, as Washington looked on.

In addition to harming the Bosnians, Clinton's vacillation disillusioned America's allies in Europe. Secretary of State Warren Christopher had announced that the U.S. wanted multilateral military action against the Serbs early in 1993. But he shuttled among the capitals of Europe with no compelling plan, and America's allies refused to get involved.

Clinton did win embarrassing praise from Serbia's president, accused war criminal Slobodan Milosevic. The *Washington Post* reported on April 9, 1993, that when its staff interviewed Milosevic, he "expressed satisfaction that the new [Clinton] administration was allowing Bosnian Serbs to consolidate their territorial grab."[6]

In an April 23, 1993, press conference, Clinton sheepishly admitted that he was taking his cues on Bosnia from the United Nations:

QUESTION: Mr. President, you continue to insist that this has to be multilateral action . . . it makes it look as if this is a state of paralysis. The United States is the last remaining superpower. Why is it not appropriate in this situation for the United States to act unilaterally?

PRESIDENT CLINTON: Well, the United States . . . even as the last remaining superpower, has to act consistent with international law under some mandate of the United Nations.[7]

Clinton later admitted his own feeble handling of the Bosnian situation. He said, "We don't need any more empty threats,"[8] presumably his, as NATO contemplated air strikes on Sarajevo in February 1994. Still, Clinton made his support for proposed NATO air strikes contingent on approval from U.N. Secretary General Boutros Boutros-Ghali. "We have placed the most critical command decision affecting our forces in the hands of a power-seeking Secretary General who has neither military experience nor capability," warned Caspar Weinberger.[9]

"On Bosnia," reported the *Christian Science Monitor*, "the president repeatedly talked tough and then backed down. For a full year he squandered a resource that is vital to any nation that plays a leadership role internationally: the sense among its friends and foes alike that it will formulate its foreign policies with care and precision, make them known unambiguously, and then follow them with maximum possible consistency."[10]

THE HAITIAN BOAT PEOPLE

Treatment of Haitian refugees was another foreign policy issue on which Bill Clinton had tried to distinguish himself from George Bush during the 1992 campaign. Under the Bush policy, the U.S. Coast Guard turned Haitian boat people away from U.S. soil. Bill Clinton denounced the Bush policy as inhumane and said, "I think . . . sending them back to Haiti . . . was an error. And so, I will modify that process."[11] The day after Clinton was elected, tens of thousands of Haitians eagerly began building boats on the beaches of Haiti.

With an estimated half-million Haitians about to pour into the United States as a result of his new policy, Clinton sobered up. A week before he took office, Clinton reversed his position: "The practice of returning those who fled Haiti by boat will continue, for the time being, after I become president. Those who do leave Haiti . . . by boat will be stopped and directly returned by the United States Coast Guard."[12]

It turned out that Clinton's attack on George Bush's Haiti policy was merely a campaign ploy to pander to black voters. To win black support, Clinton had cynically raised the hopes of desperate Haitians who dreamed of new lives in America. "On Haitian refugee policy, Bill Clinton is a liar," wrote a disgusted *Boston Globe* reporter. "Now that he [Clinton] no longer needs African-American and liberal votes, he has revealed to the world that he agreed with Bush's policy on the refugees all along."[13]

"RESTORING DEMOCRACY" IN HAITI

The history of Haiti reveals how foolish it was for Bill Clinton to shout "quick fix" solutions during his campaign.

In the eighteenth century, Haiti was the wealthiest country in the Western hemisphere—it accounted for 40 percent of the trade of prerevolutionary France. Now, it is the poorest. Its history is pitted with slavery and voodoo. A stab at democracy in Haiti brought about the 1990 election of Jean-Bertrand Aristide as president. But Aristide, after a short and bloody reign, was ousted in a military coup in September 1991, following which he has lived in exile in Washington. Meanwhile, turmoil in Haiti produced the "boat people" that figured in the 1992 presidential election.

Although Aristide's regime had a record of violence, the Clinton administration approved disbursements of about $1.8 million per month to allow him to operate in exile and pay his Washington lobbyists.[14]

These payments became increasingly outrageous as information about Aristide's ultra left-wing past and history of support for violence became better known. In September 1991, for example, Aristide told a mob that if they should see "a faker who pretends to be one of our supporters . . . just grab him. Make sure he gets what he deserves."[15] As for necklacing—the practice of hanging gasoline-soaked tires around enemies' necks and lighting them—Aristide said, "It smells good and wherever you go, you want to smell it."[16]

Ignoring Aristide's record, the Clinton administration promoted him as the answer to Haiti's troubles. On July 3, 1993, Aristide and his political opponent, Haitian armed forces commander Raoul Cedras, signed a U.N.-brokered agreement in which General Cedras agreed to resign by October 15, 1993 and allow a U.N.-sponsored group to organize a new Haitian police force. President Clinton guaranteed Aristide's safe return to Haiti on October 30, 1993.

As the deadlines for Aristide's return approached, Haiti was in chaos. Regardless, Clinton sent the U.S.S. *Harlan County* to Haiti to prepare for Aristide's return. But the U.S. warship was turned back by a gang of hoodlums gathered at the dock. "We're ready to die!" shouted one protestor. "We don't want Aristide back!"[17] Humiliated, Clinton had to order the U.S. ship back to base at Guantanamo, Cuba.

As the world sniggered at this soap-opera buffoonery, news surfaced that Clinton and his advisors had ignored reports provided by U.S. intelligence warning that U.S.

troops would be met with just such opposition in Haiti. According to the *Washington Post*, senior Clinton officials said that due to "defects in the administration's decision making, the intelligence reports either did not reach the right people or failed to make a sufficient impact."[18] For his part, Secretary of State Christopher was surprised by the angry mobs: "We had every reason to think they [U.S. troops] would be well received, we thought there was going to be a greeting party."[19]

One year into his presidential term, Bill Clinton had done nothing right on Haiti. First, he deceived the boat people. Next, he gave aid to exiled President Aristide despite Aristide's record of support for violence. Then Clinton orchestrated the agreement that made the U.S. responsible for Aristide's safe return to Haiti, which ended in the ridiculous scene of the ship being turned away by an angry mob. Finally, Clinton scaled back his support for Aristide and enforced a U.N. embargo that only adds to the suffering of the Haitian people.

In a letter to the editor of the *Washington Post*, an American citizen living in Haiti wrote, "The embargo on Haiti is the most merciless, inhumane thing I have seen or experienced in my 60 years of life."[20]

STARVATION IN SOMALIA

Somalia became a focal point of world attention in the years following the January 1991 ouster of Somali dictator Mohammed Siad Barre. In fights that ensued among rival Somali clans, food became a primary weapon. This tragic picture of starvation eventually reached American televisions and in December 1992, President Bush announced Operation Restore Hope. "To the people of Somalia," Bush said, "I promise this: *We do not plan to dictate political outcomes*. I can state with confidence we come to your country for one reason only: to enable the starving to be fed."[21]

To the American people, President Bush said: "Our mission has a limited objective, to open the supply routes, to get the food moving, and to prepare the way for a U.N. peacekeeping force to keep it moving."[22] President Bush forecast that America's food relief efforts would last through February 1993.

When Bill Clinton took office, Americans thought that the Somali crisis was all but over. But when February came, Clinton had no plan for the return of U.S. troops. Instead, he oversaw the evolution of U.S. food relief efforts into participation in U.N. Boutros-Ghali's plans for "nation-building." Clinton's U.N. ambassador, Madeleine Albright, praised this new effort as "an unprecedented enterprise aimed at nothing less than the restoration of an entire country as a proud, functioning, and viable member of the community of nations."[23]

It did not take long for President Clinton's careless expansion of the U.S. role in Somalia to collapse into tragedy.

"NATION-BUILDING" IN SOMALIA

As part of its U.S.-supported "nation-building" efforts, the United Nations called for disarmament of Somali clans and the installation of a new government. But Somali warlord Mohammed Farah Aideed refused to comply. On June 5, Aideed's forces ambushed U.N. peacekeeping forces, killing 25 and wounding 60. In response, the U.N. intensified its efforts and Boutros-Ghali's top advisor in Somalia, U.S. Admiral Jonathan Howe, announced a $25,000 reward for Aideed's capture: "He is a menace to public safety. He's a killer."[24] U.N. helicopters dropped leaflets publicizing the reward, and U.N. Ambassador Albright said those who were responsible for the ambush "would pay a heavy price."[25] On June 16, President Clinton applauded a U.N. attack on Aideed's compound: "The military back of Aideed has been broken. A warrant has been issued for his arrest."[26]

But Aideed's back had not been broken. After several failed attempts to capture Aideed, U.S. forces got word that he was meeting with his Somali lieutenants in a building in Mogadishu. In a 15-minute raid on October 3, 1993, Delta Force commandos stormed the building and took 24 Somalia prisoners. Although Aideed himself escaped, the American soldiers captured two of his top aides.

But the 15-minute raid turned into a 16-hour nightmare, with "the most intense combat by U.S. infantrymen since Vietnam."[27] The Somalis downed a Black Hawk helicopter whose pilots were killed and crew stranded. Army Rangers were deployed to defend the crash site until a successful rescue could be completed.* Meanwhile, other U.S. soldiers were killed as they convoyed through bulletfire to collect the Somali prisoners.

Then a second Black Hawk helicopter was shot down, leaving four wounded Army Rangers stranded. Although two Delta snipers came to the rescue, Somali gunmen outnumbered the Americans and killed five of the six U.S. soldiers at the site.†

---

*The Rangers were initially unable to retrieve the body of a dead co-pilot, Chief Warrant Officer Clifton P. Wolcott, from under the wreckage. Though aware that lingering at the crash site would put their own escape at risk, the Rangers refused to leave Wolcott's body behind. They knew that just weeks earlier Somali mobs had defiled the corpses of other dead American soldiers. Although the Army does not require soldiers to retrieve the dead in such situations, "there was no question in anybody's mind that we were going to stay until we got him," said Lt. Col. Danny McKnight, the commander of the Ranger battalion.[28]

†The fallen U.S. soldiers were subsequently defiled by a Somali mob. The lone

As night fell, the commander of conventional U.S. forces in Somalia, Maj. Gen. Thomas M. Montgomery, was urgently trying to scratch up armored personnel carriers from Pakistani and Malaysian commanders to rescue stranded U.S. soldiers. But the belated help was hampered by Somali ambushes and by confusion due to the language difficulties inherent in multinational forces. It was not until morning that the surviving U.S. forces were retrieved.

In all, 18 U.S. soldiers died, and more than 80 were wounded. "An unmitigated disaster," said U.S. Sen. Richard Lugar (R-Ind.).[29]

ASLEEP AT THE SWITCH

In the aftermath of the Battle of Mogadishu, top civilians in the Clinton administration scrambled for political cover.

Outraged Congressmen wanted to know why General Montgomery had to rely on foreign armored personnel carriers and why air support had been withdrawn from Somalia. Why hadn't the U.S. troops been able to rescue their fellow soldiers immediately? It soon surfaced that General Montgomery had made repeated requests for armored vehicles, and General Colin Powell had twice questioned Secretary of Defense Les Aspin about the armor request. All requests had been denied.

Not surprisingly, President Clinton had little consolation for Americans, or for the families of the dead U.S. troops.* He was too busy pinning the blame on the United

---

survivor, Chief Warrant Officer Michael Durant, was taken captive and remained a prisoner for 11 days before returning to the United States a hero.

*Rep. Henry J. Hyde (R.-Ill.), a senior member of the House Foreign Affairs Committee, wrote in the wake of the Battle of Mogadishu: "When American soldiers die in battle, the most sacred obligation of their commander in chief

Nations: "I mean we were asked to come in and in effect be the police officer in this thing," he said, "and then the U.N. shifted course and said we ought to stay there until nation-building takes place."[32] But the Clinton administration had *voted for* the U.N. plan. President Clinton had publicly supported the shift in course. And U.N. Ambassador Albright had gushed about Boutros-Ghali's grand "nation-building" goals.

After the Mogadishu disaster, Clinton was, predictably, full of denials. He said he didn't know U.S. troops were still trying to catch Aideed. "It is not our job to rebuild Somalia's society, or even to create a political process that can allow Somalia's clans to live and work in peace,"[33] Clinton said in a televised address, after months of trying to do just that.

Even the *New York Times* was incredulous over Clinton's back-pedaling: "Mr. Clinton has gone so far as to say he was not even aware United States forces were still trying to capture Aideed."[34] Secretary Aspin could only say, "Had I known at that time what I knew after the events of [October 3], I would have made a different decision."[35] In an astonishing admission, Secretary of State Christopher added, "We were not sufficiently attentive . . . the policy was being managed by the deputies committee."[36] In other words, the President, the Secretary of Defense, the Secretary of State, and the National Se-

---

is to explain to their family and friends and the rest of the country what cause was served by their sacrifice. There are 18 families in this country whose sons, fathers, husbands, and brothers were killed in Somalia in battle October 3 while attempting to arrest warlord Mohammed Farah Aideed. No one has yet heard a convincing explanation from either the president or his administration for why these soldiers gave up their lives."[30] Indeed, according to leading Vietnam Veteran John Wheeler, Clinton "has ignored the request to meet with families of Rangers killed in Mogadishu."[31]

curity Council put U.S. troops in danger in a distant country without being fully briefed on the military situation.
They were satisfied to allow this dangerous U.S. effort to
be conducted by subcabinet-level personnel.

The public was in an uproar over the gross disregard
for the welfare of U.S. troops. Congress called Secretary
Aspin to Capitol Hill for an explanation. "Never have I
heard a more confused, disjointed, vague defense of
American foreign policy in my professional career,"[37]
raged Rep. James Walsh (R-N.Y.) after Aspin's visit. Arizona Sen. John McCain, a former Vietnam prisoner of
war, said, "We need to find out how many lives were lost
because of the refusal of the civilian leadership in the
Pentagon to listen to the military leadership."[38]

In response, Clinton announced he would send additional troops to reinforce the U.S. forces in Somalia, and
that these troops would be "under American command."[39]* Clinton then promised that all U.S. troops
would be home by March 31, 1994.

But the Somalia debacle continued: in a bizarre policy
reversal following the Battle of Mogadishu, the Clinton
administration flew Aideed to peace talks in Ethiopia with
other clan leaders. "Aideed has gone from being the object of manhunts and air strikes to being a leader worthy
of protection by American troops," charged Rep. Curt
Weldon (R-Penn.). "This is further proof of an administration in disarray. We should be ashamed of ourselves.
Aideed is a tyrant and a thug. He should be captured and
arrested, not coddled and protected."[40]

Clinton's foreign policy mistakes in Somalia were inex-
cusable. First, he unwisely expanded U.S. goals there.

---

*In a controversial May 1993 decision, Clinton had approved putting U.S. troops
under foreign command.

Next, he failed to ensure that the U.S. military presence was adequate to pursue his ambitious political objectives. Then he put U.S. troops under foreign command, which failed them in a fatal mission. Afterward, he tried to deny the political expansion of the Somalia mission, and he blamed subordinates for the disaster. And finally, he extended protection and legitimacy to the very man who in one way or another was responsible for the deaths and public desecration of American soldiers.

Following the disaster in Somalia, U.S. Sen. Richard Lugar (R-Ind.) warned of the "virtual collapse of presidential leadership in [foreign] matters. The roof has fallen in. There is no significant congressional support for the president's policy in any of the three countries [Bosnia, Somalia and Haiti], and it's his own fault."[41]

CLINTON'S ASIAN MISADVENTURES

The Clinton administration has made other foreign policy missteps—potentially disastrous—in Korea and China.

Several factors have combined to raise tensions on the Korean peninsula higher than they have been since the Korean War. In recent years, North Korea has faced new hardships with a declining economy and the cessation of aid from its former communist ally, the Soviet Union. Its communist ruler, Kim Il-sung, is 82 years old. Nonetheless, North Korea apparently has two nuclear bombs and a still-whet appetite for South Korea, the staunch American ally and linchpin of stability in the region. "It is our nation's supreme task to reunify in the '90s and hand down a reunified country to generations to come," wrote the communist *Pyong-yang Times* in a January 1994 editorial.[42] Most significantly, North Korea has refused to allow inspections of its nuclear sites, in violation of the Nuclear Non-Proliferation Treaty.

"I hope we are not headed toward a full-blown crisis [with North Korea]," said Bill Clinton unassuringly. "I hope we can avoid one, but I am not positive that we can."[43] Rather than face down Kim Il-sung and nip the problem in the bud, Clinton has vacillated and even tried to appease the militant dictator. For such weakness, Bill Clinton may go down in history as the president who failed to prevent a second—and possibly nuclear—Korean War.

To make matters worse, the Clinton administration chose to alienate China at the very moment it needed its help controlling its bordering communist neighbor. "If anyone can deter North Korea from the perilous game of nuclear brinksmanship," said Asian specialist Jacques Pradel, "it's China."[44] Pradel charged that the Clinton administration has failed "the elementary diplomatic test of appreciating how policies directed toward one country may have a significant bearing elsewhere."[45]

Indifferent to this reasoning, Warren Christopher traveled to China in March 1994 threatening to withdraw its most favored nation trading status because of human rights abuses. But the wimpish Secretary of State didn't in the least faze the Chinese. His trip was described by columnist Charles Krauthammer as a "diplomatic mugging . . . Christopher went to China breathing fire and brimstone about its need to improve its human rights. The Chinese greeted him with contempt . . . Christopher's aides, report[ed] the *New York Times*, were 'shocked and bewildered' by the Chinese behavior."[46]

"Once again," Krauthammer concluded, "the classic pattern of Clinton foreign policy: It first indulges in high-flown humanitarianism, then when the time comes to make the downpayment on its moralism, it flinches."[47]

STROBE TALBOTT AND HIS RUSSIA FIXATION

Perhaps President Clinton's most revealing step in foreign policy was the appointment of his old Oxford roommate Strobe Talbott as "ambassador-at-large to the new independent states of the former Soviet Union." As a powerful "Friend of Bill," Talbott within the year became the number two man at the State Department.*

Prior to joining the Clinton administration, Talbott had worked at *Time* magazine for 22 years and served as the magazine's Washington bureau chief. Talbott's new career as Clinton diplomat has been controversial for four reasons: (1) he has no diplomatic or governmental experience; (2) his views on Russia stem from personal passion rather than sound professional judgment; (3) his writings at *Time* betray a strong anti-Israel bias†; and (4) his advocacy of a "global nation" calls into question his allegiance to a strong, independent United States.

At *Time*, Talbott ridiculed Ronald Reagan for calling the Soviet Union an "evil empire." He opposed Reagan's protection of NATO with Pershing II missiles and his plan to build a strategic defense to protect the United States from Soviet missiles. And he "assign[ed] no credit for the end of the Soviet Union to the long struggle waged by the dissidents and the refuseniks, or the Afghan rebels and the Polish workers."[50] In glorifying Mikhail Gorbachev as

---

*Like Bill Clinton, Strobe Talbott had pulled strings to avoid the draft. Talbott got a medical deferment, a move about which he says he now feels "a moral discomfort bordering on guilt."[48]

†When asked by the Senate Foreign Relations Committee to provide an example of where the U.S.-Israeli alliance has helped the United States, Talbott failed to do so. When asked to assess Israel's value in the Cold War, or Israel's value today, Talbott again failed to do so. In one of his many *Time* attacks on Israel, Talbott wrote that the U.S.-Israeli relationship was characterized by "mistrust, misunderstandings and misconceptions . . . starting with the delusion that Israel is, or ever has been, primarily a strategic ally."[49]

Time's "Man of the Decade," Talbott declared, "the Soviet threat is not what it used to be. The real point, however, is that it never was. The doves in the great debate of the past forty years were right all along."[51]*

Blinded by his pro-Russian obsession, Talbott has single-mindedly supported Russia to the detriment of other new independent states such as Ukraine. Moreover, Talbott and Clinton rebuffed the longing of Poland, Hungary, and the Czech Republic to join NATO. They further alienated the new independent states by sending aid to Russia and supporting it as the *only* force for stability in the region, despite Russia's use of economic and political subversion, and even armed warfare, to force these countries back into line.

Moreover, the Clinton administration's aid to Russia has not helped build a free market. Rather, it has reinforced Russia's old guard with a positions-command economy similar to that which plagued the Soviet Union. Even more irresponsibly, Clinton has attached no conditions on money sent to Russia. The aid, for example, was not made contingent on Russia halting its empire building or its aggressive spying against the United States.

THE TALBOTT DOCTRINE

"I'll bet within the next hundred years," Strobe Talbott wrote in one of his last columns for *Time*, "nationhood

---

*In fact, the doves were wrong, as former top Soviet officials admitted at a February 1993 conference at Princeton University. Former Soviet Foreign Minister Alexandr Bessmertnykh said that SDI "made us realize we were in a dangerous spot."[52] And Russia expert Dimitri Simes said that it had become "practically conventional wisdom in Moscow . . . that the arms buildup, SDI, and policies like resisting the Soviet invasion of Afghanistan and the decision to deploy INF convinced the Soviet Union that the Cold War could not be won."[53]

as we know it will be obsolete; all states will recognize a single, global authority . . . The internal affairs of a nation used to be off limits to the world community. Now the principle of 'humanitarian intervention' is gaining acceptance."[54]

This assertion—that humanitarianism makes nationhood irrelevant and even dangerous—has become known as the Talbott Doctrine. To Talbott's way of thinking, it is *in* our national interest to *give up* our national interests. President Clinton embraced the Talbott Doctrine in his Inaugural address, declaring that "there is no longer a clear division between what is foreign and what is domestic."[55]

The Talbott Doctrine is not always recognizable; it masks itself through indirect and confusing measures. Former U.N. Ambassador Jeane Kirkpatrick explained that "the reason the Clinton administration's foreign policy seems indecisive is that multilateral decision-making is characteristically complicated and inconclusive."[56]

Still, a gradual but distinct pattern has emerged that shows President Clinton ceding U.S. national authority to the United Nations:

- In May 1993, Undersecretary of State Peter Tarnoff, in remarks not meant for attribution, said the United States would operate "under new rules of engagement" in the post-Cold War world.[57] He said the United States had neither the leverage nor the will to use military force by itself.
- In June 1993, U.N. Ambassador Madeleine Albright told a Senate subcommittee that the Clinton foreign policy was one of "assertive multilateralism." She said, "The time has come to commit the political,

intellectual, and financial capital that U.N. peace keeping and our security deserve."[58]

- In July 1993, an interagency meeting within the administration approved a classified draft of Clinton's Presidential Decision Directive 13 (PPD-13), which would commit the United States "politically, militarily and financially" to U.N. military operations. The *Washington Post* said the draft of PPD-13 "would formalize the president's acceptance of U.N. command over U.S. troops, a significant milestone."[59] The administration put the controversial draft on hold when it became public.

- By year's end, the new chairman of the Joint Chiefs of Staff, General Shalikashvili, issued "Draft 5" of the *U.S. Army Field Manual* outlining a new command structure for U.S. troops on multinational missions. These troops would no longer take orders from their own commander-in-chief, as provided by the U.S. Constitution, but rather from the unelected politicians and generals of the United Nations.[60]

Although it has been gradual and subtle, abolishing the distinction between "what is foreign and what is domestic" is one of the most radical developments of the Clinton administration. As surely as night follows day, U.S. moral authority and willpower will dissipate under this relativist doctrine. Indeed, a profound companion development has already begun under Bill Clinton: military disarmament.

1. Jeane Kirkpatrick, "Where is Our Foreign Policy?"; *Washington Post*; August 30, 1993.
2. Bill Clinton, Inaugural Address; January 20, 1993.
3. Bill Clinton quoted by Ann Devroy and R. Jeffrey Smith in "Clinton Reexamines a Foreign Policy Under Siege"; *Washington Post*; October 17, 1993.

4. Richard Boucher quoted by Mary Curtius in "Christopher's U.N. Visit Seen Symbol of Priority"; *Boston Globe*; February 1, 1993.

5. Jeane Kirkpatrick, *supra* endnote 1.

6. Slobodan Milosevic quoted in Editorial, "Praise from Mr. Milosevic; *Washington Post*; April 9, 1993.

7. President's News Conference; April 23, 1993.

8. Paul Bedard and Rowan Scarborough, "For the 10th Times, Clinton Warns Serbs"; *Washington Times*; February 8, 1994.

9. Caspar W. Weinberger, "Bosnia—America's Shame"; *Forbes*; March 14, 1994.

10. "U.S. Voters Did Not Intend White House Bungling Abroad" (unsigned); *Christian Science Monitor*; March 18, 1994.

11. Bill Clinton quoted in "Clinton Meets the Press"; *Washington Times*; November 13, 1992.

12. Bill Clinton quoted by Ruth Marcus in "Clinton Beseiged about Policy Shifts: Promises Not Broken, He Insists"; *Washington Post*; January 15, 1993.

13. Derrick Z. Jackson, "Clinton's Haiti Lies"; *Boston Globe*; January 17, 1993.

14. Scott Shepard, "Aristide Freely Spends Frozen Haitian Funds"; *Washington Times*; November 30, 1993.

15. Lally Weymouth, "Haiti's Suspect Savior"; *Washington Post*; January 24, 1993.

16. *ibid.*

17. Ed McCullough, "Haitian Militants Force U.S. Troops to Retreat"; *Washington Times*; October 13, 1993.

18. R. Jeffrey Smith and Ann Devroy, "Handling Global Trouble Spots"; *Washington Post*; October 17, 1993.

19. Warren Christopher quoted by R. Jeffrey Smith and Ann Devroy, *supra* endnote 18.

20. Cecilia Manness; "Letter to the Editor"; *Washington Post*; March 14, 1994.

21. Text, 1992 Almanac, page 42-E, quoted in "A Somalia Chronology," by Jennifer S. Thomas; *Congressional Quarterly*; October 16, 1993 (emphasis provided).

22. Paul Alexander, "Somalis Fire on U.S. Helicopters"; *Washington Times*; October 21, 1993.

23. Madeleine Albright quoted by *New York Times* News Service; *Chicago Tribune*; March 28, 1993.

24. Paul Alexander, *supra* endnote 22.
25. Warren Strobel, "White House Policy on Aideed Comes Full Circle"; *Washington Times*; October 21, 1993.
26. Paul Alexander, *supra* endnote 22.
27. Rick Atkinson, "The Raid That Went Wrong"; *Washington Post*; January 30, 1994.
28. Michael R. Gordon, "Fateful Decision: Staying to 'Guard a Pilot's Body"; *New York Times*; October 25, 1993.
29. U.S. Senator Richard Lugar, quoted by Paul Gigot in "Clinton Abroad Resembles Bush at Home"; *Wall Street Journal*; October 8, 1993.
30. Henry J. Hyde, senior member of the House Foreign Affairs Committee, "Is the White House in Charge of Foreign Policy Decisions?" *Washington Times*; November 11, 1993.
31. John Wheeler, "Clinton Has Yet to Shed His Anti-Military Bias"; *Los Angeles Times*; January 5, 1994.
32. Bill Clinton quoted by Ann Devroy and John Lancaster in "Clinton to Add 1,500 Troops in Somalia, Considers a March 31 Withdrawal Date"; *Washington Post*; October 7, 1993.
33. Bill Clinton quoted by Associated Press in "I Am Committed to Getting This Job Done in Somalia"; *Washington Post*; October 8, 1993.
34. Michael R. Gordon with John H. Cushman, Jr., "Missing in Somalia"; *New York Times*; October 18, 1993.
35. Les Aspin quoted by Thomas E. Ricks in "Defense Secretary Aspin Draws Heaviest Fire as Criticism Mounts over U.S. Role in Somalia"; *Wall Street Journal*; October 8, 1993.
36. Warren Christopher quoted by R. Jeffrey Smith and Ann Devroy, *supra* endnote 18.
37. Rep. James Walsh (R-N.Y.), quoted by Thomas E. Ricks, *supra* endnote 35.
38. U.S. Senator John McCain (R-Ariz.) quoted by Bill Gertz, "Aspin Decision Probed"; *Washington Times*; October 13, 1993.
39. Bill Clinton by Associated Press, *supra* 33.
40. Representative Curt Weldon (R-Penn.) quoted by Rowan Scarborough in "Once Targeted Somali Warlord Gets U.S. Escort"; *Washington Times*; December 3, 1993.
41. Richard Lugar quoted by R. W. Apple, Jr. in "Policing a Global Village"; *New York Times*; October 13, 1993.

42. *Pyong-yang Times*, quoted in "North Korea's Nuclear Cloud"; *Wall Street Journal*; January 24, 1994.
43. Bill Clinton, quoted by Jeffrey H. Birnbaum in "Clinton 'Not Positive' U.S. Can Avoid Crisis in Showdown with North Korea"; *Wall Street Journal*; December 9, 1993.
44. Jacques Pradel, quoted by Bernard D. Kaplan; *Washington Times*; March 25, 1994.
45. *ibid.*
46. Charles Krauthammer, "Major Embarrassment in China"; *Plain Dealer*; March 20, 1994.
47. *ibid.*
48. Strobe Talbott quoted by Charles Lane in "The Master of the Game: Strobe's World"; *The New Republic*; March 7, 1994.
49. *ibid.*
50. Charles Lane, *supra* endnote 48.
51. Strobe Talbott quoted by Charles Lane, *supra* endnote 48.
52. Alexandr Bessmertnykh quoted by Morton M. Kondracke; *Roll Call*; January 13, 1994.
53. Dimitri Simes quoted by Morton M. Kondracke, *supra* endnote 52.
54. Strobe Talbott, "The Birth of the Global Nation"; *Time*; July 20, 1992; page 70.
55. Bill Clinton, *supra* endnote 2.
56. Jeane Kirkpatrick, *supra* endnote 1.
57. Daniel Williams and John M. Goshko, *Washington Post*; May 27, 1993.
58. R. Jeffrey Smith and Julia Preston, "U.S. Plan Wider Role in U.N. Peace Keeping"; *Washington Post*; June 18, 1993.
59. Barton Gellman, "Wider U.N. Police Role Supported; Foreigners Could Lead U.S. Troops"; *Washington Post*; August 5, 1993.
60. Bill Gertz, "Army Manual Says GIs Will Follow U.N. Orders"; *Washington Times*; December 15, 1993.

DOWNSIZING DEFENSE

"Our forces are the finest military our nation has ever had, and I have pledged that as long as I am president, they will remain the best-trained, the best-equipped, and the best-prepared fighting force on the face of this earth."[1]
 —Bill Clinton,
  State of the Union Address, 1994

"Strategic airlift in this country today is broken. I'm not sure it is workable today for one major regional contingency."[2]
 —Marine Corps General Joseph P. Hoar
  United States Central Command

"If the U.S. military ever becomes a paper tiger, it will be a call to arms for every megalomaniac in the world."[3]
 —Robert H. Burger, Letter to the Editor
  Newsday, February 3, 1994

It is easy for Americans to take for granted the strength and prestige of being the number one superpower in the world. The position comes naturally to a people who are independent and proud.

But it is well to remember that America's leadership, brought about through its military strength, is a relatively recent phenomenon.

Before World War II, the United States was not among the top military powers of the world. Although the U.S. Navy was strong, America's active Army ranked only 15th worldwide, and its active Air Force eighth.[4] To stop the Axis menace, Americans worked hard to build up their military. During the Cold War, U.S. superiority was repeatedly challenged by the Soviet Union.

In 1985, at the height of the Reagan military build-up, U.S. military forces were the finest in history. America had 27 Army divisions, 37 Air Force wings, and 542 Navy ships.[5] There was an active research and development program to maintain the technological edge, active procurement of new weapons, and an effective program to ensure supply of spare parts. America was in a constant state of readiness, and the Strategic Defense Initiative (SDI) promised a new security for the whole country.

With the end of the Cold War, then-President George Bush and his Secretary of Defense, Dick Cheney, knew that some cuts in U.S. defenses could be achieved safely. The Bush administration proposed a 30 percent reduction in U.S. defense spending, and Congress dug further still. Thus, the program handed to Bill Clinton had already made the largest cuts possible without compromising security.

Nonetheless, once in office, Clinton doubled the defense cuts he had called for in his campaign and began a rapid, massive disarmament of American forces. The Clinton defense cuts will leave the United States with 15 Army divisions, 20 Air Force wings, and 346 Navy ships. That's 12 Army divisions, 17 Air Force wings, and 196 Navy ships fewer than America had at its peak under Reagan.[6] "Clinton wants to cut the defense budget to one of its lowest points since before Pearl Harbor," wrote the *National*

Journal, "a move that will require a sweeping reorganization of federal priorities."[7]

Unsurprisingly, morale in U.S. armed forces has plummeted since Bill Clinton became Commander-in-Chief. Aware that he is viewed as hostile to the military, Clinton has nonetheless pushed to install homosexuals in the military, appointed anti-military personnel in his administration, and called for a freeze in military salaries. He has also compromised America's position in the world with his *Bottom-Up Review* and irresponsible defense cuts; established an imprudent relationship with Russia that ignores its continuing military capabilities; abandoned SDI; and allowed U.S. defense research laboratories to become ghost towns.

All of which proves the wisdom of a bumpersticker seen on an increasing number of American cars: "Never, *ever,* trust a draft dodger."

DRAFT DODGER IN COMMAND

Bill Clinton is the first person since Franklin D. Roosevelt to become president without having served in the nation's military. (Roosevelt did serve as Assistant Secretary of the Navy.) When his country called him to duty in Vietnam, Clinton absconded to the gardens at Oxford; he wrote to a fellow Rhodes scholar that he felt he was "running away from something maybe for the first time in my life."[8]

During the 1992 presidential election, Clinton evaded questions about his draft dodging. "Almost everyone concerned with these incidents is dead," he said. "I have no more comments to make."[9]

But Clinton's former ROTC commander, Col. Eugene Holmes, was alive and did have some comments to make:

"Since I may be the only living person who can give a first-hand account of what actually transpired, I am obligated by my love for my country and my sense of duty to divulge what actually happened," Holmes wrote in a 1992 affidavit.[10]

Colonel Holmes recalled that Bill Clinton had asked him in 1969 to help him join the ROTC, a move that would allow Clinton to avoid the draft and study as a Rhodes scholar. But after Clinton was safely enrolled at Oxford, he broke his commitment to Colonel Holmes by eschewing service. Clinton wrote thanking Holmes for "saving" him from the draft and he confessed that he had a "loathing" of the military.[11]

"I was not 'saving' [Bill Clinton] from the draft," Holmes later protested, "I was making it possible for a Rhodes scholar to serve in the military as an officer." Knowing he had been duped, Holmes wrote that Clinton had "purposely deceived" him in order to avoid the draft.[12]*

The mistrust, even revulsion, of Clinton for the military became mutual after he was elected president. Less than a week into Clinton's presidential term, Lt. Gen. Barry R. McCaffrey, a decorated hero from Vietnam and the Persian Gulf, passed a Clinton aide at the White House and greeted her with a "good morning." "I don't talk to the military," the aide shot back.[13] In addition to this exchange, rumors abounded for months that Clinton

---

*Colonel Holmes served 32 years in the Army, surviving the Bataan Death March and three and one-half years as a Japanese prisoner-of-war in World War II. His decorations include the Silver Star, 2 Bronze Stars, 2 Legions of Merit and the Army Commendation Medal. Both Bill Clinton's letter to Colonel Holmes, and Colonel Holmes's 1992 affidavit, are printed in full in "SLICK WILLIE": *Why America Cannot Trust Bill Clinton* (Annapolis-Washington Book Publishers, 1992).

administration officials had asked military officers not to wear their uniforms to work at the White House.[14]

Then, when the administration announced base closings in March 1993, Clinton attempted to soften the news with a visit to the *USS Theodore Roosevelt*. But the trip bombed. "Ambivalence is no frame of mind for a warship," wrote the *Washington Post* reporter covering the visit. "But there seemed to be no better word for the mood that filled the hangar deck here today."[15] Disrespectful troops couldn't help mocking their draft-dodging Commander-in-chief: "Maybe we can call this his military service," jeered an executive officer of one of the *Roosevelt*'s strike fighter squadrons.[16]

In a similarly embarrassing incident, Clinton's Memorial Day appearance at the Vietnam Wall triggered protests. "Damn you, you coward!" someone shouted from the crowd.[17] The *Washington Post* reported that Clinton "was nearly drowned out by shouts and boos."[18]

To make matters even worse, Clinton tried to freeze military pay in his defense appropriations bill. It was only due to Congressional intervention that the 2.2 percent military pay raise was restored.[19]

CLINTON'S DEFENSE APPOINTMENTS

Far from compensating for his own weak stature as Commander-in-Chief, Bill Clinton appointed to his defense staff, and to his administration in general, men with little or no military experience, or worse, known opponents of the military.

The choice of Les Aspin as Secretary of Defense showed Clinton's ignorance of the most important post at the Pentagon. Although Aspin was a reputed defense expert during his many years in Congress, his record consisted of passing legislation and pontificating. Aspin was a theorist whose sole management experience consisted of directing his congressional staff.

From the start, Aspin floundered in an institution that demands precision and strong leadership. The Secretary dumbfounded uniformed officers with his casual, unfocused meetings, for which he was routinely late.

"Aspin is a typical Beltway creation," charged an *Orlando Sentinel* reporter, "a mouthy intellectual who loves to run on endlessly about this theory or that theory but whose actual knowledge of the real world is virtually nil."[20] Larry E. Joyce, the father of an Army Ranger who died in the Battle of Mogadishu, wrote in *USA Today*, "Why is Les Aspin our Secretary of Defense? Why is a man who made a career of criticizing and reviling our military put in charge of the military? . . . [Aspin] is too uncaring and too incompetent to command the most precious resource this nation has."[21]

Although Aspin was fired two months after the Battle of Mogadishu, it was clear, as defense commentator Morton Kondracke observed, that he was "a scapegoat for the administration's own lack of foreign policy coherence."[22]

Aspin's replacement, William J. Perry, is little better. Perry is a leading advocate of selling "dual-use" technology, goods that have both commercial and military purposes, to practically anybody who wants to buy them. Perry told the U.S. Senate, "It only interferes with a company's ability to succeed internationally if we try to impose all sorts of controls in that area."[23]

"Astonishing though it may seem, decontrol is already underway," reported the *Washington Post's* Lally Weymouth in February 1994, "The administration is presiding over a massive decontrol (for export purposes) of sensitive dual-use technologies—including computers, machine tools and telecommunications equipment. These are the very technologies that rogue states require for the indigenous development and production of weapons of mass destruction."²⁴ With Perry at the helm at Defense this process will only accelerate.

Moreover, despite Bill Clinton's repeatedly stated intention of making his administration "look like America," he seldom appointed military veterans to high positions in his administration. The *Washington Post* reported the research of Vietnam veteran John Wheeler—that "of the first 66 men named to the [Clinton] White House staff, only three had served in Vietnam, and only seven ever had been in uniform."²⁵ Aside from the Pentagon and the Veterans Administration, Wheeler discovered that only two of 213 male appointees had served in uniform, both of them before Vietnam.*

"The Clinton administration," Wheeler concluded, "is largely a networked clique of people who were antimilitary and antiwar during the 1960s and carry their biases with them still."²⁶

THE BOTTOM-UP REVIEW

The Clinton Pentagon's most dubious policy achievement to date is its report on America's military, *The Bottom-Up Review: Forces for a New Era*. Announced by then-Secretary of Defense Les Aspin on September 1, 1993, the *Bottom-Up Review* reexamines America's military strategy and defenses.

The purported goal of Aspin's review was to consider U.S. military needs from the "bottom up," instead of from the top down with arbitrary budget figures and politically determined priorities. But the exact opposite occurred:

---

*John "Jack" Wheeler chaired the fund that built the Vietnam Veterans Memorial Wall. He supported Bill Clinton for president.

the *Bottom-Up Review* became a political cover for Clinton's staggering defense cuts. "What is noteworthy," said a memorandum from the Republican staff of the House Armed Services Committee, "is that while the Cheney Base Force and Aspin Bottom-Up Review strategy objectives are very similar, *the available force structure and budget resources are significantly different.*"[27] In other words, while the Clinton administration agreed with the Bush-Cheney threat assessments, it called for *far fewer resources and personnel* to combat those global threats.

During the Bush administration, America was ready to fight and win two major regional conflicts, such as Desert Storm and a war in Korea, *simultaneously.** This strategy was known as "win-win."

The early Clinton-Aspin proposal, in contrast, held that instead of fighting two wars *simultaneously*, the United States would be prepared only to fight two wars *sequentially*. This Clinton strategy was known as "win-hold-win." In other words, the second war would be put on "hold" until the first war was won. (The President and the Secretary of Defense failed to disclose how the United States would gain the cooperation of the second aggressor in this scenario; presumably the enemy would wait politely while the U.S. finished its first war and regrouped.)

The Clinton-Aspin "win-hold-win" proposal "sent shock waves through the diplomatic community."[28] In an attempt to calm concerns about the *Bottom-Up Review*, Aspin announced that a revision would be made to allow the United States to fight two *nearly simultaneous* wars, instead of two *sequential* wars. But a comparison of the force structures recommended under the two models

---

*Even this Bush proposal was a watered-down version of the Reagan strategy, which required readiness to fight two and one-half wars at the same time.

showed that they were virtually the same.[29] The Secretary of Defense was just playing word games to try to distract detractors of his plan.

The truth about the *Bottom-Up Review* is that the Clinton administration plans to reduce America's military to a level that would not allow it to sustain two regional operations at once. "It was tough enough to carry out the win-win strategy with the forces envisioned by the Bush administration," said Zalmay Khalilzad, a Rand Corporation analyst who served as head of the Pentagon's office of policy planning under Bush. "The question is can [America] really do win-win with a reduced force structure?"[30]

"HOLLOW FORCES"

In an interview with the *Los Angeles Times*, retired colonel and defense analyst Robert W. Gaskin recalled an experience he had in the 1970s as a young Air Force pilot. Visiting a base in Arizona, Gaskin passed a row of freshly painted fighter aircraft: "If you looked through their intakes, you could see daylight coming from their tailpipes," he said. "None of them had any engines inside. They'd all been cannibalized for spare parts, and there was no money around to replace them. It was a perfect example of the 'hollow force.' "[31]

The ominous phrase "hollow forces" dates to a warning issued by General Edward C. Meyer when he was Army Chief-of-Staff under Jimmy Carter. "Basically, what we have is a hollow army," Meyer told then-Commander-in-Chief Carter at a 1979 Camp David retreat.[32]

Talk of hollow forces has resumed under President Clinton. Although during his campaign he called for $60 billion in cuts to America's military, Clinton proposed $123 billion in cuts once elected. "Dozens of military bases are closing, and weapons production lines are slowly grinding

to a halt," reported the *National Journal* in August 1993.
"A variety of planes, tanks, submarines, missiles, and
helicopters are being mothballed as the Pentagon shrinks
its high-tech arsenal."[33]

It's not just that Clinton is slashing the defense budget,
but *where* he is slashing it. Recruiting, training, maintenance, and procurement all suffer under Clinton's heavy
hand. Already, the Navy has 150 warplanes, 250 aircraft
engines, and three ships overdue for maintenance. And
more than 1,000 Army tanks are in need of repair. As for
combat training, both the Air Force and the Marines have
had to cancel this essential exercise in order to finance
Clinton's global peace-keeping missions.[34]

The Navy had to dip into $25 million of its maintenance
budget to fund its activities in Somalia, and the Marines
were forced to divert more than $100 million of their read-
iness budget to pay for peacekeeping and humanitarian
missions in Somalia and Bangladesh. For the first time in
ten years, the Marine Corps reports that less than 90 percent of its equipment is ready to go to war.[35] A billion
dollars has been cut from the Army modernization
budget.[36]

"In spite of the efforts of our services," warned U.S.
Sen. John McCain (R-Ariz.), a former Navy pilot and
POW, "we are going hollow."[37]

During the Gulf War, Americans watched in awe and
admiration the perfect planning and execution of strikes
against Iraq. But the ability to conduct such missions is
costly. The immense airlift capability required for that
effort put hundreds of thousands of miles on aging air
transports. Those planes cannot be replaced in the Clinton
budget, nor can the diminished stocks. "If we adopt Clinton's plan," warns former Secretary of Defense Caspar

W. Weinberger, "we will not be able to fight and win one war like Desert Storm."[38]

Perhaps worst of all, Bill Clinton has done away with America's ultimate defense program: the Strategic Defense Initiative (SDI). Soon after taking office, Clinton renamed SDI, calling it the Ballistic Missile Defense program (BMD), and cut its budget by more than half, killing its most important component in the process.

Under Presidents Reagan and Bush, missile defenses were designed to protect the people and territory of the United States from accidental or deliberate nuclear missile attack originating from any spot in the world. To achieve this, the SDI program emphasized the strategic— that is, the long-range or global—component of ballistic missile defense by developing space-based defenses; due to America's geographic location in the world, only *strategic* defenses offer true protection. ("Strategic" defenses can be used against intercontinental attack, while "theater"-type defenses are used against regional attacks. The Patriots used in the Gulf War against Iraqi Scuds, for example, were short-range theater missiles.)

The last Bush SDI budget for fiscal years 1995-1999 totaled $40.9 billion, with $17.7 billion earmarked for strategic defenses. The equivalent Clinton budget is $17 billion, with only $3 billion earmarked for strategic defenses. Clinton's proposal effectively kills development of America's space-based strategic defenses, and cripples its program of ground-based theater defenses.

"This colossal Clinton mistake," wrote former Secretary of Defense Weinberger, "will deprive the U.S. of the ability to protect itself against nuclear missiles that are, or shortly will be, in the hands of at least four countries not all that friendly to us or our allies."[39]

RUSSIAN THREAT STILL EXISTS

While disarming America, the Clinton administration has failed to verify that Russia, whose armed forces probably are not under civilian control, is following suit as promised. Even worse, despite the apparent continuing development of weapons of mass destruction by Russia, and its willingness to sell them to terrorist regimes, President Clinton has agreed to send about $1 billion to Russia to dismantle its old weapons. Astonishingly, this largesse is not predicated on verification of how the money will be spent. Indeed, it is likely that Russia is using U.S. taxpayer dollars to develop and deploy new high-tech weapons.

Afraid to rock the boat, the Clinton administration appears willing to give the Russians whatever they want. "The Clinton administration," wrote the *New York Times*, "which has touted its support for Mr. Yeltsin as its principal foreign policy success, has played down the problems it has encountered in trying to persuade the Russians to meet the arms control commitments they inherited from the Soviet Union."[40]

Evidence backed by dissident Russian scientists shows that Russia is forging ahead with a covert program, codenamed Novichok, to deploy a new lethal nerve gas that is said to be five to ten times deadlier than any chemical weapons already developed. These scientists further maintain that U.S. aid earmarked for destruction of Russia's old chemical weapons stocks is being diverted to pay for this poison gas research.[41]

Vil Mirzayanov, a nerve gas scientist, exposed the Novichok program in 1992, for which he suffered persecution and imprisonment.[42] Mirzayanov has stated that the Russian military is using U.S. cash and technology to develop new poisons. "Our generals raised an outcry alleging that Russia would not manage to destroy its chemical weapons unaided and that we need at least $600 million [from the U.S.]," Mirzayanov told *Moscow News*. But the Russian generals' real objective, Mirzayanov added, was "to finance the destruction of obsolescent stocks and to carry on the development of binary weapons."[43]

Andrei Zheleznyakov, a scientist who was poisoned in a Novichok lab accident and subsequently died, had told a Russian magazine, "The generals cannot be trusted with the destruction of chemical weapons. The money received from the Americans for this purpose will definitely be channeled into the development of new and more powerful toxic substances."[44]

A similar story may be unfolding with regard to the vast nuclear arsenal of the former Soviet Union. In order to destroy tens of thousands of nuclear missiles, the Russian military has demanded that the United States send financial aid and help pressure other former Soviet republics to return their missiles to Russia. The Clinton administration, by complying with these demands, has put America in a dangerous position.

Significantly, while the actual Soviet missiles, many of which are deteriorating and need to be dismantled anyway, are destroyed under the watchful eye of American inspectors, their *nuclear warheads are preserved*. American inspectors have no means of determining what Russia does with the warheads. Moreover, Moscow is building a new generation of high-tech strategic missiles to replace the old ones the U.S. is paying to dismantle. These new missiles will be mobile and therefore difficult for U.S. intelligence to monitor.

In a special December 1993 series on the Russian military, the *New York Times* reported that, "even as they accept hundreds of millions of dollars in American aid, Russian officials have declined to provide Washington with information about the [dismantling] effort."[45] Concerns about Russia's new missiles prompted U.S. Sen. Ted Stevens (R-Alas.) to sponsor an amendment that would prohibit sending U.S. funds to dismantle weapons in countries that continue developing such arsenals.[46]

For his part, Bill Clinton has been content to leave America vulnerable to nuclear threats from Moscow by supporting Russia's development of dangerous new weapons and, at the same time, halting the SDI program designed to defend the United States against such weapons.

And that's not all. The Clinton administration, again at the insistence of the Russian government, asked Congress to repeal statutes that keep lawmakers and the American public informed about the nuclear threat to the United States. These repealed statutes concern Moscow's compliance with arms control and an annual presidential report to Congress on arms control strategy, which includes "a comprehensive data base on the military balance" between Washington and Moscow.[47]

If history has taught anything, it is that weakness invites trouble, and appeasement of aggressive military powers backfires. Bill Clinton is nonetheless disarming America's military forces and catering to a still bellicose Russia. Clinton's promise to give Americans "the best-trained, best-equipped, and the best-prepared fighting force on the face of the earth" is turning out to be one of history's monumental lies.

Surrendering American superiority and leaving the nation vulnerable may well be the Clinton administration's most lasting legacy.

1. Bill Clinton, in his State of the Union address; January 25, 1994.
2. General Joseph P. Hoar, quoted by Eric Schmitt in "Cost-Minded

Lawmakers are Challenging a 2-War Doctrine"; *New York Times*; March 10, 1994.

3. Robert H. Burger, Letter to the Editor; *Newsday*; February 3, 1994.

4. *The 1940 World Almanac and Book of Facts*; Scripps-Howard; New York, NY; page 849.

5. Department of Defense data chart, published in Heritage Foundation Backgrounder "Thumbs Down to the Bottom-Up Review"; No. 957; September 24, 1993; page 4.

6. *ibid.*

7. Lisa Corbin, "The Buying Game"; *Government Executive*; August 1993.

8. David Maraniss, "Bill Clinton and Realpolitik U."; *Washington Post*; October 25, 1992.

9. Bill Clinton, quoted by Col. Eugene Holmes in 1992 affidavit published as Appendix H in Floyd G. Brown's "SLICK WILLIE": *Why America Cannot Trust Bill Clinton*; Annapolis-Washington Book Publishers; Annapolis, MD; 1992; page 146.

10. Col. Eugene Holmes, quoted in his 1992 affidavit, published as Appendix H in Floyd G. Brown, *supra* endnote 9.

11. Bill Clinton, quoted in his December 1969 letter to Col. Eugene Holmes, published as Appendix G in Floyd G. Brown, *supra* endnote 9, page 141.

12. Col. Eugene Holmes, quoted in his 1992 affidavit, published as Appendix H in Floyd G. Brown, *supra* endnote 9.

13. Anonymous Clinton aide, quoted in "Clinton's Quick Steps to Better Relations"; *Washington Post*; April 6, 1993.

14. Mark Thompson, "President, Military in Quiet Disharmony"; *Dallas Morning News*; March 28, 1993.

15. Barton Gellman, "Warship Gives Clinton a Not-So-Hail to the Chief"; *Washington Post*; March 13, 1993.

16. Commander Bill Gortney, quoted by Barton Gellman, *supra* endnote 15.

17. Anonymous protester, quoted by Ruth Marcus in "Jeers, Cheers Greet Clinton at the Wall"; *Washington Post*; June 1, 1993.

18. Ruth Marcus, *supra* endnote 17.

19. Pat Towell, "Military Gets 2.2% Pay Raise"; *Congressional Quarterly*; November 13, 1993.

20. Charley Reese, "From the Start, Les Aspin was the Wrong Man for Secretary of Defense"; *Orlando Sentinel*; January 6, 1994.

21. Larry E. Joyce, "Did My Son Have to Die?"; *USA Today*; October 20, 1993.
22. Morton Kondracke, *Roll Call*; December 20, 1993.
23. William Perry, quoted by Lally Weymouth in "Good News for Rogue States"; *Washington Post*; February 4, 1994.
24. Lally Weymouth, *supra* endnote 23.
25. David S. Broder, "No Veterans Preference in This Administration"; *Washington Post*; December 26, 1993.
26. John Wheeler, quoted by David S. Broder, *supra* endnote 25.
27. House Armed Services Committee Republican Staff, "Memorandum"; September 7, 1993; page 2 (emphasis added).
28. *ibid.*
29. Bill Gertz, "Military Proposal Called a Retread"; *Washington Times*; September 3, 1993.
30. Zalmay Khalilzad, quoted by Michael R. Gordon in "Pentagon Seeking to Cut Military"; *New York Times*; September 2, 1993.
31. Robert W. Gaskin, quoted by Art Pine in "Military Haunted by a Paper Tiger"; *Los Angeles Times*; June 13, 1993.
32. Gen. Edward C. Meyer, quoted by David C. Morrison in "Ringing Hollow"; *National Journal*; September 18, 1993.
33. Lisa Corbin, *supra* endnote 7.
34. Art Pine, *supra* endnote 31.
35. Gen. Carl E. Mundy, Jr., commandant of the Marine Corps, in statement to the Senate Armed Services Committee; May 19, 1993.
36. "$1 Billion of Army Modernization Plans Unfunded"; *Inside the Pentagon*; July 7, 1993.
37. U.S. Sen. John McCain (R-Ariz.), quoted by David C. Morrison, *supra* endnote 32.
38. Caspar W. Weinberger, "Winning Two Wars—Or Losing One?"; *Forbes*; October 11, 1993.
39. *ibid.*
40. Michael R. Gordon, "Moscow is Making Little Progress in Disposal of Chemical Weapons"; *New York Times*; December 1, 1993.
41. J. Michael Waller, "U.S. May be Funding Russian Secret Weapon"; *Houston Chronicle*; January 11, 1994.
42. *ibid.*
43. Vil Mirzayanov, quoted by Leonard Nikishin in "Vil Mirzayanov: The Goal is to Develop New Binary Weapons"; *Moscow News*; No. 22; May 28, 1993.

44. Andrei Zheleznyakov, quoted by Oleg Vishnyakov in "I Was Making Binary Bombs"; *New Times*; No. 50; December 1992.
45. Michael R. Gordon, *supra* endnote 40.
46. Elizabeth A. Palmer and Pat Towell, "After Much Debate, Little Change, Senate Approves Defense Bill"; *Congressional Quarterly*; October 23, 1993.
47. H.R. 3000, 103rd Congress, 1st session; October 15, 1993; Section 403; "Annual Reports on Arms Control Matters."

HEALTH CARE:
THE *REAL* CRISIS

"The debate about the Clintons' health care plan is, literally, a matter of life and death. If anything like that plan becomes law, there will be much unnecessary premature death and other suffering."[1]
—George F. Will
Newsweek; February 7, 1994

"There's nothing compassionate about a program that will result in massive growth in government, a sure increase in taxes and a significant decrease in jobs."[2]
—Gary Bauer
Family Research Council

Talk about promising the moon. When it comes to health care, Bill Clinton says his government plan would provide universal coverage for top quality care at low costs. "A fantasy," cried Sen. Daniel Patrick Moynihan (D-N.Y.), chairman of the Senate Finance Committee.[3] Even Rep. Dan Rostenkowski (D-Ill.) admitted that there is no "health fairy," and that citizens have "ample reason to wonder whether a broad tax increase will be required" to finance Clinton's promised coverage.[4]

The fact is, the Clinton Plan would precipitate the largest tax increase in U.S. history. To pay for the Clinton plan, Congress would have to either double the budget deficit, roughly double the corporate income tax, increase individual income taxes by roughly 50 percent, ration health care to citizens, or some combination of the above.[5]

In the words of humorist P.J. O'Rourke, "If you think health care is expensive now, just wait until it's free."

Implementation of the Clinton system would amount to nothing less than government coercion. Under the Clinton Plan, all American citizens would be herded into large health-care collectives that would extract heavy payroll taxes and dispense medical treatment as bureaucrats see fit. Contravening the U.S. Constitution, the federal government would compel every citizen to join its health care system, and heavy fines and jail sentences would be enacted on those who disobeyed the Clinton rules. Citizens who failed to sign up, for example, would be fined a minimum of $5,000.[6]

Hillary Rodham Clinton said the debate about America's health care system "is not just a debate about how we finance our health care. It's bigger than that. It's a debate about what kind of country we are and intend to be."[7] In the country of Rodham Clinton's dreams, a massive new health care bureaucracy would be set up as follows:

1) A National Health Board, comprised of seven presidentially-appointed individuals, would determine a mandatory "standard benefits package" for every American citizen, and make an annual national health care budget;

2) Each state would be required to establish and monitor one or more Regional Health Alliances (RHAs) within its borders;

3) The Regional Health Alliances themselves would serve as health insurance collectives for all inhabitants of each alliance;

4) Large corporate employers (those with more than 5,000 employees) would be allowed to substitute their own health plans for Regional Health Alliance plans only if their policies complied fully with the National Health Board guidelines; and

5) Employers with 5,000 or fewer employees would be forced into the Regional Health Alliances. Since large employers will be allowed to self-insure under the Clinton Plan, small and mid-sized employers and their employees would bear most of the burden for those who are unemployed, on welfare, or in retirement.

THE SECRET TASK FORCE

The framework for the government takeover of one-seventh of America's economy was hammered out in secret during the first few months of the Clinton administration by Hillary Rodham Clinton, presidential advisor Ira Magaziner, and their health care task force.

This secret task force was a complex web of working groups and committees that numbered 511 claimed members. (This figure later was to be challenged as topping 1,000.)[8] Suspicions about the composition and activities of the secret task force led three groups to file suit in February 1993 to open meetings to the public. The Association of American Physicians and Surgeons, the American Council for Health Care Reform, and the National Legal and Policy Center, represented by Kent Masterson Brown, argued that pursuant to the 1972 Federal Advisory Committee Act (FACA), the task force meetings must be made open to the public because Rodham Clinton was not a federal employee. (FACA prohibits private sector individuals from meeting with federal officials in secret.) In March, U.S. District Judge Royce C. Lamberth made a compromise decision: the task force had to open its meetings whenever it was conducting "fact-gathering" sessions, but could keep them closed when it was formulating advice to give the President.

The Clinton administration appealed Lamberth's decision, and in May the federal appeals court determined that Rodham Clinton did qualify as a federal employee.

Legal questions next shifted to whether or not the records of the task force should be made public. In June, Judge Lamberth responded to a *Washington Times* report that the task force was destroying its files. The judge ordered that no files be destroyed and requested "a name and address of who's going to be held in contempt if there are any records destroyed."9

As it became known that nongovernment consultants and representatives of various special interests had served on the task force, attorney Brown insisted that the task force's records be made public. In November, a frustrated Judge Lamberth threatened the White House with contempt if papers concerning membership and activities were not produced. The task force's Justice Department lawyer, Jeffrey Gutman, offered the feeble excuse that he couldn't assemble the documents because, "We had hundreds of people meeting for thousands of hours over several months."10 The task force was in such disarray that the total membership couldn't even be determined, to say nothing of reports on travel expenses and financial disclosures. "[This is] so much government gobbledygook," complained Judge Lamberth, "I can't understand it all."11 For his part, attorney Brown wanted to know how the task force could draw up a health plan if no one kept records.12

"It is insulting to Congress and the American people," said Rep. William F. Clinger (R-Penn.) "that the government now claims that these records are not available. At best, the White House had tried to slip through legal loopholes to avoid the production of these records. At worst, laws may have been violated, and statements to a federal court may have been perverted."[13]

When attorney Brown finally procured some task force records under the court order, he uncovered a hornet's nest. Brown charged that the secret task force had spent "$4 million on consultants and possibly $16 million in consulting fees, salaries and expenses,"[14] sums far in excess of the White House charter that estimated $100,000 in expenses. Some outsiders, it turned out, had been paid $300 an hour in consulting fees. Travel and expense papers had been backdated. Conflicts of interest abounded. More than half the working-group members, it turned out, were outsiders paid by universities and private foundations, a revelation that showed the task force should never have been secret in the first place. Most troubling of all was the discovery that representatives of institutions such as the Robert Wood Johnson Foundation and the Henry J. Kaiser Family Foundation were influential in the writing of the Clinton health care plan.[15] These foundations could reap fortunes under the Clinton health system.*

"It becomes clear," said attorney Brown, "that large, well-heeled nonprofit foundations invented this bureaucratic, yet secretive, means of achieving 'change' in the delivery of health care in the United States by directly influencing the government decision-making processes from the inside to achieve their goal of promoting their own well-planned agendas."[17]

The fact that non-government outsiders had served on

---

*The question arises whether these special interests actually wrote themselves into the Clinton Plan. Title I, Subtitle D, Section 1301 of the Clinton proposal specifically defines "regional alliance" as a "non-profit organization, an independent state agency, or an agency of the State."[16]

the task force contradicted sworn court testimony given by Ira Magaziner, who stated on March 3, 1993, under penalty of perjury, that only federal employees had participated in the task force.[18]

These court disclosures were not the only embarrassments for the Clinton administration. Even some task force members were disdainful of the group's secret efforts. "A waste of time," said Thomas Pyle, a health care expert who had resigned from the task force.[19] "Too big, too secret, too rushed, too eggheady," complained Arthur Caplan, bioethics professor at the University of Minnesota.[20]

Moreover, Hillary Rodham Clinton's position as head of the secret task force and her sermons against "profiteering" in the health care industry were compromised by reports that she maintained a $97,500 investment in Value Partners. This investment fund sold health stocks "short"—that is, made bets that the price of those stocks would fall—during the time the First Lady was attacking pharmaceuticals. This means Rodham Clinton was positioned to benefit financially as the price of drug stocks dropped in response to her health care proposals.

Another compromising revelation, as reported in a June 1993 *Des Moines Register* article, was that the Rose Law Firm had spearheaded a 1988 profit-making scheme concerning the sale of Beverly Enterprises nursing homes in Iowa. The *Register* reported, "When Hillary Rodham Clinton complained in a recent speech about profiteering in the health care industry, she could have found a ready example in the role one of her former Arkansas law partners [William H. Kennedy III] played in an Iowa nursing-homes deal that made millions for the deal-makers."[21]

The Rose Law Firm made hundreds of thousands of dollars in what one Iowa lawyer who officially investigated the situation called the "worst case of profiteering" he'd seen in 20 years.[22] As a result of the deal orchestrated by the Rose Law Firm, debt for the nursing homes was eventually "shouldered by the old people, who saw their daily charges go up by as much as 14 percent."[23]

CLINTON "CARE"

Although the public has been denied information about the secret meetings of Hillary Rodham Clinton's task force, the product of those meetings can speak for itself. "The average American who never quite got through college and who doesn't know what a Rhodes scholar is understands that there is something very odd with any program that is outlined in 250 pages and demands many thousands of pages of legislation and supplementary regulations," wrote Irving Kristol in the *Wall Street Journal*.[24] And indeed, the plan's architect, Ira Magaziner, has a reputation for promoting complex theories that don't hold up in real life. The *New Republic* described Magaziner as "lack[ing] an awareness of how the systems he designs can go askew in practice."[25]

The Clintons' final legislative proposal, which would inevitably lead to a national single-pager system, numbered 1,364 pages. This Health Security Act details how treatment would be provided or refused to patients in the following areas of health care: "hospital services"; "services of health professionals"; "emergency and ambulatory medical and surgical services"; "mental health and substance abuse services"; "family planning services and services for pregnant women"; "hospice care"; "home health care"; "extended care services"; "ambulance services"; "outpatient laboratory, radiology, and diagnostic services"; "outpatient prescription drugs and biologicals"; "outpatient rehabilitation services"; "medical equipment and prosthetic and orthotic devices"; "vision care"; "dental care"; "health education classes"; and "investigational treatments."[26]

Under the Clinton Plan, the availability and costs of these services would be dictated to citizens by a federal government board in Washington, D.C. Citizens would be forced into a "one-size-fits-all" health plan run by government bureaucrats sitting at computer terminals. And, although the system would provide "universal coverage," this does not mean it would provide universal *treatment*. In other words, if a patient needs bypass surgery, the operation would be *covered*. But that's only if the patient *gets the operation in the first place*. First, he must qualify for the procedure under government guidelines, and wait his turn in line.

The details of the Health Security Act reveal just how rigid the government guidelines would be. For example, women age 20 to 39 would be allowed "pap" smears for cervical cancer every three years, and cholesterol tests every five years. For women age 40 to 49, the "pap" smears would come every two years; and for women age 50 to 64, "pap" smears and mammograms would come every two years.[27]

The Clinton Plan's standard benefits package *does not provide for mammograms for women under the age of 50*,[28] despite the fact that breast cancer is one of the leading causes of death for women under 50, and breast cancer patients under 35 have the poorest survival rate of any age group.[29]

While many basic services would be limited or even denied under the Clinton Plan, individuals of any age would be eligible for inpatient and outpatient "mental health and substance abuse treatment, including case management, screening and assessment, [and] crisis services."[30] In addition, the Clinton Plan's standard benefits package would provide "contraceptive devices" and "services for pregnant women," that is, abortion.[31]

In other words, a woman in her twenties, thirties, or forties, who has a strong history of breast cancer in her family, would be denied a mammogram before the age of 50. At the same time, however, she would be forced to help pay for treatment for irresponsible drug users, or for contraceptives or even *abortions* for other women. And, although healthy women could have "pap" smears only every three years, they would have to pay for annual "pap" smears for women with venereal diseases.[32] This is just one example of the warped regulations with which the Clinton Plan is rife.

FINANCING "CLINTON CARE"

The financing of the Clinton Plan is every bit the bureaucratic nightmare as the delivery of treatment. The plan calls for states to create and monitor giant new government bureaucracies called Regional Health Alliances, a requirement that effectively turns the states into federal agencies.

Each Regional Health Alliance would collect taxes from every working citizen within its region to pay for health care for everyone in the region. Specifically, every employer within a Regional Health Alliance would be forced to pay up to a 7.9 percent tax on the salary of each of its employees, and the plan includes provisions for even higher rates.

While the Clinton Plan gives the illusion that employees are receiving virtually free health care, it is they, in fact, who would wind up paying most, if not all, of the tax. The Clintons ignore the fact that employers, when faced with these burdensome payroll taxes, would have to make up their losses by cutting wages for employees, freezing hiring, or even eliminating jobs. When warned that small businesses would suffer tremendously under the Clinton Plan, Hillary Rodham Clinton couldn't be bothered. "I can't go out and save every undercapitalized entrepreneur in America," she said.[33]

Another illusion is the Clintons' claim that patients would have choices under their plan. This simply is not so. Every citizen in the country, employed or not, would have to enroll in a government-approved health insurance plan. When there is room for a person in the insurance program of his choice, the Regional Health Alliance would allow the enrollment. But if the person's program of choice is full, the Regional Health Alliance would unilaterally place that person in an insurance program of *its* choosing. Patients would be restricted to treatment only by the government-appointed doctors and hospitals available through the plan they wind up in, with exceptions made only in cases of medical emergency.

Insurance plans, for their part, would be forced to accept for coverage any person within a Regional Health Alliance at pre-established prices, regardless of that person's age, occupation, prior medical history, or engagement in risk-laden behavior, including drug use, sexual promiscuity, and homosexual activity. The Clinton Plan specifically stipulates that health insurance plans "may not terminate, restrict, or limit coverage for the comprehensive benefit package in any portion of the plan's service area for any reason, including nonpayment of premiums."[34] This means insurance plans would not only have to shoulder the burden for expensive care of irresponsible members of their programs, but they would have to absorb the costs of patients who don't pay their "premiums."

What the Clintons refuse to admit is that consumer

demand for health care would skyrocket as medical treatment becomes an *entitlement*. Despite what the Clintons say, putting things like alcohol and drug treatment, mental health services, and elective abortions in an insurance policy guarantees that instances of their use will soar. Promising care for individuals who don't pay also encourages delinquency.

Because the Clinton Plan guarantees universal coverage for all citizens, those individuals who cannot pay would be subsidized by higher taxes on those who can. Gerrymandering, the term used to describe the manipulation of boundaries for congressional districts, would acquire new meaning as communities fight to position themselves in economically advantageous Regional Health Alliances. Suburbs would try to form collectives with other wealthy areas, and they would protest boundaries that align them with the inner cities, where medical costs are high due to conditions like drug addiction, violent assault, mental illness, and AIDS. America's cities would continue to decline as wealthy citizens flee to lower-cost suburban alliances rather than foot the bill for full emergency rooms and unemployment in the inner cities.

Just how much would all this treatment cost? The Clintons say that the national health care plan would cost $331 billion from 1994-2000. They also make the preposterous claim that the National Health Board's centralized budgeting practices would reduce the nation's deficit by $58 billion during the same time period. Although President Clinton uses these optimistic figures publicly, he still tried to move his health plan "off budget," so he could duck responsibility with voters when the real costs materialize. But this proposal was rejected by the Congressional Budget Office (CBO), which concluded that "the financial transactions of the health alliances should be included in the federal government's accounts,"[35] or put "on-budget." The CBO Director further said that, rather than decreasing the nation's deficit, the Clinton Plan would add $74 billion to the burden. When confronted with this serious challenge to his proposal, President Clinton dismissed it without a thought. "Washington policy wonk," he said. "No serious person out here in the real world will be too troubled by it."[36]

By refusing to admit the inevitability of budget shortfalls under their plan, the Clintons ignore concerns about price controls, rationed care, and massive deficits. But the Clinton Plan itself indicates that shortfalls are anticipated. Why else would it call for the establishment of "Guaranty Funds" that would hold taxpayers responsible for bailing out failing Regional Health Alliances? According to the Health Security Act, "Each participating State shall ensure that there is a guaranty fund that meets the requirements established by the Board under section 1505(j)(2), in order to provide financial protection to health care providers and others in the case of a failure of a regional alliance health plan."[37] Just as taxpayers were left holding the bag for the S&L deposit insurance scandal, the Clintons would make them responsible for bailing out their health care system.

BIG BROTHER IS IN CHARGE

Under the Clinton Plan, the federal government would have power to compel specific actions from citizens, and would punish citizens for failing to abide by its decrees. It is nothing less than Big Brother government.

The Health Security Act, for example, demands that individuals' medical records be put under government control. "As part of the health information system," the Act stipulates, "the National Health Board shall oversee the establishment of an electronic data network consisting of regional centers that collect, compile, and transmit information."[38] Doctors would be required to record all patient information in this electronic data system, except in cases where they receive permission to record information on "uniform paper forms."[39]

When President Clinton waves a copy of the "Health Security Card" he wants issued to every citizen, he says it would offer patients "security" and help "streamline" the health care system. In fact, these cards, which could hold up to 1,600 pages of information about the cardholder, would radically undermine citizens' privacy and create a system conducive to government tyranny. According to the Clinton Plan, these cards could hold "any . . . information the National Health Board determines to be necessary."[40] Information for the government data banks would be collected from the individuals themselves, the individuals' employer(s), and the doctors and nurses who treat them.

And if patients ever submitted false information to a doctor, or tried to keep private information out of the federal data bank, they would be liable for fines and up to *five years in jail*.[41] Meanwhile, the Clinton Plan prescribes no punishment for government bureaucrats who might betray patient confidentiality. In other words, a taxpaying citizen could go to jail for not answering questions from a government bureaucrat, but nothing would happen to the bureaucrat if he decided to disclose private information to anyone he wants.[42]

Jail sentences are also prescribed for patients who try to seek medical care not offered in the Clintons' standard benefits package. For instance, if a woman under age 50 decided she needed a mammogram, or an extra cholesterol test, she would have to pay a doctor for this unsanctioned service. But under the Clinton Plan, this would constitute "bribery" and could result in a *two-year jail sentence*. Any doctor who agrees to accept payment outside of the Clinton system would be subject to a *15-year jail sentence*.[43]

In addition to controlling patient care and records through the National Health Board, the federal government would create a National Council to preside over medical education, teaching hospitals, and medical research facilities. This National Council would dictate to aspiring doctors, for example, which medical field they could enter. The Clinton Plan says, "In the case of each medical specialty, the National Council shall designate for each academic year the number of individuals nationwide who . . . are authorized to be enrolled in eligible [graduate medical education] programs."[44] The National Council would direct most medical students into primary care, and when it selected students for coveted specialty positions, it would consider "the extent to which the population of training participants in the program includes training participants who are members of racial or ethnic minorities."[45] In other words, the National Council would use racial quotas for medical specialties.

AMERICA AT A CROSSROADS

Bill and Hillary Rodham Clinton have staked their national political careers on the premise that America has a health care "crisis." They offer as a cure a federal government takeover of the nation's health care system, a move that would have profoundly negative medical, economic, and political consequences.

In order to win support for their plan, the Clintons have engaged in aggressive, deceptive promotion. They have kept secret the activities of the task force; they have mis-

represented costs; and they have subordinated the interests of patients to a Leviathan federal government.
Seeking approval from important political constituencies,
the Clintons have:

- Enticed large corporations to support their plan by
  including provisions that would allow them to create
  their own health plans. In addition, these large corporations would be let off the hook when it comes to
  paying for health care for early retirees, under the
  Clinton Plan, all taxpayers would pay for these retirees, a tab that the corporations would otherwise
  have to pay themselves;[46]
- Satisfied pro-abortion feminists by including provisions for taxpayer-funded abortions;[47]
- Won support from the powerful postal unions by ex-
  empting them from rigid provisions of the plan;[48] and
- Treated trial lawyers with kid gloves by failing to address the problem of exploding medical malpractice
  suits. (The only recommendation the Clinton Plan
  makes in this regard is the establishment of a "pilot
  program"—a typical bureaucratic non-answer—to ex-
  plore resolutions of medical malpractice liability.[49])

But perhaps the most revealing aspect of the Clinton
Plan is that it *exempts Congress and federal government
employees*. Instead of being herded into the Regional
Health Alliances with the rest of the country, Washington's politicians and bureaucrats would be allowed to
maintain their own elite health care system. Will Americans tolerate this?

The philosophy behind the Clinton Plan is antithetical
not only to the U.S. system of limited government and
individual liberties, but to the tradition of civilized med-

icine that began with Hippocrates more than 2,000 years ago. Swiss medical philosopher Ernest Truffer discerned an unsettling trend when he wrote about the "rejection of the medical ethic—which is to care for a patient according to the latter's specific [medical] requirements—in favor of a veterinary ethic, which consists in caring for the sick animal, not in accordance with its specific medical needs, but according to the requirements of its master and owner, the person responsible for meeting any costs incurred."[50]

Under the Clinton Plan, a federal bureaucracy would become the "master and owner" identified in the Truffer analysis. This is the *real* crisis.

1. George F. Will, "The Clintons Lethal Paternalism"; Newsweek; February 7, 1994.
2. Gary Bauer, quoted on Family News in Focus Radio; September 23, 1993.
3. Sen. Daniel P. Moynihan (D-N.Y.), quoted by Donald Lambro in "What's Broke"; *Washington Times*; October 1, 1993.
4. Rep. Dan Rostenkowski (D-Ill.), quoted in " 'Health Fairy' Tales"; *Wall Street Journal*; May 5, 1994.
5. *"A Billion Dollars a Day,"* Joint Economic Committee Report; January 24, 1994; page 39.
6. Grace-Marie Arnett, "Cops and Doctors"; *Washington Post*; December 19, 1993.
7. Hillary Rodham Clinton, quoted in the *Washington Times*; March 16, 1994.
8. "Key Players in the Health Care Debate"; *Reuters*; September 23, 1993.
9. Judge Royce C. Lamberth, quoted by Michael York and George Lardner, Jr. in "Preserve Health Files"; *Washington Post*; June 16, 1993.
10. Jeffrey Gutman, quoted by Paul Bedard in "Hillary's Task Force Lacks Records"; *Washington Times*; October 21, 1993.
11. Judge Royce C. Lamberth, quoted by Paul Bedard, *supra* endnote 10.

12. Paul Bedard, *supra* endnote 10.
13. Rep. William F. Clinger (R-Penn.), quoted by Paul Bedard in "Hillary's Panel Short on Papers"; *Washington Times*; October 22, 1993.
14. Kent Masterson Brown, quoted by Paul Bedard in "Lies by Panel"; *Washington Times*; March 24, 1994.
15. Paul Bedard, *supra* endnote 14.
16. Health Security Act (HSA), S1753, HR3600, Title I, Subtitle D, Section 1301 (emphasis added).
17. Kent Masterson Brown, quoted by Paul Bedard, supra endnote 14.
18. Declaration of Ira Magaziner; March 3, 1993; Civil Action #93-399; U.S. District Court for the District of Columbia.
19. Thomas Pyle, quoted by Judi Hasson in "For Task, Glow of Accomplishment Fades"; *USA Today*; April 5, 1994.
20. Arthur Caplan, quoted by Judi Hasson, *supra* endnote 19.
21. Jonathan Roos, "Iowa Deal Raises Question of Profits"; *Des Moines Register*; June 13, 1993.
22. Micah Morrison, "Another Arkansas Tale"; Wall Street Journal; May 2, 1994.
23. Alexander Cockburn, "Beat the Devil"; *The Nation*; March 14, 1994.
24. Irving Kristol, "Too Clever by Half"; *Wall Street Journal*; October 12, 1993.
25. Jacob Weisberg, "Dies IRA"; *The New Republic*; January 24, 1994.
26. HSA, *supra* endnote 16, Title I, Subtitle B, Section 1101.
27. *ibid.*, Title I, Subtitle B, Section 1114.
28. *ibid.*
29. "A New Look at Breast Care"; *U.S. News & World Report*; February 1, 1993.
30. HSA, *supra* endnote 16; Title I, Subtitle B, Section 1115.
31. *ibid.*, Title I, Subtitle B, Section 1116.
32. *ibid.*, Title I, Subtitle B, Section 1114.
33. Hillary Rodham Clinton, quoted by George F. Will in "Came the Revolution . . . "; *Newsweek*; February 21, 1994.
34. HSA, *supra* endnote 16, Title I, Subtitle E, Section 1402.
35. "An Analysis of the Administration's Health Proposal," Congressional Budget Office; February 8, 1994; page xv.
36. Bill Clinton, quoted by Karen Riley and J. Jennings Moss in

"Health Numbers Disputed"; *Washington Times*; February 9, 1994.
37. HAS, *supra* endnote 16, *ibid.*, Title I, Subtitle C, Section 1204.
38. *ibid.*, Title V, Subtitle B, Section 5103.
39. *ibid.*, Title V, Subtitle B, Section 5102.
40. *ibid.*, Title V, Subtitle B, Section 5105.
41. *ibid.*, Title V, Subtitle E, Section 5433.
42. *ibid.*, Title VI, Subtitle B, Section 6041.
43. *ibid.*, Title V, Subtitle E, Section 5434.
44. *ibid.*, Title III, Subtitle A, Section 3012.
45. *ibid.*, Title III, Subtitle A, Section 3013.
46. *ibid.*, Title I, Subtitle G, Section 1606.
47. *ibid.*, Title I, Subtitle B, Section 1116.
48. *ibid.*, Title I, Subtitle D, Section 1113.
49. *ibid.*, Title V, Subtitle D, Section 5312.
50. Ernest Truffer, quoted in the *Wall Street Journal*; February 14, 1994.

"WHITEWATERGATE"

"We did nothing improper and I have nothing to say about it—old story."[1]
> —Bill Clinton on "Whitewatergate"
> November 3, 1993

"I cannot speak to that in any detail."[2]
> —Hillary Rodham Clinton, on the secret removal of Whitewater documents from Vincent Foster's office soon after his death.

"If there is nothing wrong, why are they hiding?"[3]
> —Wall Street Journal
> January 11, 1994

"I would certainly expect that before this investigation is over that I would question both the President and the First Lady and that it would be under oath."[4]
> —Special Counsel Robert B. Fiske, Jr.
> January 20, 1994

Most Americans started hearing about Whitewater in the fall of 1993, when federal investigations that had been going on quietly since before the presidential election intensified. Pundits dubbed the controversy "Whitewater-gate," because it was the Whitewater Development Corporation that directly linked Bill and Hillary Rodham Clinton to the wheeling and dealing that reached a peak in the 1980s in Arkansas.

The activities of the Clintons and their associates suggest political bribery; illegal campaign contributions; conflicts of interest; tax evasion; and massive fraud, often committed at taxpayer expense. Moreover, developments during Bill Clinton's presidency have called into question the propriety, and even legality, of the behavior of top White House officials.

"In a nutshell," explains Rep. James Leach (R-Iowa), the ranking Republican on the House Banking Committee, "Whitewater is about the arrogance of power."[5] At the least, the unfolding scandal shows Bill Clinton to be the ultimate hypocrite: it was Clinton who denounced the "ripoff artists [who] looted our S&Ls";[6] it was Clinton who campaigned for reform and responsibility in government; it was Clinton who promised to defend the little guy and represent those who "work hard and play by the rules."

In his book *Putting People First*, Clinton wrote, "It's important to remember that the most irresponsible people of all in the 1980s were those at the top . . . not the hard-working middle class, but those who sold out our savings-and-loans with bad deals and spent billions on wasteful takeovers and mergers."[7]

But one year into office, it was Clinton who was being lambasted on the floor of the House of Representatives as the worst type of offender of the rules of ethics he claimed to represent. Representative Leach, one of the least partisan members of Congress, listed five points outlining the scope of the Whitewater scandal:

"One, Whitewater may have begun as a legitimate real estate venture, but it came to be used to skim, directly or indirectly, federally insured deposits from an S&L and a small-business investment corporation. When each failed, the U.S. taxpayer became obligated to pick up the tab."

"Two, the family of the former governor of Arkansas received value from Whitewater well in excess of resources invested."

"Three, taxpayer-guaranteed funds were in all likelihood used to benefit the campaign of the former governor."

"Four, the independence of the U.S. government's regulatory system has been flagrantly violated in an effort to protect a single American citizen."

"Five, Congress and the executive are employing closed-society techniques to resist full disclosure of an embarrassing circumstance with unfortunate, precedent-setting ramifications."[8]

Throughout, Bill and Hillary Rodham Clinton have maintained their innocence. In a presidential press conference, Bill Clinton said their participation in Whitewater was "a perfectly honorable thing to do."[9] What follows is only the *known* record of the Clintons' "perfectly honorable" performance.

THE PLAYERS

The participants in the unfolding Whitewater drama include those who were involved in the web of deals in Arkansas, and those who are trying to sort them out today. They include—

Bill Clinton: President of the United States; former Governor of Arkansas; former Whitewater Development

Corporation partner; former Attorney General of Arkansas.

Hillary Rodham Clinton: First Lady of the United States; former Rose Law Firm senior partner; former Whitewater Development Corporation partner.

James B. McDougal: former Madison Guaranty Savings and Loan owner; former Bank of Kingston part owner; former Madison Financial Corporation president; Whitewater Development Corporation partner.

Susan H. McDougal: former Master Marketing president; former Whitewater Development partner.

Jim Guy Tucker: Governor of Arkansas (D); former Lieutenant Governor of Arkansas; former Mitchell, Williams, Selig, Jackson, and Tucker Law Firm partner; former Castle Grande investor; former Castle Water & Sewer president; former Southloop Construction president; former Bank of Kingston co-owner.

Webster L. "Webb" Hubbell: former Associate Attorney General; former Rose Law Firm managing partner.

Seth Ward: father-in-law of Webster L. Hubbell; former Madison Financial Corporation officer; former Castle Grande investor.

Vincent W. Foster: deceased; former Deputy White House Counsel; former personal attorney to Bill and Hillary Rodham Clinton; former Rose Law Firm partner.

Thomas F. "Mack" McLarty III: White House Chief of Staff; former chairman of Arkla, Inc.

J. William Fulbright: retired; former Democratic U.S. Senator from Arkansas.

Sarah J. Worsham: former Madison Guaranty senior vice president; former Federal Home Loan Bank Board examiner.

W. Maurice Smith: former Clinton-appointed Arkansas State Highways and Transportation executive director; former Bank of Cherry Valley owner; former Clinton campaign aide.

David L Hale: grand jury witness in the investigation of Special Counsel Robert B. Fiske, Jr.; former Clinton-appointed municipal judge; former Capital Management Services owner.

Beverly Bassett Schaffer: former Clinton-appointed State Securities Commissioner; former Mitchell, Williams, Selig, Jackson and Tucker Law Firm attorney; former Clinton campaign worker.

Charles Peacock: former member, Madison Guaranty board of directors.

Kenneth Peacock: son of Charles Peacock; alleged donor of $3,000 Clinton campaign contribution.

Stephen A. Smith: former Communications Co. owner; former Bank of Kingston president; former Clinton aide.

Chris Wade: realtor and developer of Whitewater Development properties.

Paula J. Casey: U.S. attorney in Little Rock, Arkansas; former Clinton campaign volunteer; former University of Arkansas Law School student of Bill Clinton.

James M. Lyons: Denver, Colorado attorney and Clinton confidant; author of the Lyons Report.

Sam Heuer: attorney to James McDougal.

David Kendall: personal attorney to Bill and Hillary Rodham Clinton.

Janet Reno: Attorney General of the United States.

Robert B. Fiske, Jr.: Special Counsel appointed by Janet Reno to investigate Whitewater; on leave of absence from David Polk & Wardell Law Firm; former U.S. attorney for Presidents Ford and Carter.

Roderick C. Lankler: New York homicide prosecutor

and head of Special Counsel Fiske's Washington office; responsible for investigation into death of Vincent Foster.

Jeremy Hedges: University of Little Rock student; Rose Law Firm courier.

Clayton Lindsey: University of Little Rock student; Rose Law Firm courier.

Bernard W. Nussbaum: former White House Counsel; recipient of Fiske subpoena.

Patsy L. Thomasson: Special Assistant to the President; former executive vice president of Lasater & Company.

Margaret Williams: Hillary Rodham Clinton's Chief of Staff; recipient of Fiske subpoena; former Communications Director of Children's Defense Fund; former Democratic National Committee press deputy.

Jean E. Hanson: Treasury Department General Counsel; recipient of Fiske subpoena.

Bruce R. Lindsey: White House Senior Advisor; point man on Whitewater and Madison matters; recipient of Fiske subpoena.

Mark D. Gearan: White House Communications Director; recipient of Fiske subpoena.

Joshua Steiner: Chief of Staff to Treasury Secretary Lloyd Bentsen; recipient of Fiske subpoena.

Jack R. DeVore, Jr.: former Treasury Department Press Secretary; recipient of Fiske subpoena.

Harold M. Ickes: White House Deputy Chief of Staff; recipient of Fiske subpoena.

Roger C. Altman: Deputy Treasury Secretary; former RTC acting head; college classmate of Bill Clinton and longtime friend of Bill and Hillary Rodham Clinton; former vice chairman, Blackstone Group; recipient of Fiske subpoena.

George Stephanopoulous: White House Senior Adviser;

former Clinton Press Secretary; recipient of Fiske subpoena.

L. Jean Lewis: senior investigator in RTC Kansas City, Missouri, office.

Sen. Donald W. Riegle, Jr.: Michigan Democrat; chairman of Senate Banking Committee.

Sen. Alfonse M. D'Amato: New York Republican; ranking member of Senate Banking Committee.

Rep. James A. Leach: Iowa Republican; ranking member of House Banking Committee.

Rep. Henry B. Gonzalez: Texas Democrat; chairman of House Banking Committee.

GETTING STARTED IN ARKANSAS

In the late 1960s, when Bill Clinton was hired as an intern for then-Sen. J. William Fulbright, he met James McDougal, another Fulbright staff member. The two rising stars in their state's Democratic establishment became friends and McDougal served as a "protective big brother" to Clinton.[10]

While Clinton became Arkansas's Attorney General in 1976, McDougal realized that his interests lay in finance. McDougal speculated on land with Senator Fulbright in the mid-1970s, and he decided in 1978 to develop vacation and retirement homes in the Ozarks. He and his wife, Susan, invited friends Bill and Hillary Clinton, who were busy campaigning in their first gubernatorial race, to join them in the Whitewater real estate venture.

The partnership made a $20,000 down payment with an unsecured loan to purchase 230 acres of property along Arkansas's White River for $203,000. In 1979, this land was transferred to the newly formed Whitewater Development Corporation. The Whitewater Development Corporation was structured so that, in return for little or no initial investment, the Clintons would receive 50 percent of all profits.* That same year, Bill Clinton began his first term as Governor of Arkansas, and he appointed Mc-Dougal Director of Economic Development for the state.

"In this venture called Whitewater," explained Representative Leach, McDougal "provided virtually all, perhaps all, the money; the Governor-in-the-making provided his name."[12]

QUESTIONS: Did James McDougal make the Clintons partners in Whitewater because of past, or in expectation of future, favors? If so, did this constitute an illegal gratuity? If not, why *did* McDougal give 50 percent of his company to the Clintons?

In 1980, after one term in office, Bill Clinton lost the Governor's seat to Republican Frank White. He spent two years out of office lawyering at Wright, Lindsey, and Jennings, and repairing his image before voters.

Meanwhile, McDougal began his banking career with the purchase of the Bank of Kingston. On December 16, 1980, McDougal lent Hillary Rodham Clinton $30,000 from that bank, accepting a Whitewater lot as collateral. The loan, which was made out to "Hillary Rodham," was deposited ten days later into a Whitewater account that showed a balance of $456.[13] The $30,000 was used to build a model Whitewater home.

QUESTION: Did James McDougal make this $30,000 personal loan to Hillary Rodham Clinton, who then channeled the money into Whitewater, to avoid the appearance of lending money to himself or one of his entities? (Although Whitewater Development Corp. made payments on this loan, the Clintons deducted $5,133 from their federal tax returns for interest payments, thereby reducing

---

*The March 26, 1994, *New York Times* reported that the Clintons' initial investment was only $500.[11]

their 1984 and 1985 tax payment by $2,156. When this illegal deduction was brought to light during the 1992 presidential campaign, the Clintons repaid the government $4,000 in back taxes and interest.[14])

THE RISE OF MADISON GUARANTY

In 1982, Clinton recaptured the governorship and McDougal bought a rural savings and loan, naming it Madison Guaranty.

At the time of purchase, Madison had assets of $6 million. During McDougal's three-year tenure as president and owner, Madison's assets jumped to $123 million, while capital reserves dropped sharply. Reported the *Washington Post*: "Loans to officers, directors and related parties had swelled from $500,000 to $17 million. Most of the money was never repaid."[15]

As early as 1983, just one year after McDougal bought Madison, state investigators were skeptical of its operations. They warned that McDougal might not be fit to run an S&L. Arkansas banking commissioner Marlin Jackson warned Governor Clinton that McDougal had made "imprudent loans" at his Bank of Kingston, and pointed out that McDougal engaged in high-risk lending and cronyism.[16] Nothing came of Jackson's warnings.

QUESTION: Was the state of Arkansas, governed by Bill Clinton, remiss in not controlling McDougal's imprudent loans? Why were Commissioner Marlin Jackson's warnings ignored?

It certainly appeared as if James McDougal and his S&L had begun receiving favorable treatment from state regulators under Bill Clinton. When Madison wanted to open a new branch in Salina County, for example, a rival bank complained. A decision was needed from the Arkansas S&L regulatory board. At the time, there was a vacancy

"There is little to suggest that the wild ride the nation took with Bill and Hillary Rodham Clinton in 1993 was a function of first year settling-in. It appears to be a way of life."

— Ann Devroy
Washington Post

Hollywood stars swamped Washington for Bill Clinton's Inauguration. Barbra Streisand gushed over Clinton at the Presidential Gala.

Roger Clinton performed rock 'n roll at the Arkansas State Society Inaugural Gala and earned the Secret Service codename "Headache."

Bill Clinton sang his theme song, "Don't Stop Thinking about Tomorrow," with pals Michael Jackson and Stevie Nicks.

Clinton made unusually poor personnel decisions. Failed nominee Admiral Bobby Ray Inman was one of at least 27 Clinton picks with a "Nannygate" problem.

Clinton proudly appointed Roberta Achtenberg as the first open homosexual to high government office. Here, Achtenberg gives thumbs up to a crowd at San Francisco's Lesbian and Gay Freedom Day Parade.

Clinton withdrew support for Lani Guinier as civil rights chief after admitting he couldn't defend her extremist views.

As Clinton's Surgeon General, Joycelyn Elders has promoted an agenda of sex education, condom distribution, and abortion. Elders wants the government to give prostitutes the contraceptive Norplant, "so they could still use sex if they must to buy their drugs."

Paula and Steve Jones said they wanted to clear her name after Arkansas state troopers reported to the press that "a woman named Paula" had rendezvoused with then-Governor Clinton at the Excelsior hotel in Little Rock.

Arkansas state troopers Larry Patterson and Roger Perry say Clinton asked them to help arrange his extramarital affairs.

When asked if the troopers' charges were true, President Clinton said: "We, we did, if, the, the, I, I, the stories are just as they have been said. They're outrageous and they're not so."

Bill Clinton and Janet Reno: true crime fighters?

President Clinton warned tyrannically after Waco, "I hope very much that others who will be tempted to join cults and to become involved with people like David Koresh will be deterred by the horrible scenes they have seen."

President Clinton announces his policy on homosexuals in the military to top military brass at Ft. McNair.

Clinton golfing partner Webster Hubbell was made the number three man at the Justice Department. But Hubbell had to resign his post when the Rose Law Firm raised ethics allegations against him. One charge under investigation is that Hubbell billed the FDIC for work when he was really golfing at the Country Club of Little Rock.

Bill Clinton wants to issue every American a Health Security Card that would allow federal bureaucrats to maintain citizen files on a national electronic data bank.

Hillary Rodham Clinton and Ira Magaziner were the power behind the secret health care task force.

President Clinton and Rep. Dan Rostenkowski (D-Ill.): You scratch my back, I'll scratch yours.

Rep. James Leach (R-Iowa), ranking Republican on the House Banking Committee, charges that Clinton business partner James McDougal ran his S&L as a "private piggy bank" for an inside group of family, friends, and politicians.

Robert B. Fiske, Jr., was named special counsel by Janet Reno on January 20, 1994.

James McDougal and his attorney carry Whitewater documents returned to McDougal by the Clintons in April 1994. The Clintons said during the 1992 campaign that they did not have the files.

Photo by Associated Press

Bernard Nussbaum resigned as White House Counsel on March 5, 1994. Nussbaum was at the center of White House controversies concerning Whitewater and the death of Vincent Foster.

Photo by Associated Press

Vincent Foster allegedly shot himself on July 20, 1993, at Fort Marcy Park.

on the board, and Governor Clinton appointed regulator Dick Fisch to join temporarily "as a special member . . . to specifically hear" the Madison case.[17] Madison's request was approved. Although it never opened the Salina County branch, "in the view of some lawyers," reported *Time* magazine, "it was unethical for Clinton to decide who should vote on an application from a business partner."[18]

As Madison grew, James and Susan McDougal achieved a sort of celebrity status in Little Rock. The McDougals flaunted their new-found wealth: Susan McDougal was renowned for wearing hot pants while riding horseback in their real estate television commercials and James McDougal's baby-blue Bentley was a well-known sight around town. As the *Washington Post*'s Howard Schneider wryly observed, "Together, they were Little Rock's answer to Donald and Ivana [Trump], a 90 percent rayon copy, perhaps, but flashy and well-heeled enough to cause a stir in the mid-1980s Arkansas."[19]

Companies controlled by Susan McDougal received $1.3 million from Madison for marketing promotions between 1983 and 1986. The *Los Angeles Times* reported that examiners found "profits had been inflated and hundreds of thousands of dollars paid in commissions and fees to McDougal's wife and other relatives."[20]

Moreover, the *Washington Post* wrote that in the mid-1980s, "tens of thousands of dollars were passing through Whitewater's accounts at Madison . . . the transactions seemed to bear no direct connection to Whitewater's lot sales or home development activity. At times the account would be overdrawn by thousands of dollars. The overdrafts were then covered with deposits from other McDougal corporations with Madison accounts."[21]

"It is apparent," said Representative Leach, "that Madison was allowed to continue in existence as a private piggy bank despite its insolvent condition."[22] Living high on the hog seemed the thing to do. "I bought clothes basically," said Susan McDougal, summing up this period in her life.[23]

QUESTION: Did James McDougal receive lenient treatment by Arkansas bank officials because of his relationship with Bill Clinton? Was it ethical for Clinton to hand-pick Dick Fisch, the regulatory official who would rule on a McDougal request? Were Madison transactions with family, friends, and the political elite of Arkansas conducted in a proper "arms length" manner, or did loans result from improper favoritism?

MADISON'S ROAD TO FINANCIAL RUIN

Like many S&Ls in the 1980s, Madison's wealth rested on a foundation of sand. McDougal made unwise real estate investments and conducted business sloppily. "Large loans were being extended to [former U.S. Sen. J. William] Fulbright and other state political figures," reported the *Los Angeles Times*.[24]

Madison suffered huge losses in 1984 after embarking on an ambitious land development scheme in New Brunswick, only to have nearly half of its purchasers cancel. McDougal violated federal land sale laws in the process, further raising the eyebrows of regulators.[25]

Still more money was lost on Castle Grande, a mobile home park north of Little Rock in which Jim Guy Tucker and Seth Ward were investors. When federal bank regulators visited Castle Grande, construction of which was never even completed, they concluded, "There is no evidence that there is a viable market for the land."[26] Madison lent Tucker's Castle Water and Sewer $1.05 million for the project, and wound up losing $861,000 on that deal alone.[27] For his part, Seth Ward defaulted on $587,793 in Madison loans.[28]

Madison also suffered when McDougal transferred bad loans from his other banks to it. Records show he made at least five such transfers in 1984.[29]

In 1985, McDougal wrote a Whitewater check for $7,322 to pay back a loan Bill Clinton had taken from the Security Bank of Paragould. Because the Whitewater account had only $12.49 in it, McDougal had to deposit $7,500 from a Madison subsidiary to cover the account.[30]

According to a financial consultant quoted by the *Los Angeles Times*, Madison Guaranty "should have been flashing bright red on the regulators' screen at least by 1984."[31]

QUESTIONS: Did Madison Guaranty operate as a "private piggy bank" for Arkansas's elite? Were Madison funds illegally diverted to pay personal and/or political debts of top Arkansas politicians, including Bill Clinton? Why did James McDougal pay Bill Clinton's Paragould loan for him?

In February 1984, Federal Home Loan Bank Board examiner Sarah J. Worsham warned that Madison had engaged in "unsound lending practices."[32] McDougal responded to this criticism by hiring Worsham as a vice-president of Madison, where she received a $65,000 annual salary; a $500 monthly expense allowance; a yearly bonus of $2,000; a $5,000 unsecured loan; and use of the S&L's $35,000 Bentley sedan.[33]

Hiring Worsham was not the only step McDougal took to protect his cozy enterprise. The same year, he retained Hillary Rodham Clinton, a partner at the Rose Law Firm.

The genesis of McDougal's legal representation by Hillary Rodham Clinton was disclosed by the *Los Angeles Times*. McDougal told the *Times* that Bill Clinton came asking for financial help during one of his early morning jogs in 1984. McDougal said Clinton complained that "things were tight" and asked him to hire his wife Hillary to give them extra cash flow.[34]

"I asked him how much he needed," McDougal recalled, "and Clinton said 'about $2,000 a month.' " McDougal said he immediately instructed one of his staff to retain Rodham Clinton for $2,000 a month. "I hired Hillary because Bill came in whimpering they needed help," McDougal said, adding that, at the time, he didn't have any particular work for her to do.[35]

"McDougal said he recalled the event vividly," the *Times* reporters wrote, "because he was so uncomfortable in the meeting, not over the retainer but because throughout that morning conference, Clinton sat sweating in McDougal's new leather desk chair, an expensive gift from his wife."[36]

McDougal wound up paying Rodham Clinton approximately $30,000 to represent Madison, even though she was not listed as one of Rose's financial experts.[37]

QUESTIONS: Did James McDougal imply or extend a job offer to Sarah Worsham before her federal loan bank board report was completed? Why did McDougal retain Hillary Rodham Clinton and pay her $30,000 to represent Madison Guaranty when she was not an expert in financial matters? Was hiring Rodham Clinton a favor for which McDougal expected reciprocity?

BILL CLINTON: STRAPPED FOR CASH

Although he had secured the $2,000 monthly retainer for his wife, Bill Clinton needed more money for his re-election campaign. So, in the fall of 1984, he sought help from Maurice Smith, a member of his staff who owned the Bank of Cherry Valley. Smith's bank lent Clinton $50,000, and Clinton contributed the money to his campaign.[38] Smith didn't ask Clinton for collateral and, in fact, Clinton had few assets at the time. (He did not own a house, for example.)

The next spring, saddled with the Smith loan, Clinton asked McDougal to "knock out a deficit" for him, namely, to pay back the $50,000 to Cherry Valley.[39] McDougal responded by hosting a lavish cocktail reception for Clinton's campaign at Madison Guaranty on April 4, 1985. This reception, attended mostly by Madison stockholders and employees, reportedly raised $35,000 to help pay off Clinton's loan.[40]

At the party, the Clinton campaign was presented with four $3,000 Madison cashier's checks. One of the central questions of current investigations is whether any of these checks, or other funds raised at this event, broke banking or campaign laws.

One of the four people whose name appears on a check, Dean Landrum, is dead. One check had Susan McDougal's name on it. A third alleged donor, former Sen. J. William Fulbright, was seriously ill, and a Fulbright aide said Fulbright had no knowledge of the check.[41] The fourth cashier's check bore the name Ken Peacock, at the time a 24-year-old college student. Peacock has denied making the contribution. Peacock's father, Charles Peacock, who was on the Madison board of directors, initially said he knew nothing about the check and, as a third-generation Republican, would never have contributed such a generous sum to a Democrat. The elder Peacock subsequently recanted this explanation and stated he had approved the check that bore his son's name.[42]

On top of the mystery surrounding these four cashier's checks, questions abound about other contributions. Madison employees, for example, have reported that a Madison executive promised to reimburse them for contributions made at this fundraiser. One senior vice president said he was reimbursed for a $500 contribution, but would not disclose who paid him.[43] Two former Madison executives told the *Los Angeles Times* that McDougal had ordered them to contribute to Bill Clinton's campaign fund.[44]

Moreover, files that would have recorded the contributions at the April 4th fundraiser are mysteriously missing from the Pulaski County Clerk's records in Little Rock. Phil Hoots, then-manager of these records, reported that all copies of campaign contribution records were microfilmed, but that some of the microfilms had been destroyed in the boiler room where they were stored. "They had all that stuff back there in the catty-combs," Hoots explained. "Bingo! It was all ruined."[45]

QUESTION: Why was Maurice Smith willing to lend $50,000 to Bill Clinton without any collateral? Who wrote the checks to the Clinton campaign at the Madison reception? Was there an illegal diversion of Madison funds into the Clinton campaign? If so, was Bill Clinton aware of it? Were any campaign contribution rules violated at this reception?

KEEPING MADISON GUARANTY ALIVE

On April 3, 1985, the day before McDougal hosted the fundraiser for Governor Clinton, Madison executives met with state regulators who were concerned about the S&L's solvency. The regulators indicated that unless Madison took immediate steps to raise capital, it would be shut down.[46]

To stave off the regulators, the S&L executives concocted a proposal to sell preferred stock in Madison, an unusual plan given that such stocks had never before been issued by an Arkansas S&L.

Because Madison was state-chartered, this irregular stock sale proposal needed a regulator's stamp of approval. The decision on the stock sale fell to Bill Clinton's newly appointed chief regulator of the state S&L industry, a woman with previous ties to both Clinton and McDougal, Beverly Bassett Schaffer.* McDougal has subsequently bragged that he personally instructed Bill Clinton to hire Bassett Schaffer because the choice "was to our advantage."[47]

When the Madison executives proposed the stock sale, some within the Arkansas Securities Department wondered why anyone would want to buy preferred stock in a failing S&L. Charles Handley, a state regulator at the time, asked, "Can they, and how could they, sell stock in a failing institution? Who would want to buy it?"[48] Handley even suggested that Bassett Schaffer seek legal advice before approving the Madison plan.

Representing Madison Guaranty to Bassett Schaffer in this case was none other than Hillary Rodham Clinton, who, of course, was on retainer with Madison per Governor Clinton's earlier request. In making Madison's case before state regulators, Rodham Clinton submitted a financial report by the accounting firm Frost and Company that claimed the S&L was solvent with $109 million in

---

*Before assuming her position as commissioner of the Arkansas Securities Department, Beverly Bassett Schaffer had been a contributor to the Clinton campaign. Her brother, Woody Bassett, had been a contributor to the Clinton campaign and had helped manage Clinton's 1984 gubernatorial re-election campaign. Her husband, Archie Schaffer, also was a major contributor to the Clinton campaign. Schaffer worked as an executive at Tyson Foods, on whose board of directors Hillary Rodham Clinton sat. Moreover, Bassett Schaffer had formerly represented Madison Guaranty when she worked at Mitchell, Williams, Selig, Jackson, and Tucker Law Firm.

assets.[49] But the Frost audit had been prepared by James Alford, who had two outstanding loans at Madison. Although Alford's report later turned out to be fraught with error, Rodham Clinton used it to establish credibility for the cash-hemorrhaging S&L. The plea worked: on May 14, 1985, in a letter addressed "Dear Hillary," Bassett Schaffer accepted the Madison preferred-stock plan.[50]

Although ultimately no investors could be found who would buy the Madison stock, Bassett Schaffer's approval gave the increasingly troubled S&L some breathing room. Or, viewed from another perspective, her approval gave the S&L more time to accumulate debt that would eventually land in the laps of U.S. taxpayers.

When controversy erupted over Bassett Schaffer's approval of the Madison plan, she denied being influenced by the Clintons. But RTC investigators point out that Bassett Schaffer should have exercised greater vigilance given her knowledge of Madison's past indiscretions. In 1984, when Bassett Schaffer was working for Mitchell, Williams, Selig, Jackson and Tucker Law Firm, which represented Madison, she called McDougal's violation of federal land law "willful."[51]

"It made an amazing tangle of interests," observed the *New Yorker*'s Peter J. Boyer. "Hillary Clinton was arguing for a rescue plan on behalf of [Governor Clinton's] business partner (and her own financial rescuer) before a state official who was also a friend, and who had been appointed by Hillary's husband, the Governor, and who had herself done work for the bank in question."[52]

QUESTIONS: Did James McDougal improperly influence Governor Clinton's choice of Beverly Bassett Schaffer? Was it a conflict-of-interest for Bassett Schaffer to rule in a decision involving a former client? Did Madison

Guaranty receive favorable treatment from Bassett Schaffer because it was represented by Hillary Rodham Clinton? Did it constitute a conflict-of-interest for the wife of the Governor to represent a troubled S&L, owned by a friend and business partner of herself and her husband, before a state regulator answerable to her husband? Did Bill or Hillary Rodham Clinton improperly use influence to keep open an S&L that was, by most indications, on the verge of collapse, thereby increasing the cost to taxpayers of the eventual bailout?

CONNECTIONS . . . CONNECTIONS . . . CONNECTIONS . . .

The Beverly Bassett Schaffer decision was not the only conflict-of-interest that cropped up during the final, failing years of Madison Guaranty.

In March 1985, during the period when Madison's operations were under heavy scrutiny by the state, and although Governor Clinton had been warned that Madison was engaged in risky business practices, he appointed Madison's chief executive officer, John Latham, to the Arkansas Savings and Loan Board. Eventually, Latham became chairman of this board.[53]*

The state of Arkansas also provided Madison with some sorely needed business. For example, the Arkansas Development Finance Authority (ADFA)† rented offices in

---

*Latham subsequently pleaded guilty to falsifying Madison records.
†ADFA was one of Bill Clinton's more notorious boondoggles. Established in 1985 to bring jobs to Arkansas, ADFA spent an average of $13,000 per job created, while the average salary for these jobs was $15,000. Clinton's consolidation of authority to issue bonds through ADFA did, however, give him important political leverage. ADFA became a vehicle through which he gave millions of dollars of business to Little Rock's business and legal elite. Seth Ward's Park on Meter, Inc. (POM), for example, received a $2.75 million bond from the

a Madison-owned building, a contract for which Mc-Dougal has openly thanked Bill Clinton.[55] According to the *Washington Times,* top state officials overruled ADFA employees who wanted offices in Little Rock's financial district. The senior officials, who reported to Clinton, insisted that ADFA put its offices in the inconveniently located Madison building. The state of Arkansas paid Madison $5,300 in monthly rent for these offices for nearly two years, even though ADFA had received five lower bids for its offices. (Some investigators question whether Madison's rent was inflated to help McDougal pay Hillary Rodham Clinton's retainer.)[56]

In addition to winning lucrative state contracts, sources say McDougal "enjoyed regular access to the Governor's office." Once, when a state official questioned a Madison venture, McDougal warned the official that if he complained to the Arkansas Attorney General, McDougal would go over his head to Clinton. "I'll be sitting in the Governor's office," McDougal chortled. The official dropped his complaint.[57]

QUESTION: Were payments from Arkansas state agencies to Madison proper, given that McDougal and the governor were business partners? Why did ADFA reject bids for lower-priced offices in favor of the Madison-owned property?

LOOTING THE FEDERAL GOVERNMENT

Despite many perks, Madison continued to bleed dollars. Then, in 1986, a new player entered the game: Judge

---

state in 1985, a deal in which Ward was represented by the Rose Law Firm.[54]

Part of Special Counsel Robert B. Fiske, Jr.'s, investigation will focus on whether McDougal, Madison, or Whitewater Development benefited improperly from ADFA loans.

David Hale. Hale was a Democrat and longtime Clinton supporter. When Clinton created Arkansas's first municipal small claims court, he asked David Hale to head it.

In addition to serving as judge, Hale was president of Capital Management Services, Inc. (CMS), a well-known Arkansas Small Business Investment Corporation (SBIC).* According to Hale, James McDougal told him in the fall of 1985 that there were "some members of the political family [of Arkansas] that had some loans that might be in question at Madison."[58] Hale said that he came to learn that "the political family" was a euphemism for an elite group that included the Clintons.[59] Hale said McDougal next confessed that he needed help "cleaning up" financial messes at Madison to keep out of trouble with regulators.[60] "I knew I had to help," Hale told the *Los Angeles Times*, "there was never any question."[61]

Hale reported that in February 1986, he encountered Bill Clinton on the steps of the state Capitol. According to Hale, the Governor asked, "David, are you going to be able to help Jim [McDougal] and me out?"[62] One month later, Hale says, he met with Clinton and McDougal to figure out how to structure CMS loans to them. "Bill said that . . . his name couldn't appear on the documents," Hale recalls.[63]

According to Hale, he, McDougal, and Clinton decided that CMS would lend to Susan McDougal, the argument being that, as a woman, she would seem a likely recipient of an SBIC loan.† Hale says that he neither met with Susan

---

*An SBIC is an investment company subsidized by the federal government's Small Business Administration (SBA) to provide venture capital to business borrowers who cannot "obtain financial and other assistance available to the average entrepreneur."

†Just months before Hale made the $300,000 loan to Susan McDougal, the

McDougal nor discussed the loan with her. But a CMS check was issued to Susan McDougal on April 3, 1986, for $300,000.*

"I knew what was going on," Hale said, "as we all did. But we were friends and that's just the way business is done in Arkansas."[65]

Bill Clinton and James McDougal have denied meeting with Hale. For her part, Susan McDougal says she doesn't remember receiving the $300,000 CMS loan. But the CMS check was deposited into a Madison account, and, on the back of the check, in lieu of a personal endorsement, is a stamped endorsement: "Deposit to the account of the named payee. Missing endorsement guaranteed by Madison Guaranty Savings and Loan."

Two things are known about this $300,000. First, more than $100,000 of it was transferred into a Whitewater account and was subsequently used to help the company buy 810 acres of property from International Paper.[66]

Second, the $300,000 CMS loan was never paid back.†

QUESTIONS: Did Bill Clinton pressure David Hale to make this or any other fraudulent loan through his SBIC? Did Susan McDougal qualify for loans made available to "disadvantaged" business people? Did Susan McDougal know that Hale made her the $300,000 loan? Did the Clintons and the McDougals illegally benefit from this $300,000 loan, which was eventually defaulted on at taxpayer expense?

McDougals had filed a joint financial statement that showed assets of more than $3 million.[64]

*See Appendix F for a copy of CMS's $300,000 check to Susan McDougal.

†Documents relating to the Susan McDougal loan were reportedly recovered by the FBI in a July 20, 1992 raid on Hale's office.

CLOSING MADISON GUARANTY

In 1986, federal bank regulators forced McDougal out of Madison Guaranty and he was hospitalized for a "florid manic episode."[67]* The S&L was shut down in 1989 at a cost to taxpayers of approximately $60 million. Accountants who looked at Madison's books shortly after McDougal's departure charged that "underlying documentation for cash disbursements . . . was often missing or incomplete, and entries [were] recorded in direct violation of regulatory and generally accepted accounting principles."[70]

After Madison was closed down, the Federal Deposit Insurance Corporation (FDIC) wanted to recover whatever money it could from the ruins. To do so, the agency decided to sue Frost and Company, the accounting firm that had prepared the 1985 audit stating Madison was financially sound.

To go after Frost and Company, the FDIC hired the Rose Law Firm, whose Hillary Rodham Clinton, of course, had used the Frost audit years earlier to convince state regulators that Madison was financially viable.

Questions remain about whether the Rose Law Firm's representation of the FDIC constituted a conflict-of-interest, given Rodham Clinton's previous work for Madison. Typically, lawyers are barred from working for the FDIC on cases involving S&Ls they previously repre-

---

*As McDougal's career collapsed, so did his marriage and his friendship with the Clintons. Susan McDougal left Arkansas in 1988. (At divorce proceedings, James McDougal said he had assets of $300.[68]) In 1990, McDougal was acquitted of bank fraud in a case concerning bonuses he paid himself out of one of his other enterprises, Madison Financial Corporation.

For her part, Susan McDougal made news for allegedly embezzling $200,000 from renowned conductor Zubin Mehta, for whom she worked in California from 1989 until July 1992.[69]

sented, and it is not clear whether the FDIC was informed of Rose's connection to Madison. The very day Madison failed, Vincent Foster wrote to the FDIC soliciting business for Rose. In his letter, Foster maintained that Rose "does not represent any savings-and-loan association in state or federal regulatory matters."[71] By writing in the present tense, Foster was able to omit the fact that Madison Guaranty had previously been a Rose client, and specifically that Rose attorneys had once endorsed the very Frost audit the FDIC wanted to sue over.

Nonetheless, the FDIC hired Rose to sue Frost and Company for negligence in preparing the audit. Although the government hoped to settle the $60 million suit for $6 million, Rose lawyers ultimately settled for only $1 million.[72] Sources reporting to the *Washington Post* claimed this settlement was several million dollars short of the limit of Frost's insurance coverage. And, after the Rose Law Firm billed the FDIC $400,000 on the case, the government's net gain was reduced to approximately $600,000, or roughly one percent of Madison's losses.[73]

After an unthorough review of its relationship with Rose Law, the FDIC found no conflict-of-interest in its handling of the Frost case. But Republican lawmakers branded the FDIC review a whitewash, and the agency agreed to reopen its probe for a conflict-of-interest. The entire matter, including the possibility of civil fraud charges against Rodham Clinton, has also become a point of investigation for Special Counsel Robert B. Fiske, Jr.

Finally, Rose Law's representation of the FDIC is a point of investigation in the allegations of overbilling against Webster Hubbell, for it was Hubbell who did most of the work on the FDIC case. Regulators from the RTC and the FDIC began a review of Hubbell's billing to them in March 1994. The regulators were concerned about a specific allegation of a $30,000 double billing, and their investigation will review billings of several hundred thousand dollars.[74]

The *Washington Times*, in its review of Rose Law's billing to the FDIC, found that Hubbell had billed the government for a full day of work, at $125 an hour, on at least two occasions when he was golfing at the Country Club of Little Rock.[75] Hubbell faces professional sanctions and/or charges of criminal fraud if allegations against him prove true.

"My nose as a legal professor smells something suspicious in the activities of the Rose firm," said Harvard law professor Alan Dershowitz. Dershowitz said he was going to teach a special class at Harvard "to make sure that no student of mine gets himself or herself into this Hillary mess."[76]

THE LYONS REPORT

In March of the 1992 presidential campaign, the *New York Times* broke the first major story on the Clintons' Whitewater partnership with James McDougal. Reporter Jeff Gerth raised questions about the possibility of a sweetheart deal between the Clintons and the McDougals; about the improper deductions the Clintons took on their 1984 and 1985 tax returns; and about the conflict-of-interest suggested by Hillary Rodham Clinton's representation of Madison before State Securities Commissioner Beverly Bassett Schaffer.[77]

In order to stem suspicions about Whitewater, Clinton asked his friend James M. Lyons, a Denver attorney, to prepare a report on his Whitewater involvement. Lyons hired Patten, McCarthy and Associates, a Denver accounting firm, to help him put together what became known as the Lyons Report, an analysis that concluded that Whitewater was a money-losing endeavor in which the Clintons had minimal involvement.

Specifically, the Lyons Report said that the McDougals had lost $92,200 and the Clintons, $68,900, and that the Clintons were "passive shareholders" in Whitewater.[78] Because the Lyons Report implied that the Clintons were not very involved in Whitewater, and that they had roughly shared losses with the McDougals, it effectively shielded candidate Clinton from further tough questioning on this issue.* (The Lyons Report did conclude that the Clintons had improperly deducted $5,133 from their 1984 and 1985 tax returns. To amend for this, the Clintons paid $4,000 to the federal government.[82])

Although the Lyons Report was treated as authoritative, it was not so by any means. Lyons admitted that he never consulted the McDougals as part of his research, and he did not have access to the documents he needed to write an accurate statement.[83] The report did not mention, for

---

*Time and time again, the Clintons pointed to the Lyons Report as exonerating them of any wrongdoing in Whitewater. "We just think that what we've said is adequate, especially with that independent accountant's report," said Hillary Rodham Clinton.[79]

It was not until 1994, as Whitewater returned to the headlines, that the Lyons Report was exposed as a sham, designed to throw the public off the trail of Whitewater during the presidential election campaign. The *Wall Street Journal* revealed that at the time the Lyons Report was issued, Patten, McCarthy, and Associates had submitted its findings as informal: "certain financial transactions could not be traced to underlying source documents or other evidential matter," warned the accounting firm. In March 1994, Lyons himself said he had overstated the Clintons' loss on Whitewater and that he now believed they only lost $46,635.[80]

The *New York Times* reported that Lyons's revised estimate only "raised new questions about how Mr. and Mrs. Clinton responded in 1992 to potentially damaging news accounts suggesting that Whitewater might have been a sweetheart deal."[81]

Materials used in preparing the Lyons Report are now in the possession of Special Counsel Robert B. Fiske, Jr.

example, Whitewater's 1986 purchase of land from International Paper, nor did it mention that Whitewater's corporate tax returns had not been filed for a three-year period.

Moreover, the Lyons Report did not explain why, if the Clintons lost nearly $70,000 on Whitewater, they did not deduct these losses from their tax returns. The Clintons were extremely thorough with other deductions, taking credit for donating items as small as socks and underwear and even an old bathing suit of Chelsea Clinton's, valued at $1.00.[84]*

Tax experts contacted by the *Washington Times* said the Clintons' losses, if legitimate, could have resulted in deductions of $3,000 a year for up to 20 years.[86]

When the Lyons Report was released, James McDougal told Little Rock attorney Sheffield Nelson, in a tape-recorded conversation, that the Clintons were lying about how much money they lost in Whitewater. "I could sink it [the claim that the Clintons lost $68,900] quicker than they could lie about it if I could get in a position so I wouldn't have my head beaten off," McDougal said. "And Bill [Clinton] knows that."[87]

Chris Wade, the real estate agent who managed Whitewater, said he thought it was profitable. "I don't see

---

*See Appendix G for an example of the thoroughness with which the Clintons searched out deductions on their income tax returns.

In a 1986 return, for example, Bill Clinton listed 17 items he donated to the Salvation Army, for which he took $555 in deductions. These items included a brown sportcoat, valued at $100; five t-shirts for $10; six pairs of socks for $9; and three pairs of underwear, valued at $6. Hillary Rodham Clinton was similarly detailed in her record-keeping. In 1988, for example, she deducted $8 for a white cotton shirt; $2 for a striped cotton dress; $1 for a pair of gloves; $30 for ten of Chelsea Clinton's used turtlenecks (including "red, white, polka dotted, flowered, white balloons, red, purple, yellow"), and $1 for a pair of Chelsea's slippers.[85]

where they could have lost money," Wade told the *Washington Post*. Wade said he made regular payments into Whitewater accounts.[88] He also said that, while public documents recorded that he bought 28 acres of land from Whitewater in 1980 for $2,000, he actually had paid $32,000.[89]

As for the claim that the Clintons were "passive investors," evidence suggests otherwise. In November 1993, the *Washington Times* reported that Hillary Rodham Clinton had sought legal control of Whitewater Development. In a letter to James McDougal dated November 28, 1988, Rodham Clinton wrote, "I am enclosing a Power of Attorney for you to sign, authorizing me to act on your behalf with respect to matters concerning Whitewater Development Corporation." The letter specified that Rodham Clinton would have power to endorse, sign, and execute "checks, notes, deeds, agreements, certificates, receipts or any other instruments in writing of all matters related to Whitewater Development Corp."[90]

Although Rodham Clinton's request was never carried out, it suggests that the Clinton involvement in Whitewater was more than "passive." Moreover, the *Times* reported that "available records show that many of the Whitewater loans, advancements and investments were signed by both the Clintons and the McDougals."[91]

QUESTIONS: Did the Clintons make or lose money on the Whitewater Development venture? If they made money, was this reflected on their income tax returns? If they lost money, why didn't they deduct losses from their taxes? If the Clintons were "passive investors," why did Hillary Rodham Clinton want power of attorney over Whitewater?

FEDERAL INVESTIGATIONS PUT WHITEWATER BACK IN NEWS

Whitewater seemed to sink from sight after Bill Clinton's election. In December 1992, Vincent Foster, acting as the Clintons' personal attorney, arranged the sale of their interest in Whitewater to James McDougal for $1,000. Foster also prepared Whitewater's missing corporate tax returns. It was not until the fall of 1993 that events converged to put the issue back in the headlines.

In September 1993, David Hale was indicted on charges of loan fraud in connection with his SBIC. Although the charges were unrelated to the $300,000 loan Hale had issued to Susan McDougal, Hale took the opportunity to make public his accusation that Bill Clinton and James McDougal had pressured him into making that fraudulent loan.

Also in September, the RTC, which had been investigating the failure of Madison for years, issued criminal referrals to the Justice Department on matters that could potentially involve the Clintons, including questions of whether checks written on overdrawn Madison accounts wound up in the Clinton campaign.* The *Washington Post* reported that the RTC had determined that during a six-month period in 1985 for which the RTC had examined records, Whitewater "had issued 10 checks for more than $70,000. Several [checks] were written to the Bank of Cherry Valley, where Clinton had a campaign account."[92] Although the RTC had not yet determined if the funds

*The Resolution Trust Corporation (RTC) was established in 1989 to clean up the S&L mess and investigate failed S&Ls for potential criminal activities. When RTC investigators, who have no prosecutorial powers, find reason to suspect criminal wrongdoing, they refer their findings to the Justice Department for further investigation and possible indictments. When RTC findings are forwarded to Justice, they are called criminal referrals.

went into a Clinton campaign account, it had discovered that the Whitewater checks were overdrafts covered by various enterprises of James McDougal.

The package RTC sent to Justice was the second round of criminal referrals on these matters.* "We have found Madison to be a very interesting institution," confirmed RTC spokesman Steve Katsanos.[93]

When the new referrals arrived in the office of the U.S. attorney in Little Rock, Paula Casey, she swung into action. Casey promptly rejected the first round of criminal referrals, citing insufficient evidence.[94] She also rejected offers from David Hale to plea bargain, significantly diminishing prospects of his cooperation in a probe of Madison.

But before Casey could rule on the second round of referrals, her close connections to Bill Clinton were exposed by the media.† Casey, it turned out, was a former law student of Clinton's and a former gubernatorial campaign volunteer. Casey's husband, moreover, had once received a Clinton-appointed job in Arkansas and, of course, Clinton had appointed Casey to her Little Rock post as U.S. attorney. In light of these close ties, Casey was forced to recuse herself from the investigation of Madison. The matter was forwarded to career attorneys at the

---

*The first round of RTC referrals was sent to the Justice Department in the fall of 1992, just before the presidential election. These referrals mentioned Bill and Hillary Rodham Clinton as principals in "shell corporations" created by McDougal. The referrals languished in the system for a year. Having received no response to these referrals, RTC officials sent a second round of findings to Justice in September 1993.

†Paula Casey was appointed U.S. attorney in Little Rock following the Clinton-Reno mass firing of U.S. attorneys in March 1993, raising suspicions that Clinton anticipated the RTC referrals and wanted a friendly U.S. attorney in place in Little Rock.

Justice Department and then turned over to Special Counsel Robert B. Fiske, Jr., in January 1994.

WHITEWATER DOCUMENTS PURLOINED

As if the Hale indictment and the RTC criminal referrals were not enough, the *Washington Times* reported on December 20, 1993, that top White House officials had clandestinely searched Vincent Foster's office the night of his death and that Whitewater documents had been removed from his office soon after. The late night search was conducted by White House Counsel Bernard Nussbaum; the First Lady's Chief of Staff, Margaret Williams; and Special Assistant to the President, Patsy Thomasson. These activities were covered up for five months before being exposed by reporter Jerry Seper in the *Times*.*

The cloak and dagger behavior of top White House officials focused national attention on Whitewater. "Television," reported the *Washington Post*, "began to pay attention [to Whitewater] when it was learned that White House officials had removed Whitewater files from the office of Deputy Counsel Vince Foster after Foster's suicide."[97]

---

*The very fact that Foster had Whitewater files in his office is suspicious to begin with, for the Clintons had long denied possession of any Whitewater records.

Susan McDougal said she had delivered the Whitewater files to the Arkansas Governor's Mansion in December 1987, per Hillary Rodham Clinton's request. McDougal said she included "every sheet of paper . . . every file . . . all the purchase agreements, all monthly payments by customers, all checks written by the corporation, all correspondence."[95] James McDougal confirmed that all files were sent to the Clintons in 1987, at which point he said the Clintons "assumed the responsibility for filing the tax returns."[96]

The presence of the Whitewater files in Foster's White House office was additionally noteworthy because he should have worked on these files in his capacity as personal attorney for the Clintons, not in his capacity as White House Deputy Counsel. That Foster held both positions simultaneously was unusual; did he work on the Clinton's private business at taxpayer expense?

Once the existence of the Whitewater papers was revealed, demands for their release quickly followed. But the Clintons stonewalled. The *Washington Post* reported that in a meeting with White House Senior Advisor Bruce Lindsey, "he said the White House did not want to release any Whitewater records to the news media because it would only raise more questions about the investment."[98]

Even as he invoked attorney-client privilege to keep secret the files found in Vincent Foster's office, President Clinton maintained publicly, "Of course, we'll do what we can to cooperate."[99] White House officials maintained the Clintons were innocent while at the same time insisting they knew nothing about the files' contents. "I don't think anybody here has any idea what stuff is in the Madison files," said White House Press Secretary Dee Dee Myers.[100]

QUESTIONS: On what authority did Nussbaum, Williams, and Thomasson search Vincent Foster's office? What exactly was in Foster's files? What else transpired during the visits to Foster's office by White House officials before it was sealed 18 hours after his death?

APPOINTMENT OF THE SPECIAL COUNSEL

As early as November 1993, Republican lawmakers began calling for investigations into Whitewater. Reps. Toby Roth (R-Wisc.) and John J. LaFalce (D-N.Y.) called for an SBA investigation into David Hale's $300,000 loan to Susan McDougal, and support grew for the appointment of a Special Counsel. Attorney General Janet Reno rebuffed the idea, however, arguing that a Special Counsel would not be viewed as truly independent.*

---

*A Special Counsel is different from an Independent Counsel. A Special Counsel, or Special Prosecutor, is chosen by the Attorney General, while an Independent

Meanwhile, Representative Leach wrote to David Kendall, the Clintons' Washington white-collar crime attorney, requesting the Whitewater files. On December 23, 1993, with Representative Leach knocking at his door, attorney Kendall secretly arranged with the Justice Department for a subpoena of the Clinton files. This subpoena, which was issued on Christmas Eve, was not made public until January 5, 1994. White House aides admitted that the subpoena was sought in order to protect "the privacy" of the Clintons' files. One official told the *Washington Post* that the subpoena was desirable "because then it becomes a crime to leak [the files]."[101]

Sen. Robert Dole (R-Kan.) called the negotiated subpoena "almost unbelievable . . . I don't know of any precedent for this. It appears the White House is running the investigation and not the Justice Department."[102] Rep. Newt Gingrich said, "It is very, very disturbing to have the White House going to the Justice Department to apparently collude to get a subpoena so the American people can't see the documents."[103]

Legal scholars agreed with the Republican lawmakers. "This is a unique bit of legal judo," said George Washington University law professor John Banzhaf. "It's certainly changing the whole purpose of a subpoena, which is to compel the protection of evidence, not to protect the defendant."[104]

At the same time the Clintons were keeping zealous

Counsel, or Independent Prosecutor, is appointed by a three-judge federal appeals court as stipulated by the Independent Counsel law Congress passed in 1978. Because the Independent Counsel Law expired in 1992, and has not yet been reauthorized, critics of the Whitewater mess called for appointment of a Special Counsel.

During the Watergate scandal, *Special* Counsel Archibald Cox was fired by the Nixon administration in the Saturday Night Massacre. *Independent* Counsel Lawrence Walsh investigated the Iran-Contra scandal.

guard over their secret files, they criticized those who were curious about the files' contents. "I am bewildered that a losing investment . . . is still a topic of inquiry," said First Lady Hillary Rodham Clinton.[105]

But Clinton administration attempts to characterize the Whitewater attacks as partisan politics collapsed on January 9, 1994, when Sen. Daniel P. Moynihan (D-N.Y.) called for release of the Clinton files and appointment of a Special Counsel. "Nothing to hide," implored the Senator, "Do it. Come on."[106] When Moynihan's call was echoed by other Democratic senators, including Bill Bradley (N.J.); Bob Kerrey (Neb.); Charles Robb (Va.); Russell Feingold (Wisc.); Jim Exon (Neb.); Joseph Lieberman (Conn.); Carol Mosley-Braun (Ill.); and Tom Harkin (Iowa), the situation became politically unbearable. Clinton could not ignore this formidable line-up and on January 12, despite his prior strenuous objections to a Special Counsel, he asked Janet Reno to appoint one.

The appointment of Robert B. Fiske, Jr., as Special Counsel came on January 20, 1994, exactly one year after Clinton's Inauguration, six months after Vincent Foster's death, and one month after the *Washington Times* reported the clandestine office search.

Fiske demanded, and received, permission to make his inquiry very broad. And Fiske himself drew up the charter of his expansive investigation: "The specific language authorizes me to investigate whether any individuals or entities have committed a violation of any federal criminal law relating in any way" to the Clintons and Madison Guaranty.[107] The Special Counsel said he anticipated taking both Bill and Hillary Rodham Clinton's testimony under oath.

Fiske opened offices in Little Rock and hired 25 FBI

agents and financial analysts, and six former federal and state prosecutors. He appointed Roderick D. Lankler, an experienced homicide investigator, to head a Washington, D.C.-based examination of Vincent Foster's death.

In March 1994, Fiske secured David Hale as a grand jury witness for his investigation. "We are significantly better off with Mr. Hale's cooperation than with having to try him as a defendant," Fiske said.[108] The *Chicago Tribune* reported that Rusty Hardin, an assistant to Special Counsel Fiske, reported a link had been made between Hale's SBIC and Madison Guaranty.[109]

When asked how he felt about the Hale plea bargain, the President said, "This is all a bunch of bull."[110]*

OBSTRUCTIONS OF JUSTICE?

Following the appointment of Special Counsel Fiske, the White House tried to deflect interest in Whitewater. "It's an investment I made 15 years ago that lost money,"

---

*Although Clinton has denied involvement with Hale, testimony has emerged that corroborates Hale's story. During a pretrial hearing for Hale, before his plea bargain with Special Counsel Fiske, Louisiana businessman Gayland Westbrook testified that Hale had spoken to him of CMS's involvement with Clinton in August 1989. That August, Westbrook and his wife had met with Hale in Little Rock to discuss a possible loan. Although the loan never materialized, Westbrook has recalled under oath that Hale spoke to him at the time of his relationship with Governor Clinton. Westbrook's wife, Doris, recalled that she was "very impressed" by Hale's connection to Governor Clinton.[111]

Also, Hale's SBIC has an established record of lending to Clinton associates in Little Rock's elite circles. Capital Management Services lent at least $300,000 to companies in which now-Arkansas Governor Jim Guy Tucker had invested; these loans were not paid back. (Tucker served as attorney for CMS.) Tommy Trantham, a former Madison president, received a $100,000 loan from Hale.[112] Yet another CMS loan went to Stephen A. Smith, president of Communications Company and former president of the Bank of Kingston. Explaining how he got the loan, Smith said, "McDougal introduced us . . . and he [Hale] gave me the loan."[113]

said the President. "It's a simple, straightforward thing, and it'll be shown to be."[114]

Although the Clintons kept insisting they had done nothing wrong, vigorous efforts were launched to prevent information about Whitewater from reaching the public. This, of course, only heightened suspicions. Whitewater could become another case of the cover-up being worse than the actual crime.

Indeed, Whitewater was no longer the story of a long-ago failed land deal in Arkansas. Fresh revelations that suggested cover-ups and obstructions of justice gave the Whitewater story new immediacy and significance.

On February 9, the *Washington Times* revealed that the Rose Law Firm reportedly had shred files bearing Vincent Foster's initials *after* the appointment of Special Counsel Fiske. "There's absolutely no doubt that the records destroyed last Thursday [February 3] were those the firm had on Whitewater," reported a Rose Law employee. "There were a lot of papers, and the process took quite a long time."[115]

A second Rose employee, who had told friends that he was "scared to death" about the shredding, would not comment publicly.[116]

These two employees were subsequently revealed as Jeremy Hedges, 20, and Clayton Lindsey, 19, both students at the University of Little Rock who worked as couriers for the firm.

Ron Clark, managing partner at Rose, denied that any improper shredding had occurred. Nonetheless, Special Counsel Fiske made the matter part of his investigation and FBI agents interviewed Rose employees, including Clark and Hedges. Hedges stood firm concerning his allegations after testifying before Fiske's grand jury; "The [shredded] files were his [Foster's]," Hedges insisted. "The files were set up, organized in one manila folder after another, with tabs saying VWF searches, VWF correspondence, and VWF pleadings."[117]

Moreover, news stories of Hedges and Lindsey's controversial shredding prompted other current and former Rose Law employees to talk to the *Washington Times* about how they too had shredded documents during Clinton's 1992 presidential campaign. The couriers told the *Times* that after the initial *New York Times* story broke about Whitewater in March 1992, Hillary Rodham Clinton instructed them to pick up records from the Governor's Mansion and shred them at the Rose Law Firm. The couriers said they made repeated "mansion runs" throughout the 1992 campaign. "A lot of papers were run through the shredder," said one employee, "I can assure you of that."[118]

When asked directly about the shredding allegations, President Clinton was evasive. "Mr. President, how do you feel about your wife's becoming a focal point of the Whitewater investigation?" asked one reporter. "The *Washington Times* quotes three couriers as testifying that she ordered the shredding of documents. . . ." Clinton replied, "Well, let me say that the only thing that I want to say on behalf of both of us is that we want to support the Special Counsel's work."[119]

Another development that hinted at an obstruction of justice was the revelation of ethically dubious meetings between White House and Treasury Department officials to discuss the RTC's criminal referrals.

At what should have been a routine congressional oversight hearing on February 24, 1994, RTC interim head Roger C. Altman, a college classmate of Bill Clinton and longtime friend of both Bill and Hillary Rodham Clinton—revealed shocking news under questioning from Sen.

Alfonse D'Amato. Altman testified that he had met with White House officials to give them a "heads-up" briefing on the RTC criminal referrals involving the Clintons.

It quickly surfaced that at least three meetings were held between RTC and White House officials, all in the office of White House Counsel Bernard Nussbaum. The first meeting was held on September 29, 1993, more than a week *before* the RTC made its referrals to Justice. According to the *Washington Post*, RTC General Counsel Jean Hanson, who had just been briefed about the criminal referrals by the RTC, "took Nussbaum aside and outside the hearing of others offered the Whitewater information"—namely, that it appeared as if criminal investigations were about to be requested that would name the Clintons as possible beneficiaries of illegal activity.[120] Nussbaum forwarded this highly sensitive information to White House Senior Advisor Bruce Lindsey.[121]

The second meeting, held October 14, was attended by Nussbaum, Hanson, Lindsey, White House Communications Director Mark Gearan, Treasury official Joshua Steiner, and Treasury spokesman Jack DeVore. The purported reason for this meeting was to discuss how to handle media inquiries about the criminal referrals.

The third reported meeting, held February 2, 1994, was attended by Nussbaum, Deputy Treasury Secretary and interim RTC chief Roger C. Altman, White House Deputy Chief of Staff Harold Ickes, and the First Lady's Chief of Staff Margaret A. Williams. (The presence of Williams seemed to indicate that Hillary Rodham Clinton might have a special interest in these matters; one regulator called the meeting "a political heads-up for Hillary."[122])

Congress and the media erupted over revelations of these meetings. "At the time this group was meeting at the White House," roared Sen. Alfonse D'Amato, "I was speaking out on the Senate floor about the RTC's failure to provide our committee with any information about its activities on the Madison/Whitewater mess. And I have yet to encounter a reporter covering this story who says he was briefed by the RTC, let alone its acting CEO, Mr. Altman!"[123]

Representative Leach warned, "Seldom have the public and private ethics of lawyers in the White House and executive branch departments and agencies been so thoroughly devalued."[124]

Although President Clinton admitted he knew about the RTC criminal referrals before they were made public, he said he couldn't remember who told him about them. Seeming to shrug the matter off, he asked the American people not to give the meetings "a second thought."[125]

But these meetings were so troubling that Special Counsel Fiske issued subpoenas to all officials involved. The FBI served the subpoenas at the White House at 7:00 p.m. on March 4, 1994. President Clinton, who was attending the musical *Grease* when the subpoenas were served, had no comment.[126]

The *Washington Post* called the subpoenas a "public disgrace." The newspaper said that they "only added to the impression that there is something not quite right about the Clinton's Arkansas political and business dealings."[127]

The RTC-White House shenanigans brought about the resignation of Bernard Nussbaum, who was denounced by the *Post* for allowing the Clinton White House to "slide into improprieties that a child of four could have figured out."[128] Lloyd N. Cutler, 76, who had served as Jimmy Carter's White House Counsel, was brought in to babysit the Clinton White House until a suitable counsel could be found.

But there was more news. Senior White House aide George Stephanopoulos admitted that he, too, had made contact with the RTC. The *Washington Post* reported that Stephanopoulos had protested to Joshua Steiner, Chief of Staff to Treasury Secretary Lloyd Bentsen, about the RTC's selection of Jay B. Stephens to handle part of its Madison investigation. (Stephens was the U.S. attorney who was investigating Rep. Daniel Rostenkowski when he, along with all other U.S. attorneys, was fired by Reno and Clinton in March 1993.) Following Steiner's rebuff of his implied, if not explicit, request to dismiss Stephens, Stephanopolous tried to excuse the matter by saying he had to "blow off steam."[129]

The *Post* also reported that Stephanopoulos and White House Deputy Chief of Staff Harold Ickes had questioned Roger Altman about his recusal from the Madison case. Although the White House denied wrongdoing, suspicions grew deeper that the White House was somehow tampering with the RTC investigation.

Representative Leach, stymied by Democrats in Congress who had cancelled scheduled hearings on Whitewater, provided the next revelation. Leach said that an official in the RTC's Kansas City office, which has jurisdiction over Arkansas, had sought protection under "whistleblower" laws after being pressured by Washington to scale back her characterization of the Madison failure as a "highly prosecutable case of check kiting."[130]

The official, L. Jean Lewis, is the senior criminal investigator in the RTC's Kansas City, Missouri, office. Outlining the Madison case in an RTC memo, Lewis concluded that the Clintons must have known something was awry in their dealings with McDougal: "If you know that your mortgages are being paid, but you aren't putting money into the venture, and you also know the venture isn't cash flowing, wouldn't you question the source of the funds being used for your benefit? Would you just assume that your partner was making these multi-thousand dollar payments out of the goodness of his heart?" Finally, Lewis asked, "Wouldn't you wonder even more if you knew that your business partner's main source of income, an S&L, was in serious financial difficulty?" Lewis said that she had uncovered evidence through her investigations that directly linked Madison losses to Whitewater.[131]

But apparently Lewis's probing questions were unwelcomed by her superiors in Washington. Lewis reported that in a February 2, 1994, meeting with Washington RTC official April Breslaw, Breslaw told her that "people at the top" would be "happier" if RTC findings "got them off the hook."[132] Although Breslaw denied any wrongdoing, Representative Leach issued a warning that "officials at the Kansas City RTC office are being gagged and possibly coerced."[133]

QUESTIONS: Why were the Clintons so determined to keep their Whitewater files secret if they merely recorded an innocuous business deal? Were Whitewater documents shredded? If so, why? Were White House officials involved in briefings with the RTC acting at the behest of Bill or Hillary Rodham Clinton? Did the Clintons in any way benefit from these meetings, or attempt to manipulate the RTC investigation of Madison?

WILL THE TRUTH OUT?

Given what is already known about Whitewater, the Clintons' repeated denials of any wrongdoing are hard to believe. "Here's a policy wonk," writes *Time* magazine's Michael Kramer, "well versed in every domestic issue that ever made a Sunday-morning talk show, a politician with near total recall of events and conversations from long ago, a meticulous record keeper capable of itemizing underwear donations to charity. Why, then, are so many vital Whitewater records missing? How is it possible that two respected lawyers like Bill and Hillary Clinton don't possess a paper trail capable of proving their innocence, unless they're hiding something? How could the products of the Watergate generation ignore the central lesson of Richard Nixon's downfall: stonewalling, and even its mere appearance, can be at least as corrosive as laying out the whole tale publicly, unless the true story transcends mere embarrassment?"[134]

As part of its investigation, Special Counsel Fiske's team will investigate more than a quarter-million dollars worth of loans made to Bill and Hillary Rodham Clinton between 1978 and 1984 from Arkansas banks. Fiske's team will also trace large sums of money lent to Whitewater by various McDougal enterprises during the time Bill Clinton sought money for his reelection campaign. Fiske has so far subpoenaed hundreds of individuals and companies, from top White House officials, to Arkansas Governor Jim Guy Tucker, to Dallas Cowboys owner Jerry Jones.

Many questions need answering: were federally guaranteed funds illegally diverted to pay Bill Clinton's personal and/or political debts? Was Madison Guaranty and/or state agencies such as ADFA used by McDougal and Clinton as their own piggy banks? Did Bill Clinton pressure David Hale to make a fraudulent SBA loan, and did the Clintons illegally benefit from that loan? Were documents pertaining to Whitewater ever destroyed as part of a coverup? Was there any impropriety or illegality to the meetings between RTC and White House officials? What were the circumstances of Vincent Foster's death, and does the death have any bearing on matters involving the Clintons?

Although Special Counsel Fiske has promised a broad probe, his findings must remain confidential except where they result in indictments. It is only through congressional hearings that Americans will learn the answers to all of these questions.

"If we fail to pursue our constitutionally given oversight responsibilities," Representative Leach wrote in protest of Representative Gonzalez's failure to hold Whitewater hearings in March 1994, "we are in effect giving a permissive green light to those who want to fudge the law or set aside ethics. Above all, Congress has an obligation to the American people to ensure that no American, whatever his or her position, is above the public accountability and the rule of the law."[135]

In a letter to Special Counsel Fiske, Representative Leach reminded him that it was only through Senate hearings that the questionable RTC-White House meetings were found out. The Congressman also pointed out that it was only through Congressional hearings in 1974 that the Watergate tapes were brought to light. The point is worth bearing in mind as America tries to sort out the Clinton presidential scandal.

1. Bill Clinton, quoted Susan Schmidt in "Regulators Say They Were Unaware of Clinton Law Firm's S&L Ties"; *Washington Post*; November 3, 1993.
2. Hillary Rodham Clinton; First Lady's Press Conference; April 22, 1994.
3. Editorial; *Wall Street Journal*; January 11, 1993.
4. Robert B. Fiske, Jr., CNN's "Inside Politics"; January 20, 1994.
5. Rep. James Leach (R-Iowa), quoted in *Washington Times*; March 25, 1994.
6. Bill Clinton; Announcement Speech for President; October 3, 1991.
7. Bill Clinton, *Putting People First*; Times Books; 1992; page 195.
8. Rep. James Leach (R-Iowa), *supra* endnote 5.

9. Bill Clinton, quoted in *Wall Street Journal*; March 25, 1994.

10. Michael Weisskopf and Howard Schneider, "Clinton Ex-Partner's Path to Bankruptcy"; *Washington Post*; November 29, 1993.

11. Jeff Gerth, "Clintons Release Tax Data"; *New York Times*; March 26, 1994.

12. Rep. James Leach (R-Iowa), *supra* endnote 5.

13. Jerry Seper, "What were the Clinton Stakes in Land Scheme?"; *Washington Times*; November 4, 1993.

14. Douglas Jehl, "Review Likely to Find Taxes were Unpaid by Clintons"; *New York Times*; March 19, 1994.

15. Susan Schmidt and Marilyn W. Thompson, "With Political Connections, Arkansas S&L Lived and Died"; *Washington Post*; January 24, 1994.

16. Michael Weisskopf and Howard Schneider, *supra* endnote 10.

17. George J. Church, "The Tangled Web"; *Time*; January 24, 1994, page 33.

18. *ibid.*

19. Howard Schneider, "The McDougals were on a Wild Ride; Then They Hit the Rocks"; *Washington Post*; January 13, 1994.

20. William C. Rempel and Douglas Frantz, "Defunct S&L's Connections"; *Los Angeles Times*; November 12, 1993.

21. Howard Schneider and Charles R. Babcock, "Clintons' Arkansas Land Venture Losses Disputed"; *Washington Post*; December 19, 1993.

22. Rep. James Leach (R-Iowa), Letter to Rep. Henry B. Gonzalez (D-Tex.), quoted by Jerry Seper in "Hill Republicans Expand Probe"; *Washington Times*; December 15, 1993.

23. Susan McDougal, quoted by Howard Schneider, *supra* endnote 19.

24. Unsigned, "Whitewater and the White House"; *Los Angeles Times*; January 16, 1994.

25. Jeff Gerth, "Head of Failing S&L Helped Clinton"; *New York Times*; December 15, 1993.

26. William C. Rempel and Douglas Frantz, *supra* 20.

27. Howard Schneider, "Gov. Tucker's Finances Become Probe Focus"; *Washington Post*; November 4, 1993.

28. William C. Rempel and Douglas Frantz, *supra* endnote 20.

29. Unsigned, *supra* endnote 24.

30. Jerry Seper, "$283,000 in Loans to Clintons Probed"; *Washington Times*; February 25, 1994.

31. William C. Rempel and Douglas Frantz, *supra* endnote 20.
32. Jerry Seper, "Hillary Clinton's S&L Ties Probed"; *Wasington Times*; January 12, 1994.
33. *ibid.*
34. William C. Rempel and Douglas Frantz, "Fallout from Collapse of S&L Shadows Clinton"; *Los Angeles Times*; November 7, 1993.
35. *ibid.*
36. *ibid.*
37. Jerry Seper, "Probe of S&L Chief Touches on Hillary's Legal Fee"; *Washington Times*; November 5, 1993.
38. Jerry Seper, *supra* endnote 30.
39. Unsigned, "What might Clintons have done Wrong?"; *Washington Times*; January 14, 1994.
40. Susan Schmidt and Charles R. Babcock, "Businessman Denies Giving Donation"; *Washington Post*; December 16, 1993.
41. *ibid.*
42. Jerry Seper, "S&L Director Gave to Clinton in Son's Name"; *Washington Times*; February 3, 1994.
43. Bruce Ingersoll, "Madison Employees Say Executive Promised Reimbursement for Contributions to Clinton"; *Wall Street Journal*; January 31, 1994.
44. William C. Rempel and Douglas Frantz, *supra* endnote 20.
45. Peter J. Boyer, "The Bridges of Madison Guaranty"; *New Yorker*; January 17, 1994, page 38.
46. Wesley Pruden, "The Skeleton that Won't Stay Dead"; *Washington Times*; January 3, 1994.
47. *Arkansas Democrat Gazette*, March 8, 1992.
48. Charles Handley, quoted by Susan Schmidt and Marilyn W. Thompson, *supra* endnote 15.
49. Jerry Seper, "Perks were Flowing While Madison S&L was Dying"; *Washington Times*; April 5, 1994.
50. *ibid.*
51. Jeff Gerth, *supra* endnote 25.
52. Peter J. Boyer, *supra* endnote 45, page 35.
53. Susan Schmidt and Marilyn W. Thompson, *supra* endnote 15.
54. Jerry Seper, "Whitewater Probe Grows to Include State Agency"; *Washington Times*; January 24, 1994.
55. William C. Rempel and Douglas Frantz, *supra* endnote 34.
56. Jerry Seper, *supra* 54.

57. Michael Weisskopf and Howard Schneider, *supra* endnote 10.
58. Michael Isikoff and Howard Schneider, "Clintons' Former Real Estate Firm Probed"; *Washington Post*; November 2, 1993.
59. William C. Rempel and Douglas Frantz, *supra* endnote 34.
60. Jerry Seper, *supra* endnote 13.
61. William C. Rempel and Douglas Frantz, *supra* endnote 34.
62. Jerry Seper, *supra* endnote 13.
63. William C. Rempel and Douglas Frantz, *supra* endnote 34.
64. Jerry Seper, "Clintons Understated Involvement in Venture"; *Washington Times*; November 4, 1993.
65. Jerry Seper, *supra* endnote 13.
66. William C. Rempel and Douglas Frantz, *supra* endnote 34.
67. Michael Weisskopf and Howard Schneider, supra endnote 10.
68. *ibid.*
69. Howard Schneider, "Woman Linked to Clintons in Land Venture Faces California Charges"; *Washington Post*; January 6, 1994.
70. Howard Schneider and Charles R. Babcock, "An Ever-Growing Paper Trail"; *Washington Post*; January 8, 1994.
71. Peter J. Boyer, *supra* endnote 45, page 36.
72. *Los Angeles Times*, *supra* endnote 24.
73. Susan Schmidt, "Regulators Say They Were Unaware"; *Washington Post*; November 3, 1993.
74. Jerry Seper and Michael Hedges, "Hubbell Resigns Post, Cites Distractions"; *Washington Times*; March 15, 1994.
75. *ibid.*
76. Alan Dershowitz, quoted by Nancy E. Roman in "Probe of First Lady"; *Washington Times*; January 8, 1994.
77. Jeff Gerth, "The 1992 Campaign: Personal Finances"; *New York Times*; March 8, 1992.
78. Jeff Gerth, "The 1992 Campaign: Candidate's Record"; *New York Times*; March 25, 1992.
79. Michael Isikoff, "Whitewater Files Were Found in Foster's Office"; *Washington Post*; December 22, 1993.
80. Bruce Ingersoll, "Critics Say Some Gaps in Report"; *Wall Street Journal*; January 4, 1994.
81. Jeff Gerth, *supra* endnote 11.
82. Bruce Ingersoll, *supra* endnote 80.
83. Jerry Seper, *supra* endnote 13.
84. Lloyd Grove, Bill Clinton's Great Skivvies Giveaway"; *Washington Post*; December 28, 1993.

85. *ibid.*
86. Jerry Seper, "Why Didn't Clintons Deduct Losses?"; *Washington Times*; January 14, 1994.
87. Jerry Seper, "Hale Emerges as Whitewater 'Piggy Bank' "; *Washington Times*; January 31, 1994.
88. Howard Schneider and Charles R. Babcock, *supra* endnote 21.
89. *ibid.*
90. Jerry Seper, *supra* endnote 13.
91. *ibid.*
92. Susan Schmidt and Michael Isikoff, "Dealings of Clinton Partners Were Referred to Justice Dept. in 1992"; *Washington Post*; November 11, 1993.
93. Susan Schmidt, "U.S. is Asked to Probe Failed Arkansas S&L"; *Washington Post*; October 31, 1993.
94. Susan Schmidt and Michael Isikoff, *supra* endnote 92.
95. Peter J. Boyer, *supra* endnote 45.
96. Michael Isikoff and Howard Schneider, *supra* endnote 58.
97. Ann Devroy and Howard Schneider, "A Damage Control Mess"; *Washington Post*; January 7, 1994.
98. Howard Schneider and Charles R. Babcock, *supra* endnote 70.
99. Bill Clinton, quoted by Jerry Seper in "Clinton Puts Limits on Offer to Help Probe"; *Washington Times*; December 23, 1993.
100. Dee Dee Myers, quoted in *Washington Times*; January 6, 1994.
101. Michael Isikoff and Ann Devroy, "Subpoena Issued for Clinton Files"; *Washington Post*; January 6, 1994.
102. Sen. Robert Dole (R-Kan.), quoted by Jerry Seper in "Dole Sees Conspiracy in Probe of Whitewater Affair"; *Washington Times*; January 7, 1994.
103. Rep. Newt Gingrich (R-Ga.) on NBC's "Today Show," quoted by Michael Isikoff in "Reno: Counsel Possible"; *Washington Post*; January 7, 1994.
104. John Banzhaf, quoted by Nancy E. Roman in " 'A Good Strategy' by Clinton's Lawyer"; *Washington Times*; January 7, 1994.
105. Hillary Rodham Clinton, quoted by Jerry Seper, *supra* endnote 99.
106. Sen. Daniel P. Moynihan (D-N.Y.), quoted by Ann Devroy in "New Whitewater Strategy May Entail Selective Release of Documents"; *Washington Post*; January 10, 1994.
107. Robert B. Fiske, Jr., quoted in *Wall Street Journal*; January 21, 1994.

108. Robert B. Fiske, Jr., quoted in *Washington Times*; March 23, 1994.

109. Tribune Wires, "Accuser of Clinton Pleads Guilty"; *Chicago Tribune*; March 23, 1994.

110. Bill Clinton, quoted by *Los Angeles Times*; March 22, 1994.

111. Jerry Seper, "Clinton Linked to SBA Deal"; *Washington Times*; March 1, 1994.

112. Tribune wires, *supra* endnote 109.

113. Howard Schneider, "Ex-Judge: SBA Loans Mocked Law"; *Washington Post*; February 15, 1994.

114. Bill Clinton, Interview with Don Imus; WFAN Radio; New York, NY; February 17, 1994.

115. Jerry Seper, "Rose Firm Shreds Whitewater Records"; *Washington Times*; February 9, 1994.

116. *ibid.*

117. Jeremy Hedges, quoted by Michaek K. Frisby and Bruce Ingersoll in "Clinton Says He Was Told in Advance"; *Wall Street Journal*; March 8, 1994.

118. Jerry Seper, "Rose Staffers Say Hillary Ordered Papers Shredded"; *Washington Times*; March 7, 1994.

119. Bill Clinton, quoted in *New York Times*; March 8, 1994.

120. Ann Devroy, "File Search Indicates Other S&L Contacts"; *Washington Post*; March 9, 1994.

121. Michael K. Frisby and Bruce Ingersoll, *supra* endnote 117.

122. Ann Devroy, *supra* endnote 120.

123. Sen. Alfonse D'Amato (R-N.Y.); "A Whitewater Whitewash"; *Wall Street Journal*; March 2, 1994.

124. Rep. James Leach (R-Iowa), "Whitewater: Public Policy and Private Ethics"; *Washington Times*; March 8, 1994.

125. Bill Clinton, quoted by Ann Devroy and Ruth Marcus in "Clinton Faults Contacts with Officials on Probe"; *Washington Post*; March 4, 1994.

126. Paul Bedard, "Whitewater Counsel Subpoenas 6 in White House"; *Washington Times*; March 5, 1994.

127. Editorial, "Mr. Nussbaum Goes, Not the Mess"; *Washington Post*; March 6, 1994.

128. *ibid.*

129. Michael K. Frisby, "Whitewater Counsel Asks Whether Aides of Clinton Targeted Foe in RTC Inquiry"; *Wall Street Journal*; March 28, 1994.

130. Michael Hedges, "Madison Prober Urged to Back Off"; *Washington Times*; March 25, 1994.
131. *ibid.*
132. *ibid.*
133. Michael Hedges, "Leach Accuses White House of Gagging Regulators"; *Washington Times*; March 12, 1994.
134. Michael Kramer, "Where It Hurts"; *Time*; January 24, 1994; page 34.
135. Rep. James Leach (R-Iowa), Letter to Rep. Henry B. Gonzalez (D-Tex.), quoted by Jerry Seper, *supra* endnote 22.

WHY DID VINCENT FOSTER DIE?

"I cannot make this point to you too strongly. There is no victory, no advantage, no fee, no favor which is worth even a blemish on your reputation for intellect and integrity."[1]

> —Vincent W. Foster, addressing the
> University of Arkansas Law School
> May 8, 1993

"Foster knew these people, and he came to the conclusion that he had to resign from life."[2]

> —U.S. Rep. James A. Leach
> January 12, 1994

Before Vincent Foster died, few Americans had heard of the Arkansas lawyer who accompanied his boyhood friend, Bill Clinton, to the White House. When history is written, however, Vincent Foster's death may well turn out to be the seminal event of the Clinton presidency.

Vincent Foster served as Deputy White House Counsel, the number two lawyer who advises the president on legal issues concerning his office and administration. On July 20, 1993, Foster's body was found in a remote park outside Washington. Ruled a suicide, Foster became the first high-ranking White House official to kill himself since former

Secretary of Defense James Forrestal committed suicide after being fired from his post in 1949.

Many aspects of the Foster death were strange. Important questions were left unanswered by the government's official investigation. In fact, the investigation itself became the target of criticism; conducted sloppily and superficially, the investigation failed to refute the possibility of foul play in Foster's death. The possibility that Foster's body had been moved after either a murder or suicide was never seriously studied. Moreover, the discovery under questionable circumstances of a note in Foster's briefcase only deepened the mystery.

While many issues remain unanswered on the Foster case, the bare facts are these: Vincent Foster served as both Deputy White House Counsel and personal attorney to the Clintons. In these capacities, he was involved in more Clinton controversies than perhaps any other individual aside from Bill and Hillary Rodham Clinton themselves. Finally, it has been established that the public was deliberately misled on important issues surrounding Foster's death, such as the secret, late-night search of his office conducted by top White House officials the day he died.

"Until the Foster death is seriously studied," wrote the *Wall Street Journal*, "a Banquo's ghost will stalk not only the independent investigation but the next three years of the Clinton administration."[3]

WHO WAS VINCENT FOSTER?

Vincent Foster was a native of Hope, Arkansas, the town where Bill Clinton spent part of his childhood. Clinton and Foster were even next-door neighbors for a while, and they attended kindergarten with Thomas L. "Mack" McLarty, now President Clinton's Chief of Staff.

Foster received his bachelor's degree in psychology from

Davidson College in 1967, went on to graduate first in his class at the University of Arkansas Law School, and scored first on the Arkansas bar exam before starting a successful career at the Rose Law Firm, becoming a partner in only two years.

During his tenure at Rose, Foster represented Stephens Inc., the powerful Arkansas investment firm that extended a $3.5 million line of credit to the Clinton campaign. And he was outside counsel for Wright, Lindsey, Jennings, the law firm from which presidential advisor Bruce Linsdey hailed. Foster also had a newspaper client and, according to the *Washington Post*, "was fond of telling reporters that he was sympathetic to their needs because he had represented an Arkansas newspaper while in private practice."[4] Foster was part of the elite Rose Law Firm clique, along with Hillary Rodham Clinton, Webster Hubbell, and William H. Kennedy III, that accompanied Bill Clinton to Washington.

During his six months at the White House, Foster was the all-purpose lawyer called upon to douse the political fires that perpetually lapped at the Clintons. He defended Hillary Rodham Clinton's position as head of the government's health care task force and was engaged in the legal battle to maintain the secrecy of the task force. He played a part in the failed nominations of Zoe Baird and Lani Guinier. And he was sufficiently concerned about his participation in the Travelgate controversy to seek private legal advice shortly before his death.[5]

As personal attorney to the Clintons, Foster was responsible for trying to straighten out their increasingly questionable involvement with James McDougal and the Whitewater Development Company. He filed delinquent corporate tax returns for Whitewater Development and arranged the sale of the Clintons' remaining Whitewater interest to McDougal. Foster was working to put the Clintons' assets in a blind trust when he died; it was a point of controversy that the Clintons had not established a blind trust prior to their arrival in Washington.

JULY 20, 1993

July 20, 1993, was a big day for the White House, and especially so for the White House Counsel's office. Louis J. Freeh was named the new FBI Director in a Rose Garden ceremony and Supreme Court nominee Ruth Bader Ginsburg completed successful testimony before the Senate Judiciary Committee. White House Counsel Bernard Nussbaum exclaimed to Foster at midday: "Hey, Vince, not a bad day. We hit two home runs."[6]

Foster ate lunch alone at his desk and left his office at approximately 1 p.m. He was never heard from again.*
At approximately 6 p.m., Foster's body was found at Fort Marcy, an isolated Civil War-era fort overlooking the Potomac River. A park maintenance worker was alerted to the dead body by an individual who has since remained anonymous. The Park Police then called the Fairfax (Virginia) County Fire and Rescue Department and, within 15 minutes, both Park Police and Fairfax County officers were on the scene. Foster's car was found in an overlook next to Fort Marcy.

The White House received positive identification of Vincent Foster's body that night while President Clinton was

---

*Inside White House source Deepwater reported that during the afternoon of July 20, Foster's office colleagues were looking for him and considered beeping him on his pager, but decided not to bother. Foster's co-workers were not alarmed by Foster's absence because he was known to leave the office for a period of several hours in the afternoon. After Foster was found dead, these colleagues wondered if the events of July 20 might have turned out differently if they had reached Foster by page and asked him to return to the office.

appearing on "Larry King Live." Upon finishing the show, Clinton was informed of Foster's death by Thomas McLarty. McLarty ordered Foster's office sealed, and he and the President left to visit Mrs. Foster at her home in Washington.

REACTION TO FOSTER'S DEATH

The initial reaction to Vincent Foster's death was one of total shock. Friends and colleagues uniformly described Foster as a strong and stable individual, the last person they would have expected to commit suicide.

The *Washington Post* reported, "At the White House, where Foster was a popular and respected figure, colleagues were stunned last night. One, calling his apparent suicide unbelievable, said Foster appeared to be 'the most normal person who worked in the White House.' "[7] President Clinton, who described Foster as his "friend for over 40 years,"[8] said, "in times of difficulty he was normally the Rock of Gilbraltar."[9] The *New York Times* quoted a senior administration official as saying, "People around here are totally devastated. They don't know what to do."[10]

Mrs. Michael Cardozo, who, with her husband, had hostessed the Fosters and the Hubbells in Maryland the previous weekend, said that Foster had "seemed relaxed and he seemed to be enjoying himself."[11] Chief of Staff McClarty reported that in the days and weeks prior to his death, Foster's "thought patterns were very clear and his counsel was still very sage."[12]

Many people naturally started to wonder why Foster would shoot himself. He didn't seem a likely candidate. Some even suggested foul play. It was hard to understand why Vincent Foster would leave behind his mother, his wife, and his three high-school and college-aged children. Why? Why would he do it?

As friends and reporters started pondering the reasons behind a Foster suicide, White House officials became tight-lipped. In a pronounced shift, statements coming out of the White House no longer praised Foster for his strength or expressed surprise over his suicide. The "Rock of Gilbraltar" line was dropped. Instead, top White House personnel started characterizing Foster as confused and overwrought. Spokesman Dee Dee Myers said, "People had noticed he was down and were worried about him."[13] And President Clinton remarked, "No one can ever know why this happened. What happened was a mystery about something inside of him."[14]

Had the White House really decided to spin control the death of a top official who had been a boyhood friend of the President? According to inside White House source Deepwater, the campaign to present Foster as "on the edge" was calculated. It was meant to deflect inquiries into the reasons behind Foster's suicide by giving the impression that his troubles were strictly personal. White House officials seemed to want to avoid the scrutiny that would follow if it were widely believed that Foster had killed himself due to work-related burdens or trouble.

Deepwater reported that Bernard Nussbaum even convened a meeting of his staff shortly after Foster's death to promote this official White House line. Nussbaum, said Deepwater, coached his staff to think and say that Foster's suicide stemmed from personal depression and personal problems.

Reporters, understandably hesitant to pry into the tragic circumstances of Foster's death, largely accepted this official version of events. One week after Foster's death, the *Washington Post* wrote that President Clinton and other senior White House officials had made "a series of statements . . . suggesting that Foster's death be viewed as a personal tragedy unrelated to his job."[15] The *New York Times* echoed: "After initially insisting that they had no idea why Mr. Foster would have killed himself, White House officials abruptly said last week that there were indications that he was depressed."[16]

But while the official White House line may have calmed media concerns, it did not jibe with statements made about Foster back in Arkansas. In Little Rock, Foster's friends were outraged by official Washington's depiction of Foster as reeling and beyond control. "He was not 'chewed up' by Washington," said Doug Buford, a Little Rock attorney who had been friends with Foster. "I resent that suggestion. Vince was such an able man. I think maybe the incredible pressure, the workload, exhausted him, and that was part of it, but ultimately something was badly askew, something so wrong it could make him think his three kids could be better off without him."[17]

David Williams, then-president of the Arkansas Trial Lawyers Association, told the *Wall Street Journal* on July 22, "I've had people call me and say he just didn't do it."[18]

When asked whether he had made statements suggesting Foster was depressed, Foster's brother-in-law, former Rep. Beryl Anthony (D-Ark.), said, "There's not a damn thing to it. That's a bunch of crap."[19]

Phillip Carroll, a senior partner at the Rose Law Firm who was Foster's mentor and is godfather to Foster's children, said that when he first heard of Foster's death he "kept saying no! That wasn't Vince Foster. He was my favorite. He was so competent. He was a very strong individual. I keep coming back to foul play. There had to be foul play involved."[20]

Carroll further reported that Webster Hubbell, then-Associate Attorney General, telephoned him the night of

Foster's death: "Webb called me at midnight the night it happened. He said, 'Don't believe a word you hear. It was not suicide. It couldn't have been.' "[21]*

Widow Lisa Foster retreated into isolation following her husband's death. Neither she nor her attorney, James Hamilton, made any public comment about the death. They declined even to say whether the gun found in Foster's hand was a family firearm.[23]

According to Deepwater, Lisa Foster began calling the White House shortly after the death seeking information from anyone who would talk to her. Mrs. Foster reportedly wanted to know what her husband had been working on, and if he had said anything to any of his co-workers that hinted at suicide. But, Deepwater reported, Foster's former colleagues would not accept Lisa Foster's telephone calls, leaving receptionists in the awkward and unhappy position of having to turn away her repeated inquiries. "Did he say *anything*?" "Did he do anything unusual?" These reported questions of Lisa Foster went unanswered. Deepwater said that receptionists dreaded to answer their telephones for several weeks following Foster's death, afraid it might be the distraught widow.

In marked contrast, Bill Clinton seemed indifferent about what drove Foster to kill himself. When asked whether he could think of Vincent Foster's motive for suicide, Clinton said, "No, and I don't think there is anything more to know."[24] On his way to Foster's Arkansas

---

*Reporter Gregory Jaynes wrote that "Carroll and Hubbell were thrown together several times the next few days, but Hubbell never voiced his doubts again." Carroll and his wife were invited by Hillary Rodham Clinton to come the next day to Washington, where they stayed in the Lincoln bedroom at the White House. Carroll recalled to Jaynes that at breakfast the next morning Clinton told his staff, "Don't let them get you. We know what they're up to, and we're not going to let them get by with it."[22]

funeral, Clinton said, "I don't think that any of us will ever know why his life ended the way it did."[25] And when asked if he thought the investigation into Vincent Foster's death would turn up any answers, he said, "I don't think anything's going to come out of it."[26]

One might have expected that President Clinton would have expressed *some* interest in finding out more about the tragic death of his close friend and advisor. But, in fact, no one at the White House seemed to share Lisa Foster's desperate curiosity about her husband's death. And despite President Clinton's statement that he and the First Lady wanted to "draw the Fosters close to their heart,"[27] Mrs. Foster wound up communicating with the White House through her attorney.[28]

Over the course of many months, even as significant developments in the Foster case surfaced, Clinton continued to dismiss talk about Foster's possible reasons for suicide. "I really don't believe there is any more to know," he said during a January 1994 appearance on the "Larry King Show." "He was profoundly depressed. You know, he left a note."[29]*

BOTCHED INVESTIGATIONS

The investigation of Vincent Foster's death was fraught with mistakes and omissions from the very outset. Because Foster's body was found on a slice of federal property over which Park Police have legal jurisdiction, it was they who assumed responsibility for investigating the death.

Almost immediately after finding Foster's body, the Park Police reported the incident as an "apparent sui-

---

*The note to which Clinton referred was, in fact, a torn-up list of dubious origin, which made no mention of suicide. It was misleading of the President to tell the national television audience that Foster "left a note," implying it was a suicide note.

cide."[30] Nonetheless, Park Police Chief Robert Langston promised that "no stone will be left unturned" in the investigation.[31]

But when Park Police investigators arrived at the White House to search Foster's office on July 21, they were barred time and again from entering it and had to schedule an appointment for the next day. Meanwhile, the White House announced that the Justice Department would be "the point of contact" for the investigation into Foster's death.[32]

On July 22, Bernard Nussbaum conducted the official search of Foster's office. Although this search was monitored by FBI agents and Justice Department lawyers, Nussbaum removed material that they were not allowed to view. Justice Department spokesman Carl Stern said officials had to take Nussbaum's word that the material he removed did not "shed any light on why Foster committed suicide."[33]

Meanwhile the Park Police, although technically the official investigators, were subordinated and denied access to Foster's office. They were made to sit outside in the hallway while Nussbaum sorted through Foster's documents. One investigator said, "We were definitely shown just what they wanted us to see. We couldn't copy anything."[34]

On the day of Nussbaum's office search, Justice Department spokesman Dean St. Dennis reassured the media that, as "part of good police work," the Justice Department would "find out what the factors were—if it was a suicide—that led to him [Foster] killing himself."[35] St. Dennis added that "everything will be done to keep in sharp focus even the remote chance that he may have been murdered."[36] But no such effort ever materialized. The Justice Department abandoned its efforts because the

White House kept insisting that Foster's death was a suicide and that there was therefore no need to investigate.

On July 26, Justice spokesman Stern casually announced, "There is no investigation being conducted by the Justice Department."[37] The *Washington Post* reported that "Stern's comments . . . appear to conflict with statements made by White House and Justice Department officials last week and raise new questions about the extent of the inquiries into [Foster's] death."[38] And indeed, in less than a week, the Department of Justice did a complete about-face, from promising a thorough investigation to claiming official uninvolvement.

Whether by accident or design, events the week following Vincent Foster's death conspired to prevent any serious probe into the matter. The Park Police were prohibited from conducting a normal police investigation by officials who claimed the Justice Department was in charge. Then the Justice Department suspended its work, leaving the Park Police to wrap up superficial formalities.

"Had this been a murder," said Park Police spokesman Major Robert Hines, "I don't know what we would have done if we ran into that kind of roadblock. But we were pretty sure we knew what we were dealing with [a suicide]."[39]

In addition to refusing Park Police investigators access to Foster's office, Bernard Nussbaum insisted that lawyers from his staff monitor Park Police interviews of White House personnel. Nussbaum said he did this to provide a "comforting effect"[40] on White House employees, but investigators reportedly felt the lawyers' presence hampered their ability to obtain candid answers to their questions.[41]

"We have said publicly that we were unhappy with the type of cooperation we got" from Nussbaum, said Major Hines.[42]

THE "FOSTER" NOTE

On Thursday, July 29, nine days after Vincent Foster's death and with questions about his motives hanging heavy, White House officials announced that a torn-up note had been found in Foster's leather briefcase on Monday, July 26. After its discovery, the White House held the note for 30 hours before releasing it to the Park Police, and waited three days before announcing to the public that it was a memo authored by Vincent Foster.

This note, and the circumstances of its discovery, are highly suspicious.

The "Foster" note was first reported by Associate White House Counsel Stephen Neuwirth, who claimed he found it in Foster's briefcase while packing up Foster's office. Neuwirth told his boss, Bernard Nussbaum, and Nussbaum informed Chief of Staff McLarty. White House officials consulted with Attorney General Janet Reno, who told them to turn the note over to Park Police investigators.

The note was found in 27 bits of torn-up paper. When the bits were patched together, it became evident that a 28th piece was missing from the lower right-hand area where a signature is usually found. An FBI fingerprint analysis found no fingerprints—"a circumstance," wrote the *New York Times*, "that some investigators have found hard to believe."[43]

Moreover, although the torn-up note was reportedly found in Vincent Foster's briefcase on July 26, a Park Police investigator said he had seen Bernard Nussbaum examining the contents of Foster's briefcase during Nussbaum's original July 22 search of Foster's office.[44] The *New York Times* wrote that when this investigator "confronted Mr. Nussbaum with his skepticism," Nussbaum said he "did not recall looking in the briefcase" during the July 22 search.[45] Pressed further, Nussbaum denied to the

Times that the investigator had even confronted him with the apparent contradiction.[46]

The *Washington Times,* in its story of the discovery of the "Foster" note, reported that a Park Police investigator said that during the July 22 search he had had a "clear view into the briefcase" and was "certain it was empty."[47]

It was not until August 10, 1993, when the Park Police officially closed their investigation of Foster's death, that a transcript of the "Foster" note was finally released. The note consisted of a list of reflections, complaints, accusations, and exonerations. It did not mention suicide.*

According to Deepwater, many inside the White House did not think the note sounded like Vincent Foster. Specifically, Deepwater believes that Bernard Nussbaum's then-Executive Assistant, Betsy Pond, had reservations about the authenticity of the note. In fact, both the public record and Deepwater's private observations indicate that Pond may know more than she has publicly admitted.

According to the Park Police report, Betsy Pond visited Foster's office the morning after his death, despite Thomas McLarty's instructions that no one enter it. Pond's early morning visit occurred just before Secret Service agents set guard outside Foster's office to prevent anyone from

---

*Although the Justice Department released a transcript of the "Foster" note on August 10, it refused to release an actual copy of the note. Moreover, it refused to release the police and autopsy reports on Vincent Foster, a procedure that should have been routine. Ignoring Freedom of Information Act (FOIA) requests filed by news organizations including the *Wall Street Journal*, the Justice Department sat on these reports until the announcement of Special Counsel Robert B. Fiske, Jr., at which point Justice officials said all materials were forwarded to him in confidence. On January 21, 1994, five months after the *Journal* filed its FOIA request, Dow Jones & Company and *Journal* editor Robert Bartley filed suit against the Justice Department for copies of these reports.

entering. When the Park Police arrived shortly after Pond's visit to Foster's office, they were barred entry.

It is not publicly known what Pond saw or accomplished while in Foster's office. Newspaper accounts have her "neatening" Foster's papers.

Pond's name also surfaced in connection with the Park Police interviews of White House officials. According to the *New York Times*, the Park Police reported that Nussbaum "burst in on the questioning of Ms. Pond, his Executive Assistant, to demand whether anything was wrong."[48] Nussbaum protested to the *Times* that he never "burst in," but merely checked on the interview to make sure things were going smoothly.[49]

Concerning the "Foster" note, Deepwater reported that Pond made a highly peculiar comment when the transcript of the note was released in August. "I was there when Betsy Pond talked about the transcript of Vince's note that was released publicly," said Deepwater. "Betsy started to say that she had seen, and then she paused, that she had seen something that was more like the beginning and the end of the note. When she was asked what she meant, she said, 'I think Vince wrote the stuff at the beginning and end, but . . .' Then she looked up and stopped talking. It was very strange. She had a puzzled look on her face, and said no more."[50]

Deepwater concluded, "Betsy Pond's words and actions when she talked about the publicly released transcript of the Vince Foster note strongly suggested that she had seen something that made her question the authenticity of the note. I believe she felt it was a forgery."[51]*

---

*When contacted at the White House for comment on March 23, 1994, Betsy Pond said before she was asked any specific questions that she couldn't comment

Deepwater's reported encounter with Betsy Pond sparks interesting observations. The "Foster" note does seem uneven in tone and grammar, and it divides neatly into beginning, middle, and end sections, a fact that supports the conjecture that Foster did not author the middle section.

The beginning and end of the "Foster" note, namely the first two phrases and the last phrase, are similar. These three phrases all begin with "I" and read like the personal reflections of a person who is sad, disturbed, and remorseful. Could these be the passages to which Betsy Pond referred when she said she thought that Foster had written "the stuff at the beginning and end" of the note?

In contrast, the phrases in between seem impersonal and even legalistic. This part of the note defends the Clintons and the White House staff at the expense of the FBI, the press, the fired travel employees, the Ushers Office employees (some of whom were subsequently fired), the Republican party ("GOP") and the *Wall Street Journal*.*

The activities of Betsy Pond, and the strange make-up of the "Foster" note, raise grave suspicions that the note itself, or its placement in Foster's briefcase, was somehow

---

on matters regarding Vincent Foster. When asked if she had reason to believe the "Foster" note was unauthentic, Pond paused, then said, "I really can't comment on that." Pond said she might call back at another time, after she "checked some guidelines."

Although Pond never called back, White House spokesman Ginny Terzano responded one week later. Terzano said the Deepwater source had "bad information," and that this was "very serious." Terzano did not, however, refute any allegations about the authenticity of the "Foster" note. Terzano said Betsy Pond would not be available for further comment, and refused herself to answer or return subsequent telephone inquiries.

*A copy of the publicly released transcript of the "Foster" note is found in Appendix I.

manipulated. The note did supply the much-desired confirmation that Vincent Foster was distressed. It defended the Clintons and their staff. And it conveniently redirected the search for blame for the death away from the Clinton White House and toward Republicans and the *Wall Street Journal*.

Did someone find an authentic Foster note, rip it up, and place the pieces in his briefcase? Why was a piece of the note missing, and what was on the missing piece? Did Nussbaum examine Foster's briefcase on July 22? If so, why didn't he find the note then? Is it possible, as Betsy Pond's comments suggest, that Foster had written a short note that was embellished by someone else after his death to include exonerations of the Clintons and their White House staff? If so, was the note forged to look as if Vincent Foster had written it?

Certainly individuals abound who were in a position to manufacture the note and who had a very strong motive for wanting to be exonerated both of wrongdoing in their work and blame for Foster's death.

CASE CLOSED?

On August 10, 1993, the Park Police officially closed their investigation into Vincent Foster's death. Breaking with normal procedure, the police and autopsy reports were not released publicly. At a press conference, Park Police Chief Robert Langston admitted that his investigators had been unable to determine where Foster spent the last few hours of his life, or who alerted the park maintenance worker to Foster's body.

Langston further baffled reporters with his inability to satisfy concerns and questions about the Park Police investigation. He apparently did not know who Kaki Hockersmith was, for example, although she is mentioned in the "Foster" note. "I believe Kaki is somebody in the White House," said Langston of the Little Rock interior decorator who was involved in a contretemps over costs for White House renovations. "That's what they speculate."[52]

Langston told reporters that his investigators did not bother to interview Bill or Hillary Rodham Clinton, even though both Clintons were in close contact with Foster. President Clinton, after initially and repeatedly denying contact with Foster before his death, had finally admitted speaking to Foster by telephone for 20 minutes on the eve of his death. Clinton said he had invited Foster to the White House to watch the movie, *In the Line of Fire*, and that they had scheduled a meeting for July 22.[53] And Hillary Rodham Clinton, although out of town the day Foster died, had an office right next to his and was working closely with him on several issues. Surely any thorough investigation of his death should have included interviews with her. But neither the President nor the First Lady was queried by police investigators.

In addition, Park Police Chief Robert Langston stated that the bullet that killed Foster was never found. He said he wasn't sure off the top of his head who the last person was who saw Foster, or even if that had been determined. Langston also admitted he didn't know if Foster had logged his car out of the White House in the early afternoon of July 20.

About the only thing the Park Police did determine was that Vincent Foster had eaten lunch. "We know that he had a full meal," said the Park Police Chief. "The medical examiner said that he had a full meal."[54]

Concerning Foster's alleged note, Langston said that when his investigators showed it to Lisa Foster, she identified the writing as her husband's. Langston also said the note had undergone analysis by "an expert in handwriting," who determined that the note was Foster's.[55]

"Chief Langston," asked one reporter, "the fact remains—you don't know, do you, who tore the note up and put it in the briefcase?" Langston responded, "No, we don't." The Chief also confirmed that no fingerprints were found on the note, although there was "one [unidentifiable] smudged palm print."[56]

"The public has a right to know why things were bungled," editorialized the *New York Times* two days after the close of the Park Police investigation.[57] But no explanations were forthcoming from the federal government. After the Park Police concluded their inquiry, it was up to the press to try to collect new information.

On December 18, 1993, the *Washington Post's* Michael Isikoff reported the existence of a previously unmentioned Foster diary. Isikoff reported that the diary was given to Foster attorney James Hamilton shortly after Foster's death, and that the diary was shown to Park Police investigators on July 28, 1993, in Hamilton's office.

Sources told Isikoff that the diary included "entries relating to the 1993 presidential campaign, a party at Clinton's gubernatorial mansion in Little Rock, Ark., and a post-election discussion of whether Hillary Rodham Clinton would receive an office in the West Wing of the White House." In addition, one Park Police source told Isikoff that he saw "paperwork" relating to James McDougal among Foster's papers in Hamilton's office.[58]

Also in December 1993, five months after the Park Police closed their investigation, the *Washington Times's* Jerry Seper reported the astonishing news that three top White House officials, in direct violation of Thomas McLarty's directive to seal Foster's office, had clandestinely visited the office the night of Foster's death. Seper further reported that documents concerning the Clinton's Whitewater involvement were removed in a subsequent visit to Foster's office.[59]

The officials who visited Foster's office the night of his death were White House Counsel Bernard Nussbaum, Special Assistant to the President Patsy L. Thomasson, and the First Lady's Chief of Staff Margaret Williams. The purported reason for the trio's trip was to look for a suicide note and protect national security secrets. But these explanations do not ring true. These were not officials involved in national security matters; in fact, Thomasson did not even have White House security clearance at the time of this search.[60]

In January 1994, the *Washington Times* had more disturbing news about the Foster case. The *Times* reported that Dr. James C. Beyer, Foster's coroner, had mistaken a murder for a suicide in 1989. This earlier case involved a man who died of knife wounds. The man's girlfriend said he had stabbed himself after an argument. Overlooking the fact that the victim had a cut on his supposed knife hand, Beyer confirmed the police report of suicide. The girlfriend passed a polygraph test, and the case was closed.[61]

But unsatisfied, the victim's mother consulted another medical examiner who ruled the victim's hand wound was "definitely ante-mortem [before death] and a classical defense wound suffered while trying to avoid the knife."[62] The mother succeeded in reopening the case, and the girlfriend was ultimately found guilty of voluntary manslaughter and sentenced to prison. "I cannot understand how any competent forensic pathologist would miss it," said the second medical examiner of Beyer.[63]

But despite this challenge to the competence of Vincent Foster's coroner, the Justice Department and Park Police continued to refuse release of Foster's police and autopsy reports.

Finally the *Boston Globe* published the unconfirmed report that Vincent Foster was left-handed—a suggestion which, if true, would make further suspicious the finding of a gun in his right hand. In his interview with the *Globe*, Park Police Chief Langston suggested that Foster could have used both hands when he shot himself.[64]

NEW YORK POST INVESTIGATES

In January 1994, sensing a cover-up, the *New York Post*'s Christopher Ruddy began a series of articles detailing his own investigation of Vincent Foster's death. Astonishingly, Ruddy discovered that the paramedics who arrived at the scene of Foster's death had never been questioned by the media about what they saw.

On January 27, 1994, Ruddy reported a description of the Foster death scene given by Fairfax County emergency worker George Gonzalez, who pointed out several "strange" aspects of the scene. First, according to Gonzalez, Foster's body was laid out "as if in a coffin."[65] Gonzalez added that Foster was still holding the gun, highly unusual in a case of suicide. Gonzalez also reported finding little blood on Foster. "Usually a suicide is a mess," he said.[66] Gonzalez was upset because the Park Police had declared Foster's death a suicide after only a cursory examination of the scene.

Ruddy quoted several experienced homicide investigators who thought that Gonzalez had described some very peculiar matters and indicated that only a thorough, professional investigation could determine whether Foster's "suicide" was genuine or staged. "In my 30 years in dealing with homicides," said one detective, "I've never seen someone shoot themselves in the mouth and still hold the gun perfectly at his side."[67]

After the *Post* story appeared, Gonzalez and his fellow emergency worker Kory Ashford were swamped with media inquiries. But Fairfax county officials made them cancel a scheduled press conference, and instructed them not to make any further public comments.[68]

In a March 7, 1994, follow-up article, Ruddy reported that his FBI and Park Police sources said investigators had committed serious blunders in their probe. For example, they failed to test the bottom of Foster's shoes for residue. Such a test could have determined whether Foster had walked, or been carried, into Fort Marcy. (One rescue worker told Ruddy that Foster's shoe bottoms were "very clean.") Ruddy further reported that the official investigators of the Foster death scene failed to conduct footprint tests in the area around Foster's body, failed to take an official crime scene photo, and failed to conduct "fiber sweeps of Foster's clothes and car."[69]

"If all this is true," said Vernon Geberth, a renowned homicide investigation expert, "this is the most sloppy death investigation I have ever heard of."[70]

Park Police Chief Robert Langston gave weak reassurance that Foster's body had not been moved. He said it would have been impossible for someone to drag Foster, who was a large man, to the spot in Fort Marcy without leaving a path on the ground or dirtying Foster's clothes. But Langston's explanation did nothing to allay the suspicion that Foster was *carried*, perhaps by more than one person.[71]

In yet another *New York Post* exposé, Ruddy reported that three White House sources told him Bernard Nussbaum sought the combination to Vincent Foster's safe the night of Foster's death. Ruddy was told White House aides were scrambling like "cats and dogs" to open Foster's safe on the night of July 20.[72]*

THE MAN IN THE WHITE VAN

Although witnesses had reported a white van at Fort Marcy near the time of the discovery of Foster's body, Park Police closed their investigation without having determined who the owner of the van was, or if he/she played any role in the events that afternoon. Could the driver of the white van have known something about Foster's death? Was he the anonymous person who approached the park maintenance worker? Or, speculating darkly, could the driver of the white van have deposited Foster's body in the park?

It was not until April 1994 that the mystery of the "man in the white van" was apparently solved. According to former FBI agent G. Gordon Liddy of Watergate fame, the owner of the white van contacted him in March, saying he was the person who notified park officials of Foster's body. The white van owner said he had been afraid to step forward publicly and had contacted Liddy because he trusted him and knew Liddy wouldn't "give me up."[73]

According to Liddy, who interviewed the driver, the

---

*One month prior to Ruddy's report that Nussbaum sought Foster's safe combination, authors Stone and Manion were approached by a friend of a woman who worked in White House security. The story related by the friend fit exactly with Ruddy's *Post* report: the night of Foster's death, Nussbaum was very anxious to get inside Foster's safe, but didn't have the combination. The White House security employee reportedly said that Nussbaum was "frantically" seeking the combination, screaming at one White House employee whom he suspected had it. (The individual at whom Nussbaum reportedly screamed reportedly did not know the combination.) After finding out that the friend had made overtures to speak to the authors and to the *Washington Post* on her behalf, the female security employee "freaked out," in the words of her friend, and said she did not want to talk to either source. "I'll wind up like Foster if I talk," the woman reportedly said.

driver was returning home from work on July 20, 1993, when he stopped at Fort Marcy because he needed to urinate. Looking for a private area, the driver came across Foster's body. At first, the driver thought Foster was sleeping, but upon close examination, he saw that Foster was dead.

The driver, according to Liddy, reported that Foster was not holding a gun. "Witness stated that he had observed both hands of the body and that neither held gun," wrote Liddy in his report on their interview. "He stated that, in his opinion, had a shot been fired [at that scene], it would have been heard by the guards across the road at the home of a rich Saudi Arabian."[74]

Liddy, who is now a successful radio talk show host, reported his interview with the driver of the white van (with the driver's permission) to Special Counsel Robert B. Fiske, Jr. and Fiske sent agents to interview the driver in early April. "My gut instinct is that this guy is real," Liddy said. "There were 14 different points established [during their interview] that indicates he's real . . . [and] remember, I was trained to interview people by J. Edgar Hoover."[75]

WILL THE TRUTH OUT?

The reasons for, and circumstances of, Vincent Foster's death on July 20, 1993 remain a mystery. But they shouldn't. "We do not think that in death [Vincent Foster] deserves to disappear into a cloud of mystery that we are somehow ordained never to understand," wrote the *Wall Street Journal*. "The American public is entitled to know if Mr. Foster's death was somehow connected to his high office. If he was driven to take his life by purely personal despair, a serious investigation should share this conclusion so that he can be appropriately mourned."[76]

The federal government promised "good police work" on the Foster case, but so far it hasn't delivered. The Justice Department said it would find out if Foster's death was a suicide, and, if it was, why. But no answers have been forthcoming. In fact, the investigators responsible for finding out the truth were seriously hampered in their efforts by the Clinton White House. "Good police work was out the window," said a Park Police investigator following the improper visits to Vincent Foster's office by Bernard Nussbaum, Patsy Thomasson, Margaret Williams, and Betsy Pond. "Any evidence we found in that room [Foster's office] could have been contaminated . . . We basically were just jumping through the hoops."[77]

Instead of hoop-jumping, Americans deserve believable answers to questions about the death of an intimate advisor to the President of the United States. The Clinton administration should release the police and autopsy reports on Foster. It should be determined with certainty if Foster or someone else pulled the trigger, where Foster's death took place, whether he authored the note attributed to him, and whether he left it torn up in his briefcase. If suicide is established, investigators should provide a "psychological autopsy" to find out why Foster took his own life.

"What terrible secret drove Vincent Foster, the Clintons' personal lawyer, to put a bullet through his head?" asked *New York Times* columnist William Safire.[78] This question weighs heavily on many people's minds.

1. Vincent W. Foster, addressing graduates of the University of Arkansas Law School; May 8, 1993.
2. Rep. James Leach (R-Iowa), quoted in the *Washington Post*; January 12, 1994.
3. Editorial, *Wall Street Journal*; January 14, 1994.

4. Ruth Marcus, "Clinton Aide Vincent Foster Dies in an Apparent Suicide"; *Washington Post*; July 21, 1993.

5. Michael Isikoff, "Foster was Shopping for Private Lawyer, Probers Find"; *Washington Post*; August 15, 1993.

6. Bernard Nussbaum, quoted by Thomas L. Friedman in "White House Aide Leaves No Clue about Suicide"; *New York Times*; July 22, 1993.

7. Ruth Marcus, *supra* endnote 4

8. *ibid.*

9. Bill Clinton, quoted by Ruth Marcus in "One of the Golden Boys"; *Washington Post*; July 22, 1993.

10. Gwen Ifill, "White House Aide Found Dead"; *New York Times*; July 21, 1993.

11. Ann Devroy and Michael Isikoff, "Handling of Foster Case is Defended"; *Washington Post*; July 30, 1993.

12. Thomas L. McLarty, quoted by Stephen Labaton in "Justice Dept. to Stay on Case of Aide's Death"; *New York Times*; July 23, 1993.

13. Dee Dee Myers, quoted by Frank J. Murray in "Clinton Called Foster Day Before his Suicide"; *Washington Times*; July 28, 1993.

14. Bill Clinton, quoted by Ruth Marcus and Ann Devroy in "Clinton Mystified by Aide's Death"; *Washington Post*; July 22, 1993.

15. Michael Isikoff, "Park Police to Conduct Inquiry"; *Washington Post*; July 27, 1993.

16. Stephen Labaton, "Autopsy on Counsel to President Points to Suicide"; *New York Times*; August 5, 1993.

17. Doug Buford, quoted by David Von Drehle in "Friends of Foster Ponder a Life and a Place"; *Washington Post*; July 25, 1993.

18. David Williams, quoted by James M. Perry and Jeffrey H. Birnbaum in "U.S. is Investigating Apparent Suicide"; *Wall Street Journal*; July 22, 1993.

19. Beryl Anthony, quoted by Frank J. Murray in "Victim of Washington?"; *Washington Times*; July 24, 1993.

20. Phillip Carroll, quoted by Gregory Jaynes in "The Death of Hope"; *Esquire*; November 1993.

21. *ibid.*

22. *ibid.*

23. Michael Hedges, "Questions Cloud Ruling of Suicide in Foster's Death"; *Washington Times*; January 28, 1994.

24. Bill Clinton, quoted by Stephen Labaton, *supra* endnote 12.

25. Bill Clinton, quoted by Jason DeParle in "President Returns Home to Bury Boyhood Friend"; *New York Times*; July 24, 1993.
26. *ibid.*
27. Bill Clinton, quoted by Ruth Marcus, *supra* endnote 4.
28. Frank J. Murray, "Foster Note was Withheld so Family Could See It First"; *Washington Times*; July 30, 1993.
29. Bill Clinton, quoted by Michael Hedges, *supra* endnote 23.
30. Ruth Marcus, *supra* endnote 7.
31. Frank J. Murray, "White House Plays Down Suicide Probe"; *Washington Times*; July 23, 1993.
32. Ruth Marcus and Ann Devroy, *supra* endnote 14.
33. Michael Isikoff, *supra* endnote 15.
34. Bruce Ingersoll and Jeffrey H. Birnbaum, "File on Clintons Real Estate Dealings is with Their Lawyer White House Says"; *Wall Street Journal*; December 21, 1993.
35. Dean St. Dennis, quoted by Ann Devroy in "Clinton Finds No Explanation to Aide's Death"; *Washington Post*; July 23, 1993.
36. *ibid.*
37. Carl Stern, quoted by Michael Isikoff, *supra* endnote 15.
38. *ibid.*
39. Major Robert Hines, quoted by Joe Davidson in "Justice Official Objected to Involvement of White House in Foster Investigation"; *Wall Street Journal*; February 7, 1994.
40. Sharon LaFraniere and Ruth Marcus, "Nussbaum Staff Monitored Foster Probe Interviews"; *Washington Post*; February 5, 1994.
41. David Johnston and Neil A. Lewis, "Report Suggests Clinton Counsel Hampered Suicide Investigation"; *New York Times*; February 4, 1994.
42. Major Robert Hines, quoted by Joe Davidson, *supra* endnote 39.
43. David Johnston and Neil A. Lewis, *supra* endnote 41.
44. *ibid.*
45. *ibid.*
46. *ibid.*
47. Michael Hedges, "Foster Letter Disputed"; *Washington Times*; February 5, 1994.
48. David Johnston and Neil A. Lewis, *supra* endnote 41.
49. *ibid.*
50. Interview with Deepwater; March 1994; see Appendix A.
51. *ibid.*

52. Robert Langston; Press Conference; August 10, 1993.

53. Frank J. Murray, *supra* endnote 13.

54. Robert Langston; *supra* endnote 52.

55. *ibid.*

56. *ibid.*

57. Editorial; *New York Times*; August 12, 1993.

58. Michael Isikoff, "Probe Pursues White House Aide's Undisclosed Diary"; *Washington Post*; December 18, 1993.

59. Jerry Seper, "Clinton Papers Lifted after Aide's Suicide"; *Washington Times*; December 20, 1993.

60. Editorial, "Who Is Patsy Thomasson?"; *Wall Street Journal*; March 10, 1994.

61. Michael Hedges, "Foster Case's Coroner Erred in '89 Killing"; *Washington Times*; March 8, 1994.

62. *ibid.*

63. *ibid.*

64. Charles M. Sennott, "Foster 'Case is Closed,' Park Police Chief Says"; *Boston Globe*; March 16, 1994.

65. George Gonzalez, quoted by Christopher Ruddy in "Doubts Raised over Foster's 'Suicide' "; *New York Post*; January 27, 1994.

66. *ibid.*

67. Christopher Ruddy, *supra* endnote 65.

68. Robert O'Harrow, Jr., "Doubts on Clinton Aide's Death Silenced"; *Washington Post*; January 29, 1994.

69. Christopher Ruddy, "Cops Made Photo Blunder at Foster Death Site"; *New York Post*; March 7, 1994.

70. *ibid.*

71. Charles M. Sennott, *supra* endnote 64.

72. Christopher Ruddy, "Foster File Shocker"; *New York Post*; March 9, 1994.

73. Robert D. Novak, "No Gun in Vince Foster's Hand"; *San Diego Union-Tribune*; April 19, 1994.

74. *ibid.*

75. G. Gordon Liddy, quoted by John McCaslin in "Inside the Beltway"; *Washington Times*; April 5, 1994.

76. Editorial; *Wall Street Journal*; February 4, 1994.

77. Michael Isikoff, *supra* endnote 5.

78. William Safire, "Foster's Ghost"; *New York Times*; January 6, 1994.

APPENDIX A

In March and April 1994, the authors conducted exclusive interviews for "SLICK WILLIE" II with an inside White House source, who must remain anonymous to ensure job and personal security. The source's codename is "Deepwater."

Individuals referred to in this interview include: Rep. Bill Clinger (R-Penn.); Patsy Thomasson (Special Assistant to the President); William H. Kennedy III (Associate White House Counsel); Ira Magaziner (Senior Advisor for Domestic Policy); John Sununu (former Chief of Staff for George Bush); David Watkins (Assistant to the President for Management and Administration); Catherine Corneliustion (former White House receptionist); Clarissa Cerda (former White House receptionist, now Assistant White House Counsel); Vincent Foster (former Deputy White House Counsel; former personal attorney to Bill and Hillary Rodham Clinton); Betsy Pond (former Executive Assistant to Bernard Nussbaum); Webster L. "Webb" Hubbell (former Associate Attorney General); Bernard Nussbaum (former White House Counsel); Stephen P. Neuwirth (Associate White House Counsel); Lisa Foster (widow of Vincent Foster).

QUESTION: Critics have pointed to the lack of seriousness and dignity of the Clinton White House. William

Bennett, for example, has compared the Clinton White House to a college dormitory. How would you describe the Clinton White House? Are these criticisms on target?

DEEPWATER: Yes, they're right on target. It really has been a circus, especially at the beginning, but it continues. These people [the Clintons and their political aides] don't believe in rules. They just do whatever they want. Of course, now they're being called to task.

I think it is fair to say that they've turned what's supposed to be a serious institution into, well, I guess you could say college dormitory—in fact, the Clinton staffers often refer to the White House complex as "the campus." But it is more than that . . . The thing that really has struck me, and others inside the White House, is how the Clintons do everything for appearance's sake. I mean *everything*. When you look at their public statements, and then what really has happened, it's just incredible what they've gotten away with.

QUESTION: Give us some examples.

DEEPWATER: Okay. Take the staff cuts for example. Bill Clinton promised to cut the White House staff by 25 percent. This was completely bogus. What they really did to achieve this was to redefine EOP [Executive Office of the President]. The EOP encompasses about a dozen offices, including OMB [Office of Management and Budget], OPD [Office of Policy Development], NSC [National Security Council], OA [Office of Administration], OVP [Office of the Vice President], OSTP [Office of Science and Technology Policy], ONDCP [Office of National Drug Control Policy], CEA [Council of Economic Advisors], USTR [Office of the Trade Representative], CEQ [Counsel for Environmental Quality], and the President's

Foreign Intelligence Advisory Board (PFIAB), and the White House Office (WHO).

Well, to give the appearance that they had achieved the 25 percent cuts, they just said, right out of the blue, "Okay, OMB isn't part of EOP any more." [OMB is one of the larger EOP offices.] In fact, they didn't even attempt to officially redefine the EOP on paper, they just said one day that this was the way it was. And the drug positions [the ONDCP] were not eliminated, they were just moved over to the Justice Department. When all this was over, they had "eliminated" so much of EOP, they didn't have to fire many people in order to make the 25 percent cut. If they hadn't used this sleight of hand, they would have had to fire hundreds more to meet their goal.

Another factor that was played for political benefit were dates. The cuts were to be made by the end of Fiscal Year 1993, which, with the smoke and mirrors I've already described, they did. However, if you look at the numbers a month earlier or, more importantly, a month or two later, I think you, as well as the public, may be surprised.

The Clintons' claim that the White House staff was cut by 25 percent is bogus.

QUESTION: It sounds bogus . . . What else?

DEEPWATER: Oh, let's see. They fired quite a few of the permanent staff at White House Correspondence. The White House Correspondence office is responsible for analyzing and responding to the president's mail. In order to make it appear that they were cutting staff, the Clintons fired some correspondents, but then they backfilled those jobs with their campaign cronies. Of course, the staffers who were let go were told that their dismissals were due to the downsizing effort. It's ironic because a lot of these staffers had voted for Clinton.

Also, they let some administrative staff go, but then contracted out through "temp firms" to fill those positions. You see, contractors were not paid out of the EOP personnel budget, so even though it looked like the EOP staff had been cut, nothing had really changed cost-wise.

The new White House phone system was a big joke, too. The old system wasn't used anywhere near capacity, but they went out and spent $40 million. They said it was $26 million, but Representative Clinger did a review and found that the White House had hired AT&T on a noncompetitive contract for $40 million. Patsy Thomasson awarded the contracts; she said it was for "national security" reasons. But I think the real reason was that the president wanted to make private phone calls and he couldn't on the old system.

QUESTION: The president couldn't make private calls? That doesn't make sense . . .

DEEPWATER: Well, his calls would have been logged on on the old system. With the new system, they aren't.

QUESTION: Tell us about the "Resumix" controversy— it was some kind of computer program to sort resumes?

DEEPWATER: Now there's an outrage. Resumix was supposed to sort through huge volumes of resumes. The software program was used by the Clinton Transition Team for a trial period, I think 60 days, for free. The deal was, if they wanted it after the Inauguration, they would have to pay for it. Anyway, after the Inauguration, Resumix had become so central to the personnel process, they had to keep using it. They were hooked on the software. So a week or so after Inauguration, they just got a truck and backed it up at the Clinton Transition Team headquarters, on a weekend, and they loaded the scanning devices on and hauled them over to the White House. Then a big fight ensued over whether or not to get the license, and in the meantime, they were using it for free, which presented a real legal problem because the government has to pay for what it uses.

Finally, they decided to do a sole source contract, which presents another problem because that meant no other software systems companies got to bid on the project. A big no-no.

QUESTION: Well, did they finally get the resumes sorted?

DEEPWATER: No, no, no. The system kept crashing— they were altering the software—so they brought in all kinds of personal laptops. Resumix was only working for about two hours every day. It was hilarious: in order to justify getting Resumix as a sole source, and it was expensive, they typed up reports on their laptops.

One day McLarty and Lindsey were coming through and the personnel office was so backed up, they had boxes and boxes of resumes that hadn't been scanned into the system. They hadn't even been touched! They were afraid to let McLarty and Lindsey see this, so they just boxed up these resumes, tens of thousands of them, and sent them down to central files. All these people who wanted to work for Clinton, they went right down memory hole.

Also, with all the personal laptops, there's no official backup. In other words, in previous administrations, if there were an order not to destroy documents, the mainframe backups could not be altered, so the documents could be saved. Now, a lot of records don't have backups. A file can be erased, and it's as if it never existed.

QUESTION: Explain how Resumix classified job applicants, how it sorted their qualifications.

DEEPWATER: Well, once a resume is received, it is scanned into the system. Then a key operator types in certain information into the software's fields, showing name, address, Social Security number, and so on. Then you can retrieve anything. If personnel is looking for a person with a PhD in sociology, for example, the searcher can enter that in and get a universe of applicants. Some of the classifications were, well, unusual. For example, they wanted to be able to retrieve resumes based on characteristics such as homosexual.

QUESTION: I don't understand; resumes don't list whether the person is a homosexual, do they?

DEEPWATER: No, but they had lists from gay and lesbian organizations throughout the country. So they could just enter it in . . . All I can say is, job applicants were tracked according to whether they were homosexual or not.

QUESTION: You've talked about the informal, or really lackadaisical, atmosphere at the White House . . . Do you mean there was just a level of unprofessionalism in the Clinton White House, or were there any serious breaches of rules or security?

DEEPWATER: Well the funniest example is [associate White House counsel William] Kennedy, who just got demoted. Here he was, sacking Clinton appointees right and left for "Nannygate" tax problems, and now it turns out that he was delinquent on his taxes! This is the hypocrisy that typifies the Clinton White House. This Kennedy episode is absolutely typical.

Then of course there's Webb Hubbell, who [apparently] overbilled the government on the FDIC case . . . the Rose Law Firm folks are certainly batting pretty low.

But more than being funny, the fact is Kennedy and others are responsible for some serious breaches of security. There's no question that White House security has been seriously compromised. I know that under previous administrations no one was allowed to begin a job—even to walk into the White House grounds as an employee—until the background checks were finished. The routine is pretty straightforward: the applicant fills out a Form 86, which includes all sorts of information that serves as a basis for an FBI background check. The FBI turns this form into the White House security office, which checks it out and makes recommendations to the White House Counsel's office. The problems they look for include drug use, prior convictions, debt, back taxes, etc.

But when the Clinton people saw how they were asked about all this information, many were reluctant to reply. They all protested! I think a lot of them were worried about drugs. Anyway, within two weeks of the Inauguration [Associate White House Counsel William] Kennedy had the security office give him all the files for the senior staff—and that's over 100 people. The security office could not make any inquiries or any recommendations. Kennedy just had all those files in his office, and no one was bounced [for security reasons].

I know this had a big impact on the attitude towards drug testing. Everyone had plenty of time, often months, to wait for drug testing, even though initial drug testing is supposed to be done prior to employment. I know it was standard procedure under former administrations that new employees had their drug tests and their background checks completed before they could start work. But that system has completely broken down under Clinton. It would be easy right now to have a job here at the White House and to be doing drugs. Standard security checks have simply been circumvented. [Rep.] Frank Wolf is onto this, he said the other day, "What is going on at the White House?" He said he'd never heard of this kind of mess at the White House.

One of the biggest security problems, by the way, came with Hillary's Health Care Task Force. They were clearing in hundreds of people every day. They had to clear in these huge numbers [of people] and they [the Secret Service] kept telling the Clintons, "Look, you can't do this." But they kept holding the meetings and they literally forced the Secret Service to submit to their "open door" policy.

QUESTION: What do you know about the meetings of Hillary's Health Care Task Force?

DEEPWATER: Oh, these people were just everywhere. The White House was packed. They had "tollgate" meetings which were held in the Indian Treaty Room, as well as other conference rooms. The make-up of the task force was ridiculous, by the way. They co-opted key staffers from the big four committees on health—Energy, Commerce, and Ways and Means in the House, and Senate Finance and Senate Labor and Human Resources. They wanted to position these staffers to prep the health care lobbyists so this bill could get shoved through. They had very few people from the health care industry, and they were really the special interests. They tried to keep those names secret, but it was clear that they only wanted people from the medical field who agreed with them.

At one point, the names of hundreds of the participants were leaked to the Hill by someone concerned about the activities of the Task Force—not me, by the way—and they were put in the *Congressional Record*. They were throwing fits inside the White House when that happened. I think it's fair to say that Hillary wasn't too happy that day.

QUESTION: What were the "tollgate" meetings?

DEEPWATER: The tollgate meetings were meetings held to assess the progress and findings of the Task Force at large. A coming together of the chairmen or principals for the various working groups—these were the really senior task force members. You see, the vast majority of the task force members didn't even know who else was working in the Task Force.

[Ira] Magaziner was a real control freak. He had everybody in separate working groups, and he would get the leaders of those groups together only in these tollgate meetings. He was very rigid and very organized. The Task Force members were kept separate from each other because Magaziner scheduled the various groups to meet at different times, different places. It wasn't like the rest of the White House, where people would kind of "hang out" and chat informally about their work. Magaziner had a tight grip on everything. He wanted to know everything that was going on. If Ira didn't know about it, he didn't want it happening. The process of having tollgate meetings suited his purpose because it was a process where all information flowed up to him, with very few exchanges below him.

QUESTION: What about the use of taxpayer money to fund non-official trips by President Clinton or his staff? Any abuses there?

DEEPWATER: From what I know, and what I've seen, the Clinton administration's actions are far worse than anything I heard about during the Bush administration with then Chief of Staff John Sununu. I remember when Sununu was raked over the coals for using official transportation to attend a stamp show in New York. In the case of the Clinton administration, our tax dollars in the form of US treasury funds are being used to pay for semipolitical trips. And there has been a big increase in the number of advance staff being used on presidential trips. See, just like any other White House official, Clinton has to determine the nature of every one of his trips—official business or political. Official expenses are taken care of by the Treasury Department, while political expenses are supposed to be reimbursed by the DNC (Democratic National Committee), and I underline *supposed to be*.

Also, certain senior staff are very lackadaisical about what are supposed to be strict White House procedures on personnel, hiring, salaries, and so forth. For example, I know that an employee was on payroll but had only been in the office for a couple of days out of a three-week period. Now, that kind of arrangement just doesn't fly at the White House; but when official administrators looked into it, they we're told, "Oh, she works at home sometimes." (Laughing) They thought that was just fine—"Oh, she works at home sometimes!" I mean we're talking about the White House! It just isn't done!

The White House is supposed to be the example of accountability for the whole government. There are very, very strict rules about this stuff. The problem is, of course, those who are in a position to know about all this aren't exactly about to make a big, public deal about it. They have their jobs to preserve, and it doesn't exactly enhance your job security if you run around asking these questions and pointing out indiscretions and even gross violations going on at the White House.

It really does boil down to what you're writing in your book—about what a farce it is that Bill Clinton promised to come to Washington to clean up politics. He's the worst offender! The *worst* offender. If the American people knew what it was really like inside the Clinton White House they just wouldn't believe it.

QUESTION: The first year of the Clinton administration was clouded by several controversies, one could even say scandals. Nannygate, Scalpgate, Travelgate, then Vincent Foster's death . . .

DEEPWATER: I know a lot about Travelgate, but let's save that. I will say this, the incredible thing about the first year of the Clinton Administration is that the first fire was put out by the second, the second by the third, and so on.

It was so incredible because everybody thought Travelgate was the biggest thing since Watergate, and I mean that in the sense that the investigation was manipulated and bungled by Clinton's senior staff. Then Vince Foster dies, and everyone seemed to forget about Travelgate. The media never went back to Travelgate. Everyone just dropped it when Vince's death hit, and now we have Whitewater.

QUESTION: Tell us what it was like inside the White House when the news arrived of Vincent Foster's death. It must have been terrible.

DEEPWATER: It was terrible. Everyone was shocked. They all said he was a rock, he was tireless, he could always be counted on in a pinch. A great guy. The morning after his death Betsy Pond [Bernard Nussbaum's executive assistant] said, "He was a rock."

QUESTION: Vincent Foster left his office at about 1 p.m. the day of this death. Do you know anything about his activities that day?

DEEPWATER: Not much. I do know that at one point that afternoon his office considered beeping him [on his pager]. But he sometimes spent hours of the afternoon out of his office—at times apparently with Webb Hubbell, so they weren't really worried about him. It had happened before. So they decided not to bother him.

After learning about his death, people in the office kept saying, "If only we'd beeped him, if only we'd brought him back to the office. Things might have turned out differently."

QUESTION: You've told us about a meeting convened by Bernard Nussbaum two days after Foster's death. What happened in that meeting?

DEEPWATER: Well as a result of Foster's death, and the office being in a state of shock, Bernie [Bernard Nussbaum] gathered his staff for a meeting. At this meeting, Bernie basically put out the official White House damage control line, which said that Vince was tired and stressed, and that he just couldn't take it and, so, he took his own life. This line became the official tone of the White House damage control spin doctors, and is still used today. It was amazing to see the same staffers who had previously idolized Vince Foster just accept this degrading spin without questioning it. Maybe it was fear on their part. Whatever the case may be, I think only Vince's wife can help you solve the mystery.

QUESTION: Nine days after Foster's death, the White House reported that associate counsel Stephe Neuwirth had found a note in Foster's briefcase, and the note was torn up into 27 bits, with the 28th piece missing. There's been a lot of attention focused on this note; the FBI, as you know, conducted a fingerprint analysis and found no prints. Tell us what you know about this note.

DEEPWATER: Well, I was there when Betsy Pond talked about the transcript of Vince's note that was released publicly. Betsy started to say that she had seen, and then she paused, that she had seen something that was more like the beginning and the end of the note. When she was asked what she meant, she said, "I think Vince wrote the stuff at the beginning and end, but . . ." Then she looked up and stopped talking. It was very strange. She had this puzzled look on her face, and she said no more.

QUESTION: What conclusions did you draw from this exchange?

DEEPWATER: I will say this, Betsy Pond's words and actions when she talked about the publicly released transcript of the Vince Foster note strongly suggested that she had seen something that made her question the authenticity of the note. I believe she felt it was a forgery or a fake.

QUESTION: Was there any talk about the possibility of the note being forged, or partly forged? Were there concerns that Foster's death may not have been a suicide?

DEEPWATER: Yes and yes. First of all, on the note, I think a lot of people wondered about its authenticity. The middle part especially just didn't sound like Vince. I think whoever did write the note overdid it a bit. I mean, it's almost a joke. I don't believe that Foster would have written the line exonerating the Clintons or accusing the ushers of impropriety, not to mention the grade-school political accusations. It just doesn't sound like Vince.

QUESTION: So you think the note was a fake?

DEEPWATER: I question the authenticity of the note. I really don't think Vince wrote it.

QUESTION: Who could have written it?

DEEPWATER: Well, I can't say. It wouldn't be right to speculate about specific people. I don't have any evidence that points to a specific individual. But it doesn't sound like Vince. It sounds like somebody else. . . . I think whoever wrote the note wanted Travelgate to die with Vince Foster.

QUESTION: Are you aware that the Park Police say they showed the note to Mrs. Foster, and that she reportedly confirmed it was in her husband's handwriting? Also, that they submitted the note to handwriting analysis that they say concluded the note was Foster's?

DEEPWATER: Yes, I am. I was surprised by the report about Lisa Foster, but my question is, under what circumstances was she shown the note? How closely did she look at it, and what was her emotional state at the time?

Don't forget, it was days after Vince's death that the note was discovered.

QUESTION: Meaning?

DEEPWATER: Meaning, they had time to get something fabricated. Look, the question is, if everything is so innocent, how come they refused to release the note publicly?* What graphologist did they use? I'd like to know who the analysts are. How come they won't submit it to independent handwriting analysis? It just doesn't add up. Why is it so darn hard to get answers? Who continues to keep the issues confusing? And why? Why has Lisa Foster been so silent? I know she's upset, but think if this happened in your family. Wouldn't you want to stop the speculation, if people were questioning something?

QUESTION: You've told us that Mrs. Foster made repeated telephone calls to the White House counsel's office in the wake of her husband's death, but that she was largely ignored. What happened there? It seems strange given this is supposed to be a very tight-knit group of friends from Arkansas . . .

"DEEPWATER": Well, we thought it was strange. Mrs. Foster began calling the White House counsel's office two or three times a day. As the calls grew increasingly frequent during that time, she would ask over and over again to talk to anyone. She wanted to know if anyone knew anything about Vince. "Did he say anything?" she would ask. "Did he do anything out of the ordinary?" She wanted to know what he was working on, she would ask anybody, and it got to the point where the higher-ups in the office didn't want to talk to her. In fact, the staff dreaded answering the phone because they were afraid it would be Mrs. Foster. Everyone was upset about this, but they didn't know what to do.

QUESTION: Do you have confidence that special counsel Fiske will get to the bottom of the Foster case and Whitewater?

---

*Although a transcript of the note has been released, an actual copy has not.

DEEPWATER: Well, I don't have any special insight on Fiske. But I'll say this, when the subpoenas came, a bunch of us really thought that was it, and maybe it is, we don't know yet. I mean people at the White House were reeling. But once things quieted back down, I realized Clinton could recover. I just think a lot of what happens inside the Beltway, sometimes for better, sometimes for worse, never makes it out to the rest of the country.

The thing that's so incredible about Bill Clinton, and we may be seeing this again, is that time after time after time after time after time, he has walked away from what looked like a killer scandal. It's what he's best at.

APPENDIX B

On February 12, 1994, the authors conducted this interview with Arkansas state troopers Larry Patterson and Roger Perry.

Individuals referred to in this interview include: Danny Ferguson and Ronnie Anderson, the two Arkansas state troopers who spoke to reporters about Bill Clinton off the record; Bill Rempel, a political reporter with the Los Angeles Times; Buddy Young, the former chief of security for Governor Clinton who secured a $92,300 federal job after Clinton's 1992 election; Gennifer Flowers, the woman who claims to have had a 12-year affair with Bill Clinton when he was Governor; Hillary Rodham Clinton; Vincent Foster, the former Rose Law Firm partner who served as Deputy White Counsel before his death on July 20, 1993; and Betsey Wright, Governor Clinton's former Chief of Staff who continues to troubleshoot for the Clintons from her perch at the Washington lobbying firm Wexler & Company.

QUESTION: Tell us who you are. You worked on Governor Clinton's security detail for several years . . .

PATTERSON: I'm Larry Patterson, I'm a twenty-seven-year veteran of the State Police. I went on the [governor's security] detail in May of 1987 and left the detail in July 1993.

PERRY: I'm Roger Perry. I was hired by the state police in January 1977, and I served two years and eight months in governor's security from January 1977 to August 1979. I was with [former Arkansas governor] David Pryor for two years and then Bill Clinton. I left governor's security in Clinton's first term, then returned to governor's security in October 1989 and served there until December 1993, when I was transferred against my wishes as a result of these stories [stories based on troopers' statements about Bill Clinton's behavior in Arkansas].

QUESTION: Mr. Perry, you headed the Arkansas Police Association for some time, correct?

PERRY: Yes, I was president of the Arkansas State Police Association. I was elected to that office in November 1990, and was reelected in June 1993. In December 1993, shortly after the story broke, I was pressured to resign from that office, and I did so.

QUESTION: Pressured by whom?

PERRY: Other members of the association. I still have a lot of support within the association, and Larry does too. But, I thought it best to resign and not let my actions as an individual reflect on such a big organization because I do have a lot of friends there.

QUESTION: How many members does the association have?

PERRY: There's 618 members.

QUESTION: They must have had confidence in you to make you their president . . .

PERRY: They elected me twice.

QUESTION: In that organization, there must have been talk for years about Bill Clinton's womanizing.

PERRY: There were a lot of jokes. It was common practice in Arkansas to sit around the coffee shop and tell Bill and Hillary jokes of a sexual nature. People knew what was going on.

QUESTION: For years, people have said that the individuals who could confirm the rumors of Bill Clinton's wild private life are the women themselves, or members of Governor Clinton's security force. Why did it take you so long to come forward and make these statements? Why didn't you say something during the 1992 campaign?

PATTERSON: We've had a lot of threats and a lot of intimidation. It was a hard decision to make. It wasn't a decision that was made by Roger Perry or myself that was made in a day or a week or even a month . . . The bottom line is that the American people have a right to know the man that is the seated President, the leader of the free world, to know what kind of man he really is.

Also, we knew that if the man wasn't elected [president], then he would have had three more years to go as a seated Governor, and we knew there would be trouble if we said anything.

PERRY: There were a few people who were thinking about it. When I was receiving calls at home from journalists, I screened my calls. People like Bill Rempel were calling from the *L.A. Times,* and people like that. We had talked about it, joked about it. But we were told that if we knew what was good for us, we wouldn't talk to the news media.

QUESTION: Told by whom, by Buddy Young [former chief of security for Governor Clinton]?

PERRY: Yes, by Buddy Young.

PATTERSON: During the [presidential] campaign I was brought in four times and counseled anywhere from 15 minutes to an hour and a half being the longest session. I was told, "If you know what's good for you, if you know what's best for you, and your career and your family, you will not say anything," or, "You know better than to talk to anybody in the news media."

PERRY: People have criticized us for not coming forward in the campaign, but you have to understand that we didn't think he was going to win [the presidential election]. We thought that these women would literally destroy him in the campaign. And if he had lost, him being governor, if we weren't fired, and we would have been fired, but if we hadn't have been fired, we would have been handed the worst assignment that the State Police Department had to offer. We would have been checking the water in batteries all over the state, car batteries that is.

QUESTION: Is there anything that the public doesn't know about the Gennifer Flowers case that would help confirm it?

PERRY: There are other troopers that are thinking about coming forward, they haven't come forward, but there are other troopers who have stories. You would sit there with your mouth open in awe if you heard them. It was just an ongoing thing.

QUESTION: What knowledge do you personally have of Bill Clinton's affairs?

PATTERSON: I took Clinton on several occasions, perhaps three to five times, to Quapaw Towers [Gennifer Flowers's apartment building]. I sat in the car waiting for him anywhere from 40 minutes to two or two and a half hours. When Bill Clinton came out he smelled of female perfume. I never saw him in the presence of Gennifer Flowers. I took him to Quapaw Towers, I let him out . . .

Also, I received several phone calls from Gennifer Flowers when she called the Governor's Mansion. She always said, "This is Gennifer Flowers, I want to speak to Bill." She didn't say, "I want to talk to Governor Clinton," or "the Governor," she said, "I want to speak to Bill." I used to buzz him in the house, tell him Gennifer Flowers was on the phone. If Hillary was in the house, he'd tell me to take a message and tell her that he'd call her back. On several occasions he'd leave the mansion, there's a physical separation between the security house and the Governor's Mansion, he would come out and go into the back office of our security office, and he'd get on the phone. Who he was calling, I do not know. I did not overhear those conversations. I did not try to overhear those telephone calls. But on several occasions when Gennifer Flowers called, within five to ten minutes, he would come out to our office and make a telephone call. The calls lasted in duration from several minutes to a lengthy period of time.

QUESTION: In the *American Spectator* you said that Bill Clinton had affairs with numerous other women, including a staffer, an Arkansas lawyer, the wife of a judge, a local reporter, a power and light employee, and a cosmetic sales clerk. How did you have knowledge of those affairs?

PATTERSON: I saw him in sexual acts with them, or took him to their residences, or saw him with them in some compromising position, or overheard compromising conversations between him and the ladies. Those people you have just mentioned, I have no doubt in my mind—none—that the man [Bill Clinton] had sexual relations with every one of those women. No doubt.

QUESTION: Is it true that you once observed one of these sexual encounters on a security surveillance camera?

PATTERSON: I saw one with my own eyes, the one with my own eyes was at Chelsea's elementary school. And I watched the other one on a 27-inch television screen. I pointed it [the security office's surveillance camera] right on them.

QUESTION: How often did Clinton meet with these various women?

PATTERSON: Depending on his schedule, maybe about three or four times a week, if his schedule was light.

PERRY: If it wasn't a campaign year, two, three, four times a week. Campaign year, once a week.

QUESTION: The television show "60 Minutes" aired a segment in the wake of Gennifer Flowers's press conference; this show is widely regarded as having saved Bill Clinton's presidential ambitions because, even though he didn't deny adulterous activities in his past, he strongly implied that he had cleaned up his act and that he was committed to his wife and his marriage. The forgiving American public accepted his statements and the campaign moved on. Do either of you have any knowledge that Bill Clinton engaged in extramarital affairs after the "60 Minutes" interview?

PERRY: Oh, there were several of them. The day he left Little Rock, for example, the day he left for Washington, which was a few days before the Inauguration, he snuck a woman by Secret Service, took her to the basement, made a trooper go stand on the top of the stairs between the basement and the main level of the house. Hillary and Chelsea were upstairs sleeping. He had sex with this woman in the basement while the trooper was standing in the stairway, then snuck her back by Secret Service, and then he left that day at two o'clock in the afternoon. This incident in the basement took place at about 4:45 a.m.

QUESTION: And you have knowledge of this because that trooper told you directly?

PERRY: Yes, that day he told me. He came in, and he said, "You're not going to believe what that stupid s*n-of-a-b*tch has done now."

QUESTION: What do you mean that they "snuck by the Secret Service?"

PERRY: Let me tell you how that worked because a lot of people thought that the Secret Service was so professional that no one could get by them. But they could not function there without us. They didn't know who was who, who the governor's staff was, but we knew all these people. There was one of us sitting there at the desk with the monitors and the telephones, and we answered all the telephones. If anyone wanted to come in, I would call out to the Secret Service to tell them who was okay to come in, and they would let those people in. They'd go by two checkpoints. We could get anybody on the grounds. We could have got you guys in.

QUESTION: Did the Secret Service know what was going on when you cleared women in?

PERRY: They knew nothing about them until that last morning when Danny Ferguson was so upset that he [Bill Clinton] did it [had a sexual encounter] that day. I mean that's putting a person on the spot. There was an ATF agent and a Customs agent sitting there. And he [Danny Ferguson] said, "Boys, I'm tired of lying to ya'll. Bill Clinton's gonna sneak this lady by in a few minutes. She's gonna be here at about 4:45, and I'm gonna take her to the basement, and Mr. President's gonna get him some." He said it sarcastically; that's exactly what Danny told me . . . He said the agents laughed about it. I mean what are you going to do; here's the ATF agent, the Customs agent, and here's the President-elect of the United States. I mean what were they going to do, go complain? Say, "Don't do this?"

PATTERSON: They would have been terminated immediately if they'd stopped her. The Secret Service could not go inside the mansion. That was a standing order, because they [the Clintons] were afraid that the Bushes had sent some Secret Service or Customs or ATF agents or IRS agents in to plant bugs so they could find out all their campaign strategies. They spent big bucks bringing people in to sweep the mansion and sweep the telephone lines.

QUESTION: You've stated that Bill Clinton actually enlisted you and other troopers to help arrange his sexual liaisons. What did he ask you to do?

PATTERSON: We'd be in a crowd and he'd walk over to me after a speech or some presentation, and say something like, "Larry, see the blonde in the green dress? She has that 'come hither look.' Go get me her name and her telephone number." On several occasions, I'd walk over and say, "I'm Larry Patterson with the state police." I'd show her my I.D. Then I'd say, "The Governor would like to meet you. He would like your name and your telephone number."

PERRY: It was common practice that he would see someone in a crowd, someone he was sexually attracted to. He would say "God, she's got big t*ts. Find out who she is; find out if she's married." He'd do things like that.

PATTERSON: After a short period of time, you learn all the buttons, all the trigger words. You know, you could turn this man around. I mean if he came out and he was in a terrible, terrible mood or he'd just been through a bad meeting and he was really down. You could turn him around 180 degrees (snap!) in a matter of a few minutes.

QUESTION: How? How would you turn him around?

PATTERSON: Just start talking about anything sexual.

PERRY: He would say things like, "Larry, Roger, are you all getting any?"

PATTERSON: Or he'd say, "Hey Larry, you dating anyone new?" And I'd say, "Yea, Gov, I'm dating this really nice lady." And he'd say, "Tell me about it. What's her name? Have you had sex with her yet?" We'd be driving down the street, just driving down the street and this man [Bill Clinton] would see an attractive woman and he'd say, "Larry, look at that. What would you like to do to her? Tell me what you'd like to do to her."

PERRY: We spent a lot of time with him, his staff, his mother, his family. We spent more time on a personal basis, like two hours in a car. You know every day we had time with him by ourselves. You have to understand, this is my opinion of what was going on: our profession is still considered maybe by our society a little macho, police officers, firemen, people like that. He wanted to be one of the guys, but he didn't know how. So he'd talk to us about things . . . He would talk these things out, his sexual fantasies . . . He wanted to hear what we would do to women, what we thought about a certain woman.

He stereotyped police officers . . . Hillary did too. Hillary Clinton has called me a thug and bar room brawler. I have never been in a fight or a conflict in a bar . . . I know Hillary stereotypes us as dumb. She thinks that police officers and people that make a career in the military are stupid.

PATTERSON: If we had been the kind of characters that we have been portrayed by the spin doctors in the Clinton administration, I wouldn't have been working 28 years, Roger Perry wouldn't be working in his 19th year . . . it's ludicrous.

QUESTION: You've said that Bill Clinton instructed you to buy gifts for his various female friends at stores such as Victoria's Secret?

PERRY: He bought the gifts and we would pick them up. Victoria's Secret and very expensive, very exclusive women's stores . . .

PATTERSON: Barbara Jean's [a women's store in Little Rock] . . .

PERRY: He would buy things there and then have troopers deliver them to the ladies.

QUESTION: What do you know about Bill Clinton helping Gennifer Flowers to obtain a state job?

PATTERSON: I heard him talk to Bill Gaddy over the phone. No name was mentioned, but it was about the job that Gennifer Flowers ended up getting. He said, "I'd like to see this person get the job." In essence, she was given a job over other career employees that had been in this department for some period of time.

QUESTION: Why have you said that Hillary Clinton had an affair with Vincent Foster?

PATTERSON: I never saw a sexual act between Hillary Clinton and Vince Foster. I did see Vince Foster put his hands on Hillary Clinton. I saw him, at Hillary Clinton's birthday party, put his hands on her breast and on her buttocks. And after each of those he gave me the thumbs up and the OK sign.

QUESTION: Were either of you ever asked to destroy any incriminating documents, or do you know about destruction of any documents?

PERRY: We had kept records of anybody that came in and out of the grounds, and all phone calls . . . There were boxes of these records, 4 or 5 boxes, and they were taken down to the old maintenance house. Well, after we got started talking about going forward with the allegations, Ronnie Anderson was curious about those phone records and he went down to the maintenance house. They were gone.

QUESTION: When was that?

PERRY: This was shortly after the election, end of November, first of December 1992.

QUESTION: Ronnie Anderson and Danny Ferguson decided not to make public statements about these issues, although they gave off-the-record statements to the *American Spectator* and the *Los Angeles Times* that confirmed your allegations. Tell us what you know about them, and tell us about the alleged offers of federal jobs in return for your silence.

PERRY: I was offered anything I wanted.

QUESTION: By whom?

PERRY: By Bill Clinton through Danny Ferguson. As a matter of fact, he [President Clinton] told Danny to have me call him and I could have anything I wanted. He offered Danny Ferguson the FEMA [Federal Emergency Management Agency] directorship, or U.S. Marshall's job in Little Rock. The FEMA Director wouldn't have been in Little Rock but he was offered those jobs. They pay more than a U.S. Marshall's job.

QUESTION: You say you were threatened . . .

PERRY: I received a call from Buddy Young in September . . . He said, "I hear a rumor that you are going to write a book about Bill Clinton," and I said, "Well, Buddy, we've talked about it and I'm still considering it." And he threatened me.

QUESTION: What did Buddy Young say?

PERRY: He said, "If you do decide to do this, you will be destroyed and your reputation will be destroyed." And in the conversation he told me that he represented the President of the United States.

QUESTION: Mr. Patterson, were you threatened as well?

PATTERSON: He [Buddy Young] sent me an article and inquired about my health. Put it this way, I've known Buddy Young since 1968, we attended troop school together, and Buddy Young has *never* inquired about my health before.

PERRY: Let me say this. I've known Larry and Buddy about the same length of time. Larry and Buddy have never liked each other. Buddy Young would never write Larry a letter. He didn't like him . . . they were afraid Larry was going to talk. I know myself that Buddy pulled him in one day and they were screaming at each other. They [Buddy Young and other Clinton supporters] were so afraid that Larry was going to go forward, they thought he was a threat.

PATTERSON: Young wrote to me, "I read this article, and I instantly thought of you—I am concerned about your health." The news article was about controlling cholesterol and artery clogging. It came with a hand-written note. At the bottom it was signed "Buddy," then, "My home phone number is, such and such. Please call, I would love to visit with you." Bill Rempel [the *Los Angeles Times* reporter] has the original letter . . . It was an article that he [Buddy Young] had cut out, and it had one of those big, yellow sticky notes with a hand-written note.

QUESTION: Betsey Wright . . .

PATTERSON: A tyrant. She's what I call a 100 percent Clintonite. She is totally, completely devoted to Bill Clinton.

PERRY: Obsessed.

PATTERSON: Heart, soul, body, and mind. She would do anything in the world for him. He fired her as Chief of Staff. He literally ran her out of the state of Arkansas, kicked her like some poor old hound dog. She comes back;

he kicks her again; she comes back again and again and again. She is obsessed with Bill Clinton.

PERRY: Let me say this about her. She knew more about the women than anybody on his staff. Probably next to the troopers, she knew more about the women because she covered a lot of it up. So when he started running for president she became a liability. And so she was taken back under his wing and when this story broke she was the first person in Little Rock trying to start the coverup, the damage control.

QUESTION: How did Betsey Wright try to cover up the story when you two and the other two troopers started talking?

PERRY: The Danny Ferguson affidavit. She took the lawyer and they revised the affidavit—five times. She would get on the phone with the White House, call them and read the affidavit to them and they'd say no, no, no, no . . . we don't want it to say that! Five different times she called. When they got the wording right then the lawyer signed it.

PATTERSON: This woman is a professional lobbyist in Washington D.C. What did Clinton say about lobbyists during his campaign? And the first time something bad comes out on Bill Clinton, who does he send back to Arkansas? A lobbyist. Miss Fix-it. Miss Fix-it is there. She goes to Danny Ferguson and Ronnie Anderson at the Governor's Mansion [where they were on duty]. She goes to Danny Ferguson's house. She called Danny Ferguson's house, they're not taking calls, but she talks to one of the children and one of the children says they're not taking calls. She [Betsey Wright] says, "I don't give a damn what they say, they're talking to me." She gets in the car and she drives to Cabot, Arkansas, to their [the Ferguson's] home, and confronts them. Next day this affidavit is done and Danny Ferguson has never signed the first single solitary thing.

PERRY: The truth is I was offered anything I wanted and he [Ferguson] was offered jobs. The way they worded the affidavit it made it look like he was retracting what he'd said. But all Danny Ferguson will tell you today is that he didn't like the words "specifically" and "silence." And Danny didn't tell me that I could have anything I wanted to be silent. It was that I could have anything I wanted if I didn't do what I was doing.

QUESTION: What are Danny Ferguson and Ronnie Anderson doing now?

Trooper: Governor's security.

APPENDIX C

What appears below is an affidavit from Paula Jones (then Paula Corbin, she has since married Steve Jones), who alleges that Bill Clinton made unwelcome sexual advances toward her on May 8, 1991.

<u>AFFIDAVIT</u>

STATE OF ARKANSAS)
)SS
COUNTY OF PULASKI)

The undersigned, Paula Jones, hereby states on personal knowledge under oath and penalty of perjury:

1.   That I am a resident of the State of California; that in May, 1991 I was a resident of the State of Arkansas; that I am of legal age; that I am making this Affidavit of my own free will without duress, coercion or threats from others; and that I have not received nor have I been promised, compensation or reward of any kind in the making of this Affidavit.

2.   That on May 8, 1991, while employed at the Arkansas Industrial Development Commission ("AIDC") an agency of the State of Arkansas, I was assigned, along with fellow employee, Pamela Blackard, to man the registration desk at the Arkansas Quality Management Governors Conference, and AIDC sponsored symposium at the Excelsior Hotel, in Little Rock, Arkansas.

3.   That at approximately 2:30 p.m on such date, a person identified as Arkansas State Trooper Danny Ferguson approached Ms. Blackard and me at the registration desk and informed me that then Governor Bill Clinton had requested that I meet with him in a certain room number in the hotel.

4.   Ms. Blackard and I then discussed the advisability of my meeting with the Governor whereupon I decided to meet with him as requested. Ms. Blackard assured me that she would tend to my duties at the registration desk during the meeting.

5.   That Trooper Ferguson escorted me from the registration desk up the elevator to the floor of the designated room number.

6.   That the Governor and I were the only persons present during the meeting. During the meeting the Governor made a series of unwelcomed sexual advances toward me, each of which were unmistakenly rebuffed. The meeting lasted approximately 10 to 15 minutes. I made no comment to Trooper Ferguson as I passed him in the hallway, as I returned, unescorted, to my work station at the registration desk.

7.   That my encounter with the Governor caused, and continues to cause, emotional distress for me and my family.

FURTHER AFFIANT SAYETH NOT.

Paula B. Jones
PAULA JONES

SUBSCRIBED AND SWORN to before me this _7th_ day of February, 1994.

[signature]
NOTARY PUBLIC

MY COMMISSION EXPIRES:

June 13, 1996

APPENDIX D

*What appears below is an affidavit from Pamela Black-
ard, a former co-worker of Paula Jones who was with Jones
the day it is alleged Bill Clinton made his advances.*

<u>AFFIDAVIT</u>

STATE OF ARKANSAS)
)SS
COUNTY OF PULASKI)

The undersigned, Pamela Blackard, do hereby state on personal
knowledge under oath and penalty of perjury:

1.   That I am a resident of the State of Arkansas; that I
am of legal age; that I have received no compensation, nor have I
been promised any future compensation, for making this
Affidavit; and that I am making this Affidavit of my own free
will without duress, coercion on threats of any kind from others.

2.   That on May 8, 1991, while employed with the Arkansas
Industrial Development Commission ("AIDC"), an agency of the
State of Arkansas, I was assigned, along with fellow employee,
Paula Corbin, now Paula Jones, to man the registration desk at
the Arkansas Quality Management Governors Conference, an AIDC spon-
sored symposium at the Excelsior Hotel, Little Rock, Arkansas.

3.   That at approximately 2:30 p.m. on such date, a person
who identified himself as Arkansas State Trooper Danny Ferguson
approached Ms. Jones and me at the registration desk and informed
Ms. Jones in my presence that then Governor Bill Clinton had
requsted that Ms. Jones meet with him in a certain room number in
the hotel.

4.   Ms. Jones and I then discussed the advisability of her meeting with the Governor, whereupon Ms. Jones stated that she would meet with the Governor and I agreed that I would assume her duties at the registration desk during her absence.

5.   That Ms. Jones was escorted toward the hotel's elevator by Trooper Ferguson.

6.   That Ms. Jones returned to the registration desk approximately 15 to 20 minutes later. Ms. Jones then stated that the Governor had made unwelcomed sexual advances, a description of which will not be recounted for the purposes of this Affidavit.

7.   That Ms. Jones expressed a full range of emotional distress in recounting her encounter with the Governor including embarrassment, horror, grief, shame, fright, worry and humiliation.

FURTHER AFFIANT SAYETH NOT.

Pamela Blackard
PAMELA BLACKARD, Affiant

SUBSCRIBED AND SWORN to before me this _7th_ day of February, 1994.

[signature]
NOTARY PUBLIC

MY COMMISSION EXPIRES:

June 18, 1994

APPENDIX E

Bill Clinton maintains that in the 1980s, "while the rich got richer, the forgotten middle class . . . took it on the chin." Not according to the IRS, whose figures show that throughout the 1980s, the income tax burden shifted toward the wealthy.

INCOME TAX BURDEN SHIFTED TOWARDS WEALTHY

Year	Top 1%	Top 5%	51-95 Percentiles	Lowest 50%
1981	17.89%	35.36%	57.22%	7.42%
1982	19.29	36.39	56.30	7.32
1983	20.73	37.71	55.18	7.11
1984	21.79	38.64	54.08	7.27
1985	22.30	39.28	53.61	7.10
1986	25.75	42.57	50.97	6.46
1987	24.81	43.26	50.67	6.07
1988	27.58	45.62	48.66	5.72
1989	25.30	44.04	50.25	5.71
1990	25.30	44.13	50.25	5.62

APPENDIX F

What appears below is a copy of the $300,000 Capital Management Services check to Susan McDougal. More than $100,000 of this money wound up in a Whitewater Development Corporation checking account, making Bill and Hillary Rodham Clinton beneficiaries. This Small Business Administration loan has never been paid back.

APPENDIX G

Bill and Hillary Rodham Clinton have always maintained that they lost tens of thousands of dollars in Whitewater Development Corporation. But why didn't these substantial losses ever turn up on their tax returns? The Clintons routinely deducted items as small as a $2.00 pair of underwear, as indicated below in Bill Clinton's itemization #12, when he deducted $6.00 for donating three pairs of underwear to the Salvation Army.

On the following page is an example of Hillary Rodham Clinton's detailed deductions.

CLOTHES DONATED TO THE BARGAIN BARN BY HILLARY RODHAM CLINTON
APRIL 10, 1985

1. Blue & Gray Fringed Shawl
2. Navy Blue Knit Skirt- Size 8
3. Light Green Poncho- Wool
4. Gray Wool Suit - Jacket- Size 7/8, Vest- Size 11/12, Pants- Size 11/
5. Light Gray Wool Skirt Size 9/10
6. Light Gray Wool Skirt - Size 9/10, Jacket- Size 6
7. Black Wool Jacket-Size 6
8. Blue/Black/Red Plaid Blouse- Size 6
9. Plum Colored Light Wool Suit - Skirt Size 6, Jacket- Size 36,
   Plum Colored Silk Blouse - Size 6
10. Purple Poncho Shawl - Wool
11. Peach Blouse
12. White Poly/Cotton Blouse
13. J.G. Hook Striped Blouse W/Bow Tie - Size 8
14. Yellow Silk Blouse
15. Bluish Green 100% Silk Blouse
16. Wine Colored Cotton Skirt
17. White Poly. Skirt
18. Brownish/Orange Linen Dress
19. Blue & Beige Cotton Sweater
20. Poly. Off-White Blouse
21. Blue Lambswool & Angora Sweater Size M
22. Beige Cotton Sweater Size S
23. White Turtleneck Sweater
24. Navy Blue Turtleneck Sweater
25. Jessieville Lions T-Shirt
26. "I'm a Ding Dong Daddy From Dumas" T-Shirt
27. 66th Ligislature T-Shirt Killer Bees
28. Singer T-Shirt
29. Vote Democrat T-Shirt
30. Vote Democrat T-Shirt
31. Navy Blue Running Suit Size L
32. Levis Blue Jeans Size ?
33. Wyoming T-Shirt
34. Nashville, Tenn. T-Shirt
35. Vote Demo. T-Shirt
36. Phillips 77 T-Shirt
37. Kakhi Pants
38. Peach Silk T-Shirt
39. White Cotton Short Sleeve Blouse
40. Pink/Beige Long Sleeve Sweater
41. Blue/Beige Long Sleeve Sweater
42. Black/Beige Sweater
43. Multi Colored Sweater Size M
44. Red Cotton Sweater Size S
45. Blue Socks
46. Gray High Heel Pumps Size 8B
47. Off White Sling Pumps
48. White Leather Heeled Sandals
49. Off White Flat Sandals

Beverly Moore
Chairman, Bargain Barn

APPENDIX H

What appears below is Hillary Rodham Clinton's November 28, 1988 letter to James McDougal asking for Power of Attorney over Whitewater Development Corporation. This letter has been cited as one indication that the Clintons were not the "passive" investors in Whitewater that they have claimed to be.

ROSE LAW FIRM

PHILLIP CARROLL
W. DANE CLAY
GEORGE E. CAMPBELL
HERBERT C. RULE, III
W. WILSON JONES
VINCENT FOSTER, JR.
WEBSTER L. HUBBELL
ALLEN W. BIRD II
WILLIAM E. BISHOP
HILLARY RODHAM CLINTON
C. BRANTLY BUCK
TIM BOE
M. JANE DICKEY
WILLIAM H. KENNEDY, III
KENNETH R. SHEMIN
RONALD H. CLARK
GARLAND J. GARRETT
JERRY C. JONES
THOMAS P. THRASH
CHARLES W. BAKER
DAVID L. WILLIAMS
CAROL S. ARNOLD
JACKSON FARROW JR.
LES R. BALEDGE

A PROFESSIONAL ASSOCIATION
ATTORNEYS
120 EAST FOURTH STREET
LITTLE ROCK, ARKANSAS 72201

TELEPHONE (501) 375-9131
TELECOPIER (501) 375-1309

U. M. ROSE
1834-1913

JIM HUNTER BIRCH
R. DAVIS THOMAS, JR.
KEVIN R. BURNS
RICHARD T. DONOVAN
RICHARD N. MASSEY
GARY N. SPEED
MICHAEL F. LAX
H. ELIZABETH GOFF
SARAH C. HOOD
STEPHEN N. JOINER
B. MICHAEL BENNETT
THOMAS C. VAUGHAN, JR.
JAMES H. DRUFF
JAY F. SHELL
GORDON M. WILBOURN
JESS ASKEW, III
AMY LEE STEWART
DAVID A. SMITH
T. CRAIG JONES
J. SCOTT SCHALLHORN

J. GASTON WILLIAMSON
OF COUNSEL

November 28, 1988

Mr. Jim McDougal
1076 Phelps Circle
Arkadelphia, AR 71923

Dear Jim:

At Chris Wade's request, I am enclosing a Power of Attorney for you to sign, authorizing me to act on your behalf with respect to matters concerning Whitewater Development Corporation. I am also enclosing a blank Power of Attorney for Susan to sign doing the same. I would appreciate it if you could ask her to do that for us. We are trying to sell off the property that is left and get out from under the obligations at both Flippin and Paragould. Chris and Rosalie Wade have been a big help to us, and I hope we'll be able to get all that behind us by the end of the year. If you have any questions or suggestions, please give me a call.

I hope things are going well for you in Arkadelphia and that you have a happy holiday season. With best regards, I am,

Sincerely yours,

HILLARY RODHAM CLINTON

HRC:ckp

Source: Jerry Seper, *Washington Times*

APPENDIX I

What appears below is the publicly released transcript of the note allegedly found in 27 bits in Vincent Foster's brief-case by Associate White House Counsel Stephen Neuwirth four days after Foster's death.

In light of information related by the inside White House source Deepwater, it is interesting to note that the phrases appearing at the beginning and the end of the note (which appear in bold) seem incongruous with the phrases of the middle segment (which appear in italics) in tone and construction.

The bolded phrases all begin with "I." They seem to reflect Vincent Foster's personal concerns at the time of his death. Foster was burdened by several on-going White House controversies, including questions about the Clintons' Whitewater investment and the Travelgate controversy.

The phrases in the middle segment of the note, however, are written mostly in the third person, and have an impersonal and legalistic tone.

An FBI fingerprint analysis of the 27 bits of paper found no prints.

I made mistakes from ignorance, inexperience and overwork

I did not knowingly violate any law or standard of conduct

*No one in the White House, to
my knowledge, violated any law
or standard of conduct, including
any action in the travel office.
There was no intent to benefit
any individual or specific group*

*The FBI lied in their report to
the AG [Attorney General Janet Reno]*

*The press is covering up the
illegal benefits they received
from the travel staff*

*The GOP has lied and
misrepresented its knowledge
and role and covered up a prior
investigation*

*The Ushers Office plotted to
have excessive costs incurred,
taking advantage of Kaki and
HRC [Little Rock interior
designer Kaki Hockersmith and
Hillary Rodham Clinton]*

*The public will never believe
the innocence of the Clintons
and their loyal staff*

*The WSJ [Wall Street Journal]
editors lie without consequence*

**I was not meant for the job or
the spotlight of public life in
Washington. Here ruining people
is considered sport.**

- **To order by mail**, please send your name, address, and telephone number, plus your check, money order, or credit card information, to:

**SW ORDERS
P.O. Box 545
Church Hill, MD 21690**

- **Prices are:**

"SLICK WILLIE"	— $8.95 per copy
"SLICK WILLIE" II	— $9.95 per copy
Shipping and handling	— $3.00 per order

- **To order by fax**, please send your credit card name (Mastercard or Visa), card number, and card expiration date, to "SW ORDERS" at 410-758-0862.

- **To order by telephone** with your Mastercard or Visa, call 1-800-31-TRUTH (1-800-318-7884).

- **Discounts are available on bulk orders.** For orders of up to 100 books, call 1-800-318-7884. For orders of more than 100 books, call 301-858-8585.

 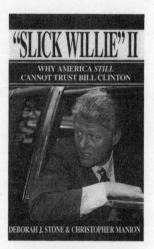

Deborah J. Stone received her MA in liberal arts from St. John's College and was a 1991 Publius Fellow at the Claremont Institute. She is a 1987 graduate of Dartmouth College, where she was editor-in-chief of the *Dartmouth Review*. Stone is president of Annapolis-Washington Book Publishers.

Christopher Manion received his PhD in political theory from the University of Notre Dame. He has taught politics, ethics, and international relations at Boston University, Catholic University, and the University of Dallas. Manion is Director for Legislation and Coalitions at the American Council for Health Care Reform in Arlington, Virginia.

Photographs appearing on the back cover of "SLICK WILLIE" II are:

• Bill and Hillary Rodham Clinton, at Bill Clinton's January 20, 1993 Inauguration. *(Photo by Sygma)*
• The coffin of Vincent Foster, Jr., proceeding from St. Andrew's Catholic Cathedral in Little Rock, Arkansas on July 23, 1993. *(Photo by Associated Press)*
• The burning Branch Davidian compound outside Waco, Texas on April 19, 1993. *(Photo by Sygma)*
• The body of a U.S. soldier, dragged down a street of Mogadishu by a Somali mob following the October 3, 1993 battle. *(Photo by Sygma)*
• Freeze frame of one of the Clinton administration's taxpayer-funded television ads for condoms.